# A MINDFUL TEEN

# PRAISE FOR *A MINDFUL TEEN*

"*A Mindful Teen* skillfully elucidates the difficulties teens face in today's world. Through mindfulness and other positive practices, the book provides a road map for creating a healthy and vibrant adolescence."
—**Frederic Luskin, PhD, director of the Stanford Forgiveness Projects and author of** *Forgive for Good* **and** *Forgive for Love*

"*A Mindful Teen* bridges the gap between understanding teenage struggles and taking mindful action. The book provides valuable tools for families navigating the complex terrain of modern adolescence using the GAIN method."—**Caverly Morgan, founder of Peace in Schools and author of** *A Kids Book about Mindfulness* **and** *The Heart of Who We Are*

"*A Mindful Teen* is an easy-to-read, accessible book for both teens and adults. The simple letters G-A-I-N can change our lives. *A Mindful Teen* is a fun and creative book filled with wisdom and loving-kindness. I will definitely be giving this to the many kids' families I coach."
—**David Matthew Brown, founder of the Underground Savages**

"*A Mindful Teen* is a road map for teachers, parents, and other adult caregivers of tweens and teens to help the teens in their life. The book demonstrates how adults in a teen's life can be instrumental in their positive growth and happiness. Great tips for everyone in the family to share!"—**Adam Avin, teen mindfulness expert and author of** *Stress Less: Mindfulness for Teens*

"A mindful approach to helping solve the unique combination of mental health issues teenagers and their parents face in today's complex world."—**Chip Conley, founder of Modern Elder Academy and** *New York Times* **bestselling author**

"*A Mindful Teen* helps us understand the issues teens face in the twenty-first century. I highly recommend this work to parents, grandparents, and mentors of our generation Z youth. Bravo!"—**Eileen Blum Bourgade, founder of Teensherpa.com**

# A MINDFUL TEEN

*Helping Today's Teenagers
Survive and Thrive through Gratitude,
Acceptance, Intention, and Nonjudgment*

**GREG HAMMER, MD**
*with*
**ERIC WENTWORTH** and **JOHN P. RETTGER, PhD**

BLOOMSBURY ACADEMIC
NEW YORK • LONDON • OXFORD • NEW DELHI • SYDNEY

BLOOMSBURY ACADEMIC
Bloomsbury Publishing Inc.
1385 Broadway, New York, NY 10018, USA
50 Bedford Square, London, WC1B 3DP, UK
29 Earlsfort Terrace, Dublin 2, Ireland

BLOOMSBURY, BLOOMSBURY ACADEMIC
and the Diana logo are trademarks of Bloomsbury Publishing Plc

First published in the United States of America 2025

Copyright © 2025 by Greg Hammer, Eric Wentworth, and John P. Rettger

All rights reserved. No part of this publication may be reproduced
or transmitted in any form or by any means, electronic or mechanical,
including photocopying, recording, or any information storage
or retrieval system, without prior permission in writing from the publishers.

Bloomsbury Publishing Inc. does not have any control over, or responsibility
for, any third-party websites referred to or in this book. All internet
addresses given in this book were correct at the time of going to press.
The author and publisher regret any inconvenience caused if addresses
have changed or sites have ceased to exist, but can accept
no responsibility for any such changes.

A catalog record of this book is available from the Library of Congress

ISBN: HB: 9798881806118
eBook: 9798881806125

Typeset by Susan Ramundo
Printed and bound in the United States of America

To find out more about our authors and books
visit www.bloomsbury.com and sign up for our newsletters.

# CONTENTS

*Introduction*     vii

**PART I: THE CRITICAL ISSUES FACING TEENAGERS TODAY**
1. Smartphones     3
2. It's All about Sex     25
3. Dealing with an Evolving World: New Anxieties     39

**PART II: PARENTING STRATEGIES**
4. The Role of Parents and Parenting     61
5. Cultivating Compassion, Forgiveness, and Empathy     77
6. Mindfulness     91

**PART III: THE GAIN METHOD**
7. Gratitude     107
8. Acceptance     115
9. Intention     123
10. Nonjudgment     129

**PART IV: PUTTING IT ALL TOGETHER**
11. The GAIN Meditation     137
12. Extracurricular Activities     149

*Conclusion*     155
*Notes*     165
*Bibliography*     185
*Index*     203
*About the Authors*     209

# INTRODUCTION

In a world where teens face unprecedented pressures and uncertainties, mindfulness could become their lifeline.

Teenagers in America are in crisis. The challenges they encounter today—many unknown to their parents' generation—are difficult to navigate without proper guidance and support. As parents and caregivers, we are the "first responders" for our children, yet we often lack personal experience with the problems our teens face.

This book introduces the GAIN method, developed by Dr. Greg Hammer, a former Stanford University School of Medicine professor. GAIN—an acronym for gratitude, acceptance, intention, and nonjudgment—provides a powerful framework for helping teens confront and manage today's challenges.

Dr. John P. Rettger, a former Stanford child and adolescent psychiatry researcher and practicing psychotherapist, and Eric Wentworth, a successful author specializing in mindfulness-based approaches, join Dr. Hammer in presenting this comprehensive guide. Together, they offer a synergistic approach to navigating the complexities of adolescence while embracing its joys.

Through this book, you will:

- Understand the critical issues facing today's teenagers
- Learn how to apply the GAIN method in daily life
- Discover practical tools for fostering resilience and emotional intelligence in your teen
- Gain insights into effective parenting strategies for the modern age
- Explore the transformative power of mindfulness for both you and your teen

By embracing these principles and helping our teens understand their power, we can provide them with an emotional health foundation valuable for the rest of their lives. In the process, we, too, will be empowered.

Mindfulness practices such as GAIN have been repeatedly demonstrated to be effective in helping us cope with complex societal problems that often harm the mental and physical health of teenagers. Teens with a secure footing in mindfulness practices can apply them to every difficult and perplexing life challenge.

Adolescence is a challenging journey, but it's also filled with potential for growth and connection. This book is your road map for guiding your teen—and yourself—through these crucial years with mindfulness, compassion, and understanding.

Start your mindfulness journey today and empower your teen to thrive amid today's complexities. The tools within these pages could make all the difference—for your teen, you, and your entire family.

# PART I

## *The Critical Issues Facing Teenagers Today*

## ONE

# SMARTPHONES

The smartphone is the digital equivalent of a Swiss Army knife. What is a smartphone?

- A phone with videophone and videoconferencing capabilities
- A camera—both still and video
- A voice recorder
- A fax
- A memo pad
- An alarm clock
- A calendar and planner
- A calculator
- A scanner
- A flashlight
- A foreign language translator
- A GPS navigation system
- A timer
- A magnifying glass
- A pedometer
- A tape measure
- A radio
- A weather forecaster
- A computer

When connected to the internet, the smartphone can access an almost unlimited amount of information.

Teenagers, who seem to be wired at birth to understand and embrace digital technologies, are understandably obsessed with smartphone capabilities.

It wasn't until the introduction of the Apple iPhone in 2007—and Android a year later—that smartphone usage skyrocketed. Around the same time, social media platforms like Facebook (launched in 2006), MySpace (2003), Instagram (2010), YouTube (2005), Reddit (2005), X, formerly known as Twitter (2006), Tumblr (2007), and others exploded on the scene. Teens now spend lots of smartphone time on newer social media platforms such as TikTok and Snapchat.

Smartphones, the internet, and social media resonated with teens immediately, opening a previously unknown and inaccessible world. This digital world quickly took over a large amount of their time and attention. Online games, chatting and texting with friends, and watching videos are other ways that teens spend their time on phones.

Combined, smartphones, the internet, and social media constitute a perfect storm of unlimited and uncontrolled access to—well—almost everything. The average screen time for teenagers has increased year over year for almost a decade. In 2015 the time spent on screens among teenagers was six hours and forty minutes per day. According to a Gallup poll as of 2024, the average teen looks at a smartphone, accesses the internet, and scrolls through social media sites an astonishing seven hours and twenty-two minutes per day—almost half of their waking hours![1]

Perhaps the single most significant factor in declining mental health among teenagers has been the introduction and rise in the usage of smartphones. Smartphones offer too much too soon for teenagers to assimilate and use responsibly. A big reason is that teens' brains are still functionally in a stage of rapid developmental growth. Teens are flooded with hormones that drive their actions and thoughts. The area of their brain that's responsible for decision making hasn't fully formed yet—and may not reach maturity until age twenty-four or twenty-five. They cannot be expected to make all the right decisions.

In just one generation, the smartphone and its access to social media have radically changed adolescent development. With their smartphones, teens have unprecedented opportunities for social interaction around the clock.

A study titled "Association of Habitual Checking Behaviors on Social Media with Longitudinal Functional Brain Development" found that the ready availability of social interaction and immediate feedback act in a Pavlovian response manner to provide a constant but unpredictable stream of social input.[2] Just as Pavlov's dogs responded automatically to the sound of a bell (a neutral stimulus) with expectations of a meal to follow (a positive stimulus), teens respond to the sound of an incoming text with the expectation of the dopamine hit a new message brings. This results in teens constantly checking their smartphones and other devices.

The data show there is an inverse relationship between time spent on social media and mental health—teens who spend more time on social media have worse mental health. The good news is that when teens have a strong relationship with their parents, their use of social media tends to decrease, and their mental health is better. Their level of social media engagement no longer predicts mental health issues.[3] More on parenting in a later chapter.

Teens are the world's first digital-savvy generation. They have never known a world without computers, tablets, smartphones, social media, and the internet. Today, more than 95 percent of teens have smartphones (compared to just 23 percent in 2011). Nearly half (46 percent) say they use their phones and the internet "almost constantly."[4]

Though the smartphone has created a new world of benefits unimaginable just two decades ago, it also comes with some potentially serious drawbacks, especially for teenagers. Despite the many positives that smartphones contribute to teens' lives, most of the media attention devoted to smartphone use by teens skews toward the negative. And the truth is there are some serious negative aspects to smartphone usage.

## SMARTPHONES: THE NOT SO GOOD

### Teens Aren't Mentally Equipped to Use Smartphones Maturely

The constant flood and unpredictable nature of the information thrust toward teens via their smartphones impacts them during a critical stage of their brain development when they are particularly sensitive to social rewards and punishments. Teens, motivated by the anticipation of social feedback, get into the habit of checking their phones frequently. This can dramatically change the way a teen's brain responds to and interacts with their environment.

If you have watched a group of teenagers lately, you likely were astonished by how they all have their phones at the ready, glancing frequently at them even when interacting with others in their peer groups. It seems that they are addicted to their smartphones, and in a way, they are.

Recent research indicates that habitually checking phones and social media can have profound consequences on the development of teen brains at an especially vulnerable time, particularly as it relates to social sensitivity. Teens are finding their way in the world, learning how to interact with their peers, and looking for guidance during their transition from children to young adults. Smartphones and social media can short-circuit the normal evolution of their brains during this period of their growth.

Teen girls seem to be especially affected by social cues from others.[5] And not only from their own circle of friends. They are bombarded by the self-serving posts of social "influencers" who appear to be leading glamorous lives. These influencers make a living based on how many followers they accrue and the number of clicks they receive on their social media forums. Many of these posts show beautiful women, dressed provocatively, doing exciting things. These are the "role models" for today's youth. It's impossible for any teen girl (or guy) to measure up.

Teenagers are emerging from childhood and transitioning into adulthood. Their lives are in a state of flux: their self-identity, how they interact with others, their newfound feelings of sexuality, and their ability to begin making their own choices. Plus, they have added responsibilities, expectations, and pressures, especially at school and extracurricular activities, that previous generations of teens did not have to navigate. And they feel pressured by the expectations of adults in their lives.

At the same time, parents and other caregivers are becoming increasingly stressed by an increasingly chaotic world. It's not easy to be a responsible adult, providing compassionate counsel and helping to steer young people in the right direction to avoid the pitfalls of our modern world. Nonetheless, adults need to step up their game. They must get current on what teens face in their world.

In early 2024, two remarkable news items alerted the public to the seriousness of the challenges posed by social media. First, US Surgeon General and Vice Admiral Dr. Vivek Murthy recommended warning labels on social media platforms suggesting that social media can be harmful to the mental health of teens, much like the cancer warnings on cigarette packaging.[6]

That's a serious warning that woke up many people, including the media, and smartphones and social media became an even hotter topic of discussion.

Shortly afterward, the Los Angeles Unified School District, the nation's second-largest school district, voted to ban cell phones during the entire school day. LA Unified School District board member Nick Melvoin told the *Wall Street Journal*, "The research is clear: the harmful effects on kids, mental health, the physical health, their academics. I'm fine to be the bad cop."[7] In response to this warning, California governor Gavin Newsom announced his support for restricting cell phone use at school.

Many schools limit the use of smartphones during school hours due to its detrimental effects on both academic performance as well as behavior. By 2020, 77 percent of US schools banned the nonacademic use of smartphones during school hours, according to the National Center for Education Statistics.[8]

That figure is almost certain to rise in the coming years as we learn more about how smartphones and social media impact students.

Some schools ban the use of personal smartphones during class hours and instead have provided students with Light phones, which are equipped with only calling and texting features (no internet).[9] Others require students to store their cell phones and earbuds in pouches that remain locked during the day except in the case of an emergency. These locking pouches are manufactured by companies including Yondr and are distributed to students at the beginning of the school year. According to Yondr's website, its pouches are used in thousands of schools in twenty-seven countries.[10] Schools address the issue in a variety of ways depending on the state or school district. A few states, like Florida, have a statewide policy that prohibits the use of phones during class hours. Yet there is no national or federal policy for how schools should handle the use of smartphones by their students. It's left up to the states, school districts, and often the individual teachers.

Many teachers, frustrated by their efforts to regain control in the classroom, praise the bans, saying that banning phones will help students focus on their schoolwork and encourage social interaction among students. In schools where smartphones are banned, students engage in conversations at lunch and play games together more often.[11]

About two-thirds of parents support phone bans, but others want their children to have them in school in case they need to reach them in an emergency. Parents also prioritize monitoring their teen's exact location, how fast they drive, and their online purchases, all of which smartphones can facilitate.

## Distraction

It turns out that multitasking is overrated—we can pay attention to only one thing at a time. Anyone who has watched a group of teens at school, the gym, or simply hanging out together will notice that some inevitably look at their phones. It's not that they need to do this, but it has become a habit—a social crutch. The constant distraction created by smartphones has caused teens to lose the ability to focus or concentrate on one thing for any length of time. Their academic performance suffers, they tend to become more socially awkward, and they are more likely to get into automobile accidents.

Teens have the highest proportion of distracted drivers involved in fatal vehicle crashes compared to other age groups, according to research by Teen Driver Source, an organization that provides extensive resources and research on teen driving safety.[12] At a time when new drivers need to focus their attention, too many are distracted by their phones. According to statistics from the National Highway Traffic Safety Administration (NHTSA), the incidence of teen drivers involved in fatal accidents is on the rise.[13] The number of fatal crashes among young drivers between the ages of fifteen and twenty increased by 18 percent from 2012 to 2021.

The NHTSA runs ongoing promotional campaigns to raise awareness about the dangers of distracted driving, highlighting the legal and financial consequences. The US Centers for Disease Control and Prevention maintains a dedicated section on distracted driving, providing resources and statistics to increase education for teens and parents to help combat the issue.[14] Every state now has laws prohibiting texting while driving for people of all ages.

It's a good idea to meet with your teen's teachers to strategize how to regulate the use of smartphones and social media, especially at school. Teachers are often the first to realize how smartphones and social media impact teenagers.

Many educators believe that smartphones are the top distraction in school classrooms. As noted elsewhere, frequent cell phone use is also linked to increased stress, anxiety, sleep deprivation, and diminished emotional and mental health. All of these factors result in poor classroom performance. Teachers note that when classrooms are free of cell phones, their students are more engaged.

A 2023 review of fifty research articles published by *BMC Psychology* showed that, in general, the more time teens spent looking at screens, the more their mental health and well-being suffered.[15] It was particularly pronounced among teen girls, whose rates of depression increased dramatically. Parents, caregivers, and teachers have noticed this increase and increasingly worry about how phones affect teens.

## Sleep Disruption

Many teens are so addicted to their smartphones and other digital devices that they use them late into the night, long after they should be sleeping. During the teen years, when so many neural connections and brain functions rapidly mature, it's especially critical that teens get adequate, restorative sleep.

Besides staying up late, the blue light emitted from smartphones can interfere with sleep patterns, making it difficult to enter deep sleep. Teens then wake up groggy and still half asleep. Teachers report students falling asleep in class because they didn't get enough rest the prior night.

As any adult knows, a poor night's sleep can lead to difficulties with concentration, cognitive function, memory retention, and alertness. Teens who do not get enough sleep and who cannot turn off their thoughts at night experience mood swings and emotional instability.

Lack of sleep also increases the risk of mental health issues. Insufficient sleep is linked to increased depression, anxiety, attention deficit disorder, and contemplation of suicide. Teens who don't get enough sleep are more likely to exhibit behavioral problems such as increased irritability and impulsivity and the inability to manage stress, which can lead to conflicts with their parents, peers, teachers, and other family members.

All these things result in poor academic performance and lower grades for teenagers. But they also contribute to several health issues, including weakened immune systems, increased risk of obesity, diabetes, and cardiovascular problems. At a time when teens should be building a good foundation for their growth and future development, lack of sleep can sabotage them.

Sleepy teens are at much higher risk of accidents, especially car accidents, due to impaired reaction times, decreased alertness, and poor judgment. Fatigue is often cited as contributing to accidents when participating in sports or engaging in physical activities.

Parents can set boundaries regarding when teens go to bed so that they are able to get the restorative and rejuvenating sleep they require to function well.

## Cyberbullying

Cyberbullying is the use of electronic communication such as the internet, texting, or social media to harass, threaten, and humiliate. The internet, social media, and smartphones provide an exponentially larger environment for bullies to do their work. The highest percentage of social media cyberbullying occurs on Instagram, with Facebook and Snapchat close behind.[16] Online avenues make it easier to target victims anonymously and relentlessly. Whereas in the past most people knew the person who was perpetrating the bullying, now anyone can be victimized by someone they cannot identify. In the past, once the school day was over, the victims of a bully had some respite. Now bullying can be inescapable.

Online bullying is common these days—according to the Cyberbullying Research Center, at least one-third of middle and high school students have reported cyberbullying.[17] The most harmful cyberbullying takes place anonymously, often by strangers. Whereas parents and teachers might intervene when bullying occurs at school, it is more difficult, and often impossible, to track down the perpetrators of online bullying. Only 40 percent of victims report it to their parents.

Cyberbullying includes a range of behaviors, including:

- Doxing—exposing private information about someone to humiliate or embarrass. In one instance, a jealous girlfriend photographed pages from another girl's diary and sent them to dozens of people in the community.
- Revenge porn—sharing intimate photos, which is often perpetrated by a former boyfriend. With sophisticated new artificial intelligence (AI) tools, images or videos can be edited to combine an innocuous photo of a teen with a pornographic photo, creating phony images that look real, not doctored. This is a serious issue that destroys lives. In one instance, a teen found a revealing, sexy photo of his teacher when she was young and sent it to students, parents, and school officials to "punish" her for a poor grade.
- Spreading malicious rumors—The internet is fertile ground for spreading lies about almost everything. Teens now often become the target of rumors and outright lies. Often, rumors spread among dozens or hundreds of people take on the patina of truth.

With the increasing popularity of generative AI, threatening or harassing messages and posts can now be created automatically and spread immediately across a wide range of online platforms.

The damage to victims of cyberbullying can be profound and enduring. Teens may experience higher levels of depression, anxiety, suicidal thoughts, self-harm, and poor self-esteem. One study reported that more than 90 percent of cyberbullying victims developed feelings of sadness, hopelessness, and powerlessness.[18] Teens may withdraw from interacting with others. They may avoid joining in group activities or sports. Bullying in general can lead to difficulty with trusting others, impacting future relationships.

If cyberbullying leads to you, or someone you know, feeling suicidal, please call 1-800-273-8255 or simply dial 988 in the United States or visit the International Association for Suicide Prevention or Suicide.org to find a helpline in your country.

Sadly, this form of harassment is a byproduct of our increasingly digital world. But there are some things parents can do to prevent their child from being cyberbullied or perhaps ease the pain of being victimized.

- It is important that neither your teen nor you respond, no matter how horrific the posts targeting your teen may be. Responding makes matters worse—and gives the bully exactly what they want. If the cyberbully is identified, it is important not to retaliate.
- Ask your teen to save the evidence of the attacks by capturing a screenshot or retaining the text message. Help them report the incident to their school. If there is sexual content or threats of harm, the police should be alerted—if the perpetrator is caught, they can be prosecuted.
- Block the cyberbully's email address and/or cell phone number, delete them from social media contacts, and "unfriend" and "unfollow" them.
- Encourage your teen to share their feelings about being victimized. Talking to parents, a teacher, a counselor, a coach, or a therapist can make a real difference in your teen's mood and self-esteem.
- Reinforce the notion that your teen should not blame themselves—it is not their fault. There is nothing to feel ashamed of or guilty about, regardless of how much they have used the social media sites in question.

A positive development occurred in September 2024, when Instagram launched "Teen Accounts" with built-in protections that limit who can contact teens and the content they can see.

Mindfulness practice can be invaluable to you and your teen for managing the stress and anxiety triggered by cyberbullying. Start by finding a quiet place to sit, even if it's for only three or four minutes. Start with slow, deep, deliberate breathing. Focus on gratitude for the benefits of having access to the online world. Accept that there are those in the world who would do us harm—unfortunately, this is a fact of life. Reinforce your intention to be more present rather than ruminating about uncomfortable or painful past experiences. Remember to allow judgment of others—even the bully and especially of oneself—to dissipate. Mindfulness will not make the problem go away, but regular practice goes a long way toward reducing the stress and anxiety associated with cyberbullying.

Many teens and young adults recognize the pitfalls of smartphones and social media apps. According to a 2024 Harris poll of Gen Z adults ages eighteen to twenty-seven, nearly half said they wished TikTok, Snapchat, and X were never invented.[19] More than one in five said they wished smartphones had never been invented. Three in five believed that social media has negatively impacted their generation, and most support parental restrictions on smartphone use until at least high school. These young adults, with more maturity, now realize the damage to their mental and physical health during their most important developmental years posed by these technologies.

However, smartphones are not all bad. Let's look at the bright side.

## SMARTPHONES: THE GOOD

Smartphones and social media have positive as well as negative effects on the emotional and intellectual development of teenagers.

To put this topic into perspective, previous generations have always been concerned about the potential negative effects of new technologies, often overly so. In the modern world, internet access and digital engagement by teens through their smartphones, computers, apps, and social media are necessary tools to accomplish important academic and developmental tasks.

Concerns regarding the possible negative impact of new technologies on younger generations have a long history. In fact, Socrates expressed concern that the invention of writing and reading might ruin teenagers' ability to use their memory (although they weren't called teenagers in 370 BC). In more recent years, adults were in a near panic about how radio and television would "rot" the minds of impressionable young people. Similarities between worries about the radio and smartphones, for example, are striking, reminding us that new technologies enter our lives accompanied by widespread concerns about their adverse effects on the most vulnerable in society.

In 1922, Americans owned six thousand radios. This number grew to 1.5 million in the following years and exploded to around 44 million by 1940. By that time, 90 percent of New Yorkers owned a radio, and children in these homes spent up to three hours per day on average listening to their radios.[20]

As with current concerns about smartphones, the internet, social media, and artificial intelligence, much of the initial focus surrounding the new radio technology concerned potential harm.

A few years ago, an article was published online with a particularly engaging title: "People Have Been Panicking about New Media since before the Printing Press."[21] A brief timeline from this and other sources[22] provides a brief review of how fears regarding new technologies span the millennia.

- 5th century BC: Athenian philosopher Plato cautioned about the use of the written word, since writing things down would surely "implant forgetfulness in men's souls."
- 1600s: Samuel Pepys, an English administrator, stopped wearing his watch because he had become addicted to checking the time.
- 1700s: As novels became increasingly popular, concerns arose about "reading addiction" and "reading mania" and their association with excessive risk-taking and immoral behavior.[23]
- 1898: The phonograph, newly invented by Thomas Edison, was so opposed by newspapers and others that Edison's safety was threatened.
- 1926: The *Charlotte News* reported that radio was "keeping children and their parents up late nights, wearing down their vitality for lack of sleep and making laggards out of them at school."

- 1936: A movement was initiated in St. Louis, Missouri, to ban car radios due to the distraction they posed, inevitably leading to an increase in car accidents.
- 1941: An article was published in a leading academic journal entitled "Children's Reactions to Movie Horrors and Radio Crime."[24] The author, who had studied hundreds of children and teens, concluded that more than half of them were addicted to radio and movie crime dramas; she observed that they "consumed" these media "much as a chronic alcoholic does drink."
- 1963: Sociologist Ernest van den Haag opined that the portable radio "is taken everywhere—from seashore to mountaintop—and everywhere it isolates the bearer from his surroundings" and alienates us "from each other, from reality, and from ourselves."
- 1971: The US Surgeon General's Scientific Advisory Committee warned of television's adverse impact on children's social behavior.[25]

There are certainly negative aspects to all these once-new technologies. But there's also a significant amount of good derived from these inventions.

## Improved Communication

This is perhaps the most important positive use of smartphones. Smartphones enable teens to stay in touch with family, friends, and other caregivers, including teachers and coaches. More communication is almost always better, reducing the stress related to not knowing where your teen is and how they are doing. They help with making appointments and changing schedules. Better communication fosters improved social engagement and a sense of security.

About nine in ten teens ages thirteen to seventeen say that they have a cellphone and use it to text friends and relatives, averaging about thirty texts per day. Nearly 100 percent of these teens use their phones to access the internet daily. Teens, often referred to as "Gen Z" and "digital natives," are the most digitally connected and digitally savvy generation in history.[26] And they are the first generation that does not know what life was like before the internet.

## Safety

When parents advocate for their children's use of smartphones, they most often cite safety as the reason. Smartphones provide a way for teens to call for help, share their location, and keep others advised about their activities. The days of parents waiting up late, worried about the whereabouts of their teens are fewer. Now, parents and teens can check in when needed.

When Devin Kowalcyzk was hiking with his family, his younger brother slipped and fell down a steep embankment. Devin called for help on his smartphone and used the GPS feature to guide rescuers to their exact remote location.

Kiana O'Neill noticed a post on social media indicating a classmate was contemplating suicide. She contacted her friend with her smartphone, offered support, and then called a trusted adult who could intervene successfully. Her actions helped prevent a tragedy.

In a scenario that happens more than five thousand times each year, a toddler at a playground was choking and turning blue. Luke Schwenke saw and used his smartphone to quickly look up instructions for performing the Heimlich maneuver on children. He was able to successfully dislodge the object from the child's throat, saving his life.

## Educational Resources

The smartphone has impacted education in ways we parents could never have imagined. Need to look up a synonym? No need to drag out a thesaurus to find one. Teens can find almost whatever they need with a couple of keyboard clicks. Need to translate French text into English? No problem. It may take as long as twenty seconds. Want to write a paper about the future potential of insects as a food staple? ChatGPT can create a draft in about fifteen seconds or less.

Teens can access apps, websites, e-books, online courses, and research materials to enhance their academic performance. With artificial intelligence, teens can use prompts to generate drafts for school assignments or do a deep dive into details about a subject they are studying. They can access YouTube for instructional videos. They get information and entertainment from Facebook, Instagram, TikTok, Reddit, and WhatsApp.

Some folks from previous generations may feel this is "cheating," but a strong case can be made that students learn significantly more using these tools. And it's way more fun for digitally savvy teens to learn this way than by wading through books and other traditional sources of information, so they likely will be more engaged in their studies. There's even an app that teens can use to take notes from the teacher's presentation, organize them, provide a summary, and create possible test questions.

Who knows? Your teen might do something as impressive as fifteen-year-old Jack Andraka, who developed a new, inexpensive method to detect pancreatic cancer. Jack used the internet to research and connect with medical professionals via email and phone. He found scientific papers and used online resources to develop his idea.

Teenage Aiden Dwyer developed a more efficient solar panel design inspired by nature. Aiden used the internet to study the Fibonacci sequence and its applications in nature, leading to a solar panel model that is patterned after tree branches.

And fourteen-year-old Emma Yang created the Timeless app using coding skills she learned online (https://www.timeless.care/). The app helps patients with Alzheimer's disease remember important information and recognize loved ones.

Finally, Ann Makosinski used her smartphone to promote her invention, the Hollow Flashlight, and crowdfund for further development.[27] Her unique flashlight is powered by body heat, providing a sustainable light source.

## Entertainment and Relaxation

Smartphones and other digital devices are the primary sources of entertainment and diversion for teens. Teens can access music, games, movies, and more to pass the time and relax. They often socialize with others via their smartphones using Facetime, Instagram, WhatsApp, Facebook Messenger, Discord, Snapchat, and TikTok, among other channels.

Teens, more than any other age group, use their digital devices to play mobile streaming and augmented reality games. They are comfortable dating online using Tinder, Bumble, and other apps as well as via texting. Teens can access streaming channels like Netflix, Disney+, Amazon Prime, and Hulu on their phones. Teens use YouTube for learning. With YouTube they can also watch videos and movies, listen to music, and quickly get the latest news.

As a result, many teens today seldom watch television, read magazines, or engage with other traditional media. They are more transactional about finding and using the information they want in their lives. And digital media enables them to do that.

As the first "digital natives," teens are far more comfortable using their phones and other digital devices to provide entertainment and relaxation than any previous generation.

## HELPING TEENS TO BE SMART ABOUT SMARTPHONES

So how can parents and caregivers help teens avoid the pitfalls of smartphones and social media? Here are some suggestions.

### Set Boundaries

Establish clear rules about when and where smartphones can be used. For example, agree on a "no phone zone," like at the dinner table or during family activities. Once the rule is in place, let it be known that breaking the rules will result in a phone time-out for a day or two.

### Monitor Usage

It isn't unreasonable to monitor the usage of apps and websites by teens who are younger than eighteen. Until that age, it is your right and responsibility as a parent or guardian to keep them safe. Let them know that if they are responsible and trustworthy about their use, there will be fewer restrictions. This means knowing the passwords for your teen's phone and apps. There are apps that track usage and block distracting and potentially dangerous sites. It is important to maintain a balance between monitoring usage and respecting their autonomy, which is a personal decision. Monitoring phone use should be more "invasive" when teens violate the rules and eased when trust is maintained. In other words, your trust can be earned.

### Encourage Balance
Work with your teen to create a plan that balances screentime with other activities such as sports, clubs and organizations, reading, studying, and good old-fashioned face-to-face socializing. As mentioned previously, smartphones and social media can be psychologically addictive. But if you can prevent this addiction or substitute healthier activities, both your teen and you will likely be better off for it.

### Discuss the Risks
Your teen may not be fully aware of the potential risks of smartphones and social media. They are just transitioning from childhood to young adults. They may not have experienced the downsides of smartphones and social media, like hacks, scams, and cyberbullying, which can put them and their family at risk.

Teens may not know that there are sophisticated bad guys out there who can clone their voice or turn a photo into a pornographic video, something that can ruin their life.

Teens may not be aware that the reason they have trouble sleeping, are feeling sad, lonely, or a sense of poor self-worth can be directly attributed to the use of smartphones and social media.

These not-so-good aspects of smartphones and the internet are reviewed earlier and in the following two chapters.

### Meet with School Officials and Teachers
Be proactive in finding out what your teen's school policies are regarding smartphone use. Meet with teachers and school administrators to coordinate your family's own decisions about how your teen will use a smartphone with the school's policy. They may have information you can use based on solid research and experience.

## Be a Good Role Model

Much of your teen's success in life depends on how successful you are as a role model. Although there are many examples of teens who go off track despite having loving, intelligent, caring parents, excellent school support, and a positive living environment, you remain the dominant factor in their development.

In some cases, you may not see how you are affecting your teen but know that you are. Often, parents and other caregivers are surprised years later when a teen they have helped raise exhibits personal behaviors they were taught.

Be a good role model in how *you* use your digital devices. Parents can model healthy smartphone use by being thoughtful about turning their phones off when there are other priorities for which their phones would be distracting. One example is during family meals (this one is a no-brainer). Everyone at the table should turn their phones off and put them away in a place other than their lap or the tabletop! Parents can set the example by turning off the ringer and leaving their phones elsewhere. Consider turning the phone off more broadly during family times, even when not all family members are present—while watching TV in the evening, attending a sibling's sporting event, or having a discussion at bedtime. Having rules governing when smartphones are not welcome and must be off and elsewhere is much more effective when we parents follow the rules.

Where and when your teen uses the phone is something you should agree on. Is it necessary for school? Can a phones-down policy after 5:00 p.m. work at home? Can you agree on time restrictions on using smartphones and social media? Is your teen okay with restrictions regarding what social media sites can be accessed? Some parents take the step of drafting an agreement with their teens, binding them to the agreed-upon terms for smartphone and social media use.

## Partner with Your Teen to Create a Win-Win Protocol for Smartphone Use

Addressing the negative aspects of smartphones, the internet, and social media has gained traction in recent years as the negative impact on teenagers and children becomes more pronounced. Several programs have emerged to teach young people how to use their digital devices and the internet wisely. There are several very useful online resources to help parents and teens prevent online harassment or worse.

Google's Be Internet Awesome program includes a curriculum and interactive games that teach young people about online safety and how to avoid harmful behaviors like engaging with or sharing inappropriate content.[28]

Common Sense Media provides resources, tools, and lesson plans for teachers and parents to help guide their kids through the safe use of technology, including instruction about dealing with cyberbullying and understanding the impact of screen time.[29]

The Social Institute (https://thesocialinstitute.com) provides programs that help students navigate social media and technology to make smart decisions about online behavior.

CyberWise is another resource for helping teens, parents, and educators deal with issues such as online privacy, cyberbullying, and healthy internet use (https://www.cyberwise.org/).

## Embrace and Model a Mindfulness Practice: The GAIN Method

As with so many aspects of our lives and that of our teens, a mindful approach to smartphone use can be very helpful. When we parents find ourselves experiencing a stress response—becoming flooded with adrenaline after discovering that our son or daughter has been misusing their smartphone by visiting pornography sites, sexting, sneaking their phone into bed, and staying up late—we can regain our composure through our mindfulness practice. We might remember to focus on slow, deep, deliberate breathing for thirty seconds or a minute. We might transition to the gratitude we feel for having our teen(s) in our lives—the joy they bring to us. Then to our acceptance of the challenges they present as well. We embrace our intention to be less reactive and to enjoy every moment we have with them; after all, they will soon move out of our homes. We remember our commitment to being nonjudgmental—they are the person they are, and we can learn to drop any comparison of them to others and to ourselves. This very accessible sequence of thoughts, experienced as we continue to breathe deeply and deliberately, constitutes the GAIN practice. We discuss this in much more detail later in the book.

These same GAIN principles can help guide us through thoughtful interactions with our teens, who will likely object to any limitations of their smartphone "privileges" and to parental access to their phone and apps. We might remind them of our gratitude for even having such devices. At the risk of sounding like dinosaurs, it is rather miraculous that the technology to access the vast realm of information and other capabilities these ingenious phones offer exists. Let's accept these devices' hazards and the fact that we parents have a responsibility to help protect our teens; they will appreciate our love even if they outwardly object and roll their eyes. We recognize that smartphones can be distracting, leading us to miss what is happening right now, right in front of us, underscoring our intention to be more present more often. As always, let's not judge each other—we are learning not to judge them for their habits and tendencies, and they can learn not to judge us for being parents and naturally protective! Little by little, these new ways of thinking will sink in and become second nature. We rewire our brains each time we embrace these mindfulness domains.

Using the principles of GAIN as a foundation for discussions with your teens, parents and caregivers can collaborate on a plan for using smartphones and social media. By weighing the pros and cons, you can agree to a protocol for using phones and social media that provides a path to responsible, mature use.

## Bottom Line

- Smartphones, the internet, and social media have upsides and downsides.
- Discuss the challenges of responsibly using smartphones, the internet, and social media with your teen, monitor their smartphone use, and set a good example by limiting smartphone use during family times.

- Meet with your teens' teachers to discuss smartphones, the internet, and social media—they may observe behaviors that parents miss.
- Consider establishing times when smartphones should be put away, such as during family meals, one or two hours before bedtime, and during class.
- Bring your mindfulness practice to bear during times of stress related to the challenges smartphones represent.

**TWO**

# IT'S ALL ABOUT SEX

Sex is a normal, healthy part of being human. It's a key ingredient in most successful, long-term intimate relationships. Sex is also a front-and-center issue for teens, for whom it may be a source of great anxiety.

The reasons teens have sex are complex. Early use of marijuana and alcohol is associated with young teens initiating consensual sexual activity.[1] At the eighth-grade level, boys may be motivated to engage in sex in their effort to attain status, whereas girls are more likely to do so to gain approval. Clearly, a multifaceted approach is needed to understand and address the issue of teen sex.

The teen years are when many boys and girls begin their sexual journey in life. Most will have intercourse for the first time before they graduate from high school, according to the National Survey of Family Growth, although there is a wide age range that extends from age twelve to age twenty-four and beyond.[2]

It's important for teens to be mindful about engaging in sex. They need to be mentally and physically prepared. Ideally, this involves open conversations with their parents beforehand. Although initial experience with physical intimacy can be a source of confidence and meaningful connectedness, it can also be traumatic. There are psychological and physical downsides to having sex during the teenage years.

## TEEN PREGNANCY

Despite declining pregnancy rates among teenage girls, at least in part due to the availability of contraception, nearly two hundred thousand teen pregnancies occur each year in the United States. The vast majority are unwanted; 35 percent of these result in abortions.[3] This is one reason that it is critical for parents and caregivers to discuss sex with their teens.

Pregnancy among teenagers involves greater risk and is associated with future adversities.

- Teen mothers are at higher risk for complications, both during pregnancy and childbirth, including preeclampsia, anemia, and preterm labor.
- Babies born to teen mothers are more likely to have low birth weight. This can lead to long-term health and developmental issues for the child. These children may have serious behavioral and cognitive problems and are at higher risk of eventually becoming teenage parents themselves.
- Unwed teenage pregnancies most often occur in poor areas of the country where maternal health care may be substandard. This includes states such as Mississippi, Arkansas, Louisiana, Oklahoma, and Texas, where there are higher rates of poverty, lower levels of education, and less access to sex education and maternal health care. Poverty rates strongly correlate with poor pregnancy outcomes.
- Teenage mothers are more likely to drop out of school due to the demands of pregnancy and raising a child. This limits their educational prospects and future job opportunities.
- Teens who get pregnant suffer from social stereotyping from their friends, family, and society, which can lead to lower self-esteem, shame, guilt, and depression.
- The stress of pregnancy—combined with the fact that teens are still developing their self-identity, evolving physically, and developing emotionally—may lead to a variety of mental health issues.
- The pressures of motherhood at a young age can lead to strained relationships with the father of the child, parents, other family members, and past and present friends.

With the Supreme Court's 2023 decision to overthrow *Roe v. Wade*, the landmark legislation in which the court ruled that the Constitution protected a woman's right to have an abortion, the number of unwed mothers is likely to rise. The personal and societal consequences of this are profound, including greater poverty, poor maternal prenatal health, rising perinatal morbidity and mortality, and a range of health issues that can follow children throughout their lives.

## SEXUALLY TRANSMITTED DISEASES

Adolescents may be inclined to take risks, such as having unprotected sex, due to their stage of cognitive development, lack of information about the hazards involved, and pressure from their peers and their partners. Maturation of the prefrontal and frontal lobes of the brain is not complete until around twenty-five years of age. Unfortunately, this is responsible in large part for teens' increased interest in sexual exploration and propensity to make risky decisions. One significant risk is the acquisition of sexually transmitted diseases, or STDs.

Millions of teenagers acquire STDs every year in the United States. Teens represent a disproportionately high percentage of new cases of STDs. Half of new cases are diagnosed in individuals aged fifteen to twenty-four years.[4] Two-thirds of these new cases are teenagers. Teens are at higher risk than adults for a variety of reasons. They may be reluctant to talk to adults—including parents, teachers, doctors, and nurses—about sex, so they may not receive information that would help keep them safe. They may not use condoms correctly—or may be too embarrassed or otherwise reluctant to use them at all. They may not know that there are tests readily available to check for STDs. They may not know that they can get STDs by having oral sex.

The most common STD in teens is chlamydia.[5] There are several reasons for this. First, 80 percent of chlamydia infections are asymptomatic—the great majority of those infected would know they had chlamydia infections only through screening. The US Centers for Disease Control and Prevention (CDC) recommends that all sexually active females under the age of twenty-five years undergo screening annually; there are no official recommendations for males. It is likely that only a minority of female teens are, in fact, tested for chlamydia. Sadly, untreated chlamydia infections can have lifelong consequences, including infertility. Chlamydia is the leading cause of infertility in the United States. Chlamydia also can lead to painful, chronic pelvic inflammatory disease in females and chronic urethritis and epididymitis in males.

Genital herpes, caused by herpes simplex virus (HSV) types 1 and 2, is common in teenagers. HSV1 and HSV2 are highly contagious and transmitted by both oral and genital contact. Remarkably, up to 80 percent of adults in the United States have had oral herpes, and one in five have had genital herpes.[6] Herpes viruses commonly remain latent in nerve fibers and can reemerge at any time, commonly during times of stress. Infection can be spread even when the "host" has no symptoms.

Another virus causing genital and oral infection is human papillomavirus (HPV). HPV infection can lead to cervical, vaginal, and vulvar cancers in females and throat cancer and genital warts in both women and men. Fortunately, the HPV vaccine provides safe, effective, and long-lasting protection against cancers caused by HPV infection. All preteens aged eleven and twelve years should get two shots of the HPV vaccine six to twelve months apart. Teens who start the vaccine series after the age of fifteen should get three injections over six months.

Other STDs in teenagers include gonorrhea ("clap"), syphilis, trichomoniasis, and HIV/AIDS.

Rates of chlamydia and other STDs continue to rise in part due to decreased condom use.[7] Even when condoms are used, they are often used incorrectly. The only foolproof way of avoiding STDs is to abstain from any kind of sexual contact—including vaginal, anal, and oral sex. It may not be realistic for parents to convince their teens not to have sex, but they can provide them with lots of information to maximize the likelihood that they use condoms, talk to their partner(s), get tested for chlamydia, and get the HPV vaccine.

As with pregnancy, it is critically important that parents talk to their teens about STDs, even if they do not think that their teens are sexually active. It is not only teens who are nervous about discussing STDs—their parents may be as well. Some parents believe that talking about sex with their teens makes it more likely that teens will want to have sex, but this is not true.

Practical information about STDs is readily available online and in doctors' offices—parents can discuss the risks of STDs with their teens and how to prevent them. Parents can influence their teens' decisions regarding sex.

## PORNOGRAPHY

According to the US Department of Justice, "Never before in the history of telecommunications media in the United States has so much indecent (and obscene) material been so easily accessible by so many minors in so many American homes with so few restrictions."[8]

Pornography, once limited and difficult to access for teenagers, is now pervasive in every society around the world. It is easy to access via the internet with smartphones and other digital devices, requiring only a couple of clicks to access the most graphic images and videos of sexual behavior of every possible variety. Much of this content is free and accessible without any parental oversight. It's reported that the largest free porn site, Pornhub, received approximately twenty-eight billion visits per year, more than 90 percent of which were accessed using smartphones.[9]

According to a 2023 report by Common Sense Media, nearly three-fourths of teens have viewed pornography online, more than half of those reported seeing it before the age of thirteen, and 15 percent accessed online pornography at age ten or younger.[10] The average age reported for first viewing pornography was twelve. Nearly half of teen respondents surveyed for the report said online pornography provides "helpful" information about sex. Interestingly, half reported that they felt guilty or ashamed after watching pornography.

James P. Steyer, founder and CEO of Common Sense Media, stated, "this research confirms that it's time for parents to have conversations with teens about pornography, the same way we talk about safe sex and drug use, to help them build better knowledge and healthier attitudes about sex. Schools also play a crucial role in teaching kids how to interpret what they're seeing online critically."[11] The report indicated that less than half of teens had discussed pornography with a trusted adult.

Many parents are unaware of how early and often their teenagers view pornography. The volume of pornography that was readily accessible just twenty-five years ago pales in comparison to what is available today. Teens now often see graphic sexual videos depicting extreme acts before they have had any real sexual experience themselves, which become their foundational sexual reference point.

The vast majority of porn actors do not use condoms. So teens are being "taught" that safe sex isn't necessary.

A study of popular pornography videos reported that almost nine in ten scenes portrayed physical violence, including spanking, gagging, and slapping, almost always perpetrated by men against women.[12] The evidence supports that pornography may contribute to a culture that promotes physical (e.g., slapping, hitting, and choking) and sexual (e.g., sexual coercion and forced penetration) violence toward women.[13]

At a time when teens are developing their identities, including sexual identities, online exposure to pornography can lead to a variety of problematic mental health issues, including mood disorders, decreased self-esteem, loneliness, and confusion.

Teen boys who watch pornography can be misled about how women want to be treated during sex. The large number of teen females who view pornography are also getting their sexual references from exaggerated, fictional depictions of sex. Porn warps their understanding of healthy sex, and it can lead to risky and abusive behavior.

In *Porn University*, author Michael Leahy reports the disturbing results of a study of twenty-nine thousand university students in America. More than half of male students and nearly a third of female students first viewed pornography when they were twelve or younger. The study also revealed that 64 percent of men and 18 percent of women students viewed pornography every week.[14]

Teens don't realize that they are being manipulated by sophisticated porn producers whose goal is to make money. Porn filmmakers know how to hook their viewers and keep them coming back for more. Teens (and adults) can easily access the voyeuristic experience of watching men have sex with beautiful, willing women; they may find it simpler than engaging with real women who must be courted.

With porn, there is no possibility of rejection. Fantasizing about sex is easier than doing it.

Viewing porn can be exciting to people of all ages because it activates a dopamine and endorphin response—the feel-good hormones that impact the brain's pleasure centers. Activating these centers can lead to addiction—there are, in fact, millions of people who are considered to be addicted to pornography and sex. Organizations like Sexaholics Anonymous, Sex and Love Addicts Anonymous, and Sex Addicts Anonymous support individuals with this problem.

Many schools provide some sex education, but this is highly variable. As of 2023, thirty states mandate that sex education meet certain requirements and minimum standards, including being medically accurate (eighteen states) and age appropriate (twenty-six states), which are open to wide interpretation. Also, forty states and the District of Columbia require parental involvement in sex and/or STD education programs. Schools and state legislators are continually updating their requirements for sex education. As of 2020, fewer than half of high schools in America teach all the essential sex education topics recommended by the CDC.

The bottom line is that many, perhaps most, teenagers aren't getting the sexual guidance they need before becoming sexually active. Although a delicate and somewhat embarrassing topic for many families, sex is a subject that parents need to address.

Many teens are unprepared for caring, lasting romantic relationships and anxious about developing them. Yet often parents, educators, and other adults provide young people with little or no guidance in developing these relationships. The good news is that a high percentage of young people want this guidance.

How can parents talk to their teens about pornography? Nonjudgment is one essential ingredient—open discussions without shame or criticism. Honesty and empathy are critical. Rather than lecturing, asking open-ended questions is helpful; for example, "What do you think is appealing about pornography?" or "How do you think porn affects the way people behave in their relationships?" Choosing the right time is important, of course—during a car ride, in the evening before bed, or while taking a walk together. Starting a dialogue is key—bringing up the topic repeatedly is a good idea. This is not a one-time conversation.

Of course, teens are often embarrassed to discuss topics related to sex, including pornography. We parents might start the conversation by acknowledging that it is awkward and difficult to discuss for all of us, and there never seems to be a perfect time for it. We can emphasize that it is an important topic to discuss, even if it does not apply to your teen. Consider mentioning that porn is entertainment and not a realistic portrayal of real-world relationships or even sex. The participants are paid actors performing in highly produced environments. The scenes represent fantasy, not reality.

## SEXTING

Teens commonly send and receive sexually explicit content through their smartphones and webcams. "Sexting" ranges from sending nude or seminude photos or videos of themselves or others to performing sexual acts. Sexting is on the rise—40 percent of males and 30 percent of females have sent or received nude images.[15]

Why do teens sext? One explanation is that many teens experience social isolation, especially since the COVID-19 pandemic. Sexting may foster feelings of intimacy with a partner and a sense of well-being. It is a form of exploring one's sexual identity. Sexting is often done impulsively, however, without due consideration of the potentially serious consequences.

As with other impulsive teen behavior, the reasons for it include:

- immaturity of the prefrontal and frontal cortex, which regulate decision making, as well as the limbic system, which governs impulsivity
- changes in hormones
- the urge to experiment and get attention from peers
- the natural tendency to separate themselves from their parents

Because teens are so familiar with smartphones, social media, and the internet, they may have a false sense of security and utilize these tools recklessly, ignoring the risks of sexting. Once the images have been sent, they cannot be recalled and may "go viral," which can lead to devastating results.

If you discover that your teen is sexting, what can you do? It is best not to shame your teen. If you invoke punishment, such as preventing them from using their phones, your teen may shut you out and figure out alternative ways to engage in sexual exploration. Teens are very industrious creatures! We cannot monitor their online activity all the time. Instead, we might understand that their curiosity is completely normal. We do not have to condone their actions, but we can be accepting and nonjudgmental (as per our GAIN understanding). We can discuss without judging the downsides of sexting, including stalking, cyberbullying, blackmail, embarrassment, and even serious legal ramifications. Importantly, let's keep the conversation going with our beloved teens.

One of the most devastating downsides of sexting is a relatively recent phenomenon called "sextortion." Sextortion is a kind of blackmail in which money or sexual favors are demanded under the threat of publicizing sexual images. A common scenario involves a teenage boy who receives a text message from someone claiming to be a female, after which a dialogue is established. The perpetrator then asks the teen to send a photo or video of their genitalia or other erotic image. There is a demand for money almost immediately—and a threat to post the material online or to alert the police if the demand isn't met. The teenager experiences extreme fear, shame, anxiety, and helplessness. Men, women, and children can be victims of sextortion. A 2022 study reported survivors' experience with sextortion, including contemplation or commission of suicide.[16]

Revenge porn is a form of sextortion in which sexually explicit or nude photos or videos are posted online without consent. A prior or current partner is often the perpetrator, but it may be a coworker or even a family member who happened to get access to private photos. Revenge porn may be in the form of blackmail, whereby there is a threat to distribute sexual images.

Of course, revenge porn, like sextortion, often results in horrific consequences for the victim. It may cause long-term psychological pain, including depression, anxiety, and suicidal ideation and attempts.[17]

There is no federal law against revenge porn; however, it is illegal in all states to share sexual photos or videos with anyone under the age of eighteen.

Revenge porn is another very good reason to refrain from sending anyone explicit photos or videos from a smartphone or computer. Parents play an essential role in helping their teens understand the hazards of doing so. No judgment—just open-minded and open-hearted communication.

Sextortion and revenge porn are "image-based" forms of sexual abuse. Another form that has emerged but is not yet on the radar of many parents is "deepfake video."

In Levittown, New York, a teenage boy cloned the images of a dozen teen girls into pornographic videos, which he distributed on the internet to humiliate and harass them. Their lives have been a nightmare ever since.

Once anything is embedded on the internet, it is virtually impossible to ever remove it completely. So these women face a lifetime of continually being demeaned and undermined in anything they attempt to do—from admission to college to finding their dream careers to dating and marriage. Their reputations have been ruined. Every victim has been seriously traumatized. Some have dropped out of school.

Deepfake videos and images have been around for years, with celebrities most often targeted. There are many examples in which a simple internet search for a popular female star eventually results in a hardcore pornographic image or video that looks all too real. It's made worse by the fact that a few big stars, like Kim Kardashian and Pamela Anderson, have had their real pornographic videos in wide distribution on the internet.

Soon, knowing what is real and what isn't will be impossible.

Deepfake videos are a growing problem, potentially reaching disastrous levels. With advances in artificial intelligence, they are easier to create and more realistic than ever. Now, anyone who has ever posted a photo or video of themselves—or their children—online is vulnerable to becoming a target.

Most people would be shocked to learn that there have already been hundreds of thousands of deepfake pornographic images generated.[18] Not only have teen girls been victimized, but boys as well; in some cases, their parents are also targets. Criminals have demanded ransoms under threat of distributing deepfake videos of their child to their friends, classmates, teachers, relatives, and more widely on the internet. Deepfake videos of parents themselves have been created to shame them in front of their children, friends, and coworkers.

Deepfake cloning extends to voices as well. Your teen's voice can be duplicated so accurately using deepfake technology that it's impossible to tell that it isn't real. Imagine receiving a phone call from someone who sounds exactly like your teen, pleading for emergency help. This has become a common scam to extort frantic parents. Using this technique, one twenty-three-year-old man swindled grandparents in Newfoundland out of $200,000.

Teens may think they are communicating with a friend or relative when, in actuality, it is a fraudster. Many teens have been victims of online romance fraud, with reported financial losses of more than $1.3 billion in 2022. Worse, some teens have been sexually assaulted or kidnapped after being lured to meet predators. Deepfake and AI technology have added a new dimension to these crimes.

So what do you do to protect your teen (and yourself) from deepfake videos, images, and voice cloning? Regrettably, identifying deepfakes is difficult and will only become more so in the future. But there are some things you and your teen can do to potentially spot them. Parents who are tech-savvy can use tools, such as InVID (https://invid tech.com/) or Forensically (https://29a.ch/photo-forensics/#level-sweep), which detect deepfakes by revealing inconsistencies or anomalies in the image, such as mismatched lighting, blurred edges, unnatural expressions, voice and lip delays, and distortions.

As with sexting, parents should engage in serious conversations with their teens to alert them to the potential life-changing nature of deepfakes. Check your teen's devices for risky apps and inappropriate content. With still-developing critical thinking abilities, teens frequently make poor choices that adults would likely never make. Make sure they delete anything that could potentially be dangerous.

If your teen uses apps such as Photoshop, Canva, Illustrator, or other content creation platforms, have them show you what they are creating that could be used against them with deepfake apps such as Reface or Zao, where their images can be misappropriated. If they use messaging apps that enable anonymous posts and messages, let them know these can be used to bully or blackmail them.

Parents will hopefully maintain honest, authentic, nonjudgmental, and open communication with their teens about these matters.

## SEXUAL ABUSE

In the United States, fully 87 percent of young women between the ages of one and twenty-four have experienced sexual harassment.[19] About one-fourth of teenage girls have been sexually abused; one in twelve have experienced rape or attempted rape. The figures for boys are lower but still very disturbing. The impact on adolescents is generally profound. Sexual violence during the teenage years is associated with poor academic performance, substance abuse, interpersonal problems, and sexual risk-taking behavior.[20] Teens who have suffered sexual assault are at risk for depression, anxiety, post-traumatic stress disorder (PTSD), anger management problems, low self-esteem, eating disorders, suicidal ideation, and suicide. For some affected individuals, mental health issues significantly improved after one or two years, but others suffer lifelong emotional consequences.

Sexual abuse may be intrafamilial—that is, perpetrated by relatives, foster care providers, or the partner of a parent. Sadly, almost half of child sexual abuse reported to police is committed by someone considered to be family by the victim. Family members may be the ones providing inappropriate sexual material, participating in sexting, inappropriately touching children—or worse. Child sexual abuse often starts at very young ages but may be initiated during the preteen and teenage years. It commonly remains unidentified, since children may fear for their own safety and even of getting the abuser in trouble. They may believe it was their fault. They may have disabilities and have difficulty reporting the abuse. Parents should be aware of signs of sexual abuse, including new or unusual fears, which sometimes involve physical contact or being alone or in a particular place, difficulty concentrating and performing in school, and changes in eating, sleeping, and hygiene habits. Parental support and psychotherapy are of paramount importance.

What can parents of teens victimized by sexual assault do? Making sure their child is safe and not in immediate danger is paramount. The police and/or child welfare services need to be involved. In California, health care professionals, teachers, and many other types of professionals who become aware of the sexual abuse of minors are mandated by law to report the abuse to child welfare services or law enforcement. If the assault is uncovered weeks, months, or even years later, suicide risk needs to be assessed, ideally by a professional therapist. A variety of hotline services are available across the United States. Once safety is confirmed, the best thing parents can do is *listen*. Ask open-ended questions. Reassure your child that what happened is not their fault. Again, nonjudgment is key—there is no blame, even if alcohol or other drugs are involved. Involve your teen in deciding what to do next—professional help can be lifesaving.

Parents may need to support *themselves*. Parents tend to blame themselves and may feel angry or ashamed. These are natural responses. Looking after our own mental health is essential; we cannot help our teens when we ourselves are in distress.

As with other instances of significant stress, a mindful meditation practice such as GAIN may be invaluable when dealing with the stress of caring for teens victimized by sexual abuse.

Detailed discussion of sexual abuse and how to deal with this tragic issue is beyond the scope of this book. Parents and teachers are encouraged to refer to the great variety of references online. There are many resources available at any time for urgent circumstances. Examples include the National Sexual Assault Hotline (800-656-4673), the National Sexual Violence Resource Center (https://www.nsvrc.org/), and the National Organization for Victim Advocacy (https://trynova.org/resources/), among many others.

## Bottom Line

- It is imperative that parents are aware of the risks of teen pregnancy, STDs, pornography, sexting, and other forms of sexual abuse.
- Parents are well served by accepting that these hazards are a part of their teens' lives—they are here to stay.
- It is also essential to have a plan to discuss all these issues with our teens in an open, nonjudgmental way.
- Parents have access to a wide variety of resources with respect to information as well as interventions and therapy when appropriate.

### THREE

# DEALING WITH AN EVOLVING WORLD

## *New Anxieties*

Although our evolving world has always been in turmoil, never before have world events created more challenges for teens.

Teens today are exposed to much more of what is happening in the world than ever before. Only a few generations ago, the news came primarily from three television networks and a handful of newspapers and magazines. Today teens are bombarded with news and information from a multitude of sources, including online platforms like TikTok, Instagram, Facebook, and LinkedIn. Online news and commentary sites, cable channels, podcasts, and media "influencers" create an enormous volume of news and entertainment posts. Teens are targeted by emails and texts with solicitations to participate in or donate to causes ranging from childhood cancer to saving the planet.

Where it was once easy to avoid much of the chaos in the world, today it is almost impossible. Teens are more connected to the media than at any time in history. They see media coverage of wars, earthquakes, floods, wildfires, terrorist attacks, horrific acts of violence, accidents, school shootings, and sex crimes. They are aware of stock market crashes and recessions. Teens face cultural changes that impact them directly, including gender identification and extreme ideological viewpoints. They see divisive politics creating tensions among their family and friends. So much media input can be overwhelming and confusing. It's difficult for mature adults to manage their emotions when exposed to these events. For teens who are just a few short years from being carefree children, it can be difficult to process.

The messages pushed to our teens often trigger emotional reactions. At best, they are a distraction; at worst, they can adversely change the way teens think and behave. Constant exposure to anxiety-provoking world events can put teens at risk for feeling overwhelmed, hopeless, and even depressed.

Stressors—including the COVID-19 pandemic, climate change, natural disasters, the great political divide, cyberbullying, and horrific suffering due to wars around the globe—can make teens understandably very anxious about their future.

## THE PANDEMIC CHANGED EVERYTHING FOR TEENS

The worldwide COVID-19 pandemic, which began in early 2020, severely altered the normal path of adolescent development. Many teens today experienced serious adverse effects of the pandemic, even if they never contracted the infection itself. And as with adults, many teens who were infected are still afflicted with long-term COVID-19.

The COVID-19 pandemic claimed the lives of more than one million Americans and significantly impacted teen mental health. More than eighteen months of lockdowns, school closures with remote learning, and social distancing came at a time of critical emotional development for adolescents. During the pandemic, teens primarily communicated with their friends and teachers using online platforms like Zoom or on their smartphones with FaceTime. At a critical stage of teen development—when socializing with others is learned—they were isolated in their family homes. However, some teens experienced positive aspects of remaining at home—those with stable family dynamics, positive role models in the home, and the ability to learn remotely may have thrived and strengthened family bonds. For others, however, the downside predominated.

COVID-19 was the lead news story nearly every day during the first two years of the pandemic. And because teens were restricted in their movements, they naturally spent much of their time on their various digital devices. Teens could not avoid the dire news about the ongoing pandemic. Many wondered, as did their parents, if the virus would ever go away.

The immediate adverse effects of the COVID-19 pandemic on teens included a myriad of issues.[1]

- Sleep disruption—absent the schedule imposed by attending school in person, normal day-night rhythms became blurred for teens and their parents; insomnia and poor-quality sleep were common and remain so even today.
- Decreased motivation—it is understandable that many teens, especially those with attention deficit disorder or attention deficit hyperactivity disorder (ADHD), found it impossible to concentrate on coursework at home amid uncertainty, lack of structure, and hours spent in front of a computer screen.
- Increased anxiety—teenagers with some baseline social anxiety suffered by remaining at home in their comfort zones without the opportunity to practice their social skills, making it even more difficult to deal with social situations. Anxiety, depression, and other emotional and psychological challenges were exacerbated by a lack of contact with role models, including teachers, counselors, and coaches.
- All the hazards of social media were amplified by increased screen time and lack of connections with the physical world (see chapter 1); more than 80 percent of teens became addicted to their screens during the pandemic.[2]

Problems that may not have received a lot of attention during the pandemic include body image and eating disorders. So much time spent on Zoom for school meant that teens were looking at themselves on their screens much of the time, even when they were supposed to be watching their teachers. Students became aware that others were looking at them as well, and they wanted to look perfect. Body image obsession can lead to eating disorders, as can other conditions associated with the pandemic, including constant access to food while at home and disordered sleeping, which can cause an imbalance of hormones that regulate appetite.

"I get daily phone calls from teachers, parents, and doctors concerning cases of bulimia and anorexia, and treatment programs are flooded," reported Dr. Shelly Ben Harush Negari, director of the Center for Adolescent Medicine at Shaare Zedek Medical Center in

Jerusalem.[3] "We see it at an earlier age, and more requests for treatment, perhaps because parents are home more and see what their kids are eating."

For many teens, struggles that began during the COVID-19 pandemic persist.

As of 2024, between 10 and 30 percent of Americans who contracted COVID-19 have experienced a variety of ongoing health issues lasting more than three months. This has been termed "long COVID." Its prevalence is difficult to confirm since many of the symptoms—including bouts of fatigue, "brain fog," joint pain, headaches, vertigo, muscle aches, insomnia or unrefreshing sleep, increased anxiety, and depression—are common among the general population. Although children and teenagers were less likely than adults to contract COVID-19 or experience severe symptoms, many were affected by the disease, with both physical and mental health issues. A meta-analysis of published studies reported that the prevalence of long COVID was 25 percent, with the most common complaints including mood symptoms (16 percent), fatigue (10 percent), and sleep disorders (8.4 percent).[4] This report and others may overestimate the true prevalence of long-term COVID-19—a more realistic figure may be closer to 10 percent. Nevertheless, long COVID is an important and impactful disorder among today's teens.

Countless teens lost a parent or other primary caretaker during the peak of the pandemic.

Young people suffered serious impacts on their education and social development. One study examined the repercussions of school closures and the shift to online remote learning, revealing significant setbacks in academic performance.[5]

Long-term impacts on the development of social skills and cognitive abilities were also identified and are being studied.

In summary, teens were the victims of a worldwide viral pandemic, the likes of which haven't been experienced in more than a century. Many will be affected for the remainder of their lives. Parents, teachers, and caregivers need to watch for signs of cognitive or physical changes in their teens that may be a result of ongoing COVID-related issues.

## GUN VIOLENCE

America's troubled love affair with guns has contributed to an environment that enables gun violence, which has left a profound and often deadly mark on the lives of adolescents, impacting their safety, mental health, and social environments.

In 2023, more than forty-eight thousand people died from gun-related injuries in the United States. Of these deaths, approximately twenty thousand were homicides, about twenty-six thousand were suicides, and the remainder were accidents.

Japan reported fewer than ten gun-related deaths in 2023. Fewer than one hundred people died of gun-related incidents in the United Kingdom. The gun death rate in Canada is one-fifth what it is in the United States. In our hemisphere, only some Central and South American and Caribbean countries have a higher rate of gun violence.

In recent years the number of mass shootings, including many at schools, has increased dramatically. Active shooter incidents in the United States tripled between 2016 and 2021. Gun interest groups and conservative politicians have thwarted efforts to enact stricter gun control laws. States with some gun control, like California, have fewer gun deaths per capita than states such as Mississippi and Texas, where gun control is minimal.[6]

Teens are also exposed to countless episodes of violent gun deaths in movies, TV, and video games. By the age of eighteen, according to Pew Research, it's estimated that the average American child will have witnessed around sixteen thousand simulated murders and two hundred thousand acts of violence on television alone.[7] Video games popular with teens often depict violence. Most of these violent acts involve the use of some form of firearm.

Exposure to gun violence in video games is a significant contributor to its normalization among teens. Some mental health professionals believe that by the time American youths reach their teenage years, they have become desensitized to gun violence. This may be particularly true in inner city areas with large populations of disadvantaged people or in states with a strong gun culture. A recent longitudinal study evaluated predictors of gun use by ethnically diverse young adults related to their exposure to violence, including violent video games.[8] The investigators found that a *greater* exposure to weapons violence between ages seven and eighteen predicts *greater* risk eight to ten years later for (1) carrying, using, or threatening to use a gun and/or other weapons, (2) being arrested for a weapons crime, and (3) believing that using a gun is acceptable in many situations. The media and video games played a role. Youths, especially those in the youngest cohort who played more violent video games more frequently as a child, showed a greater propensity as young adults to carry a gun, to use a gun, or threaten to use a gun on someone, and to believe that using a gun is acceptable in many situations. Violence, in any form, begets violence.

Americans are divided about laws controlling the use of guns. This isn't likely to change soon, despite the horrific school shootings at Sandy Hook (twenty-seven dead), Uvalde (twenty-one dead), Parkland High School (seventeen dead), and the mass shooting at a Las Vegas music concert in 2017 (fifty-eight dead and more than five hundred injured). The possibility of being killed by a gun is a very real concern for teenagers.

Teens are not only at risk of being killed or injured by gun violence, but this aspect of American culture also impacts them in several other ways, according to mental health professionals and educators.

- Exposure to gun violence, either directly or indirectly, including video games and the media, has likely exacerbated increased rates of anxiety, depression, post-traumatic stress disorder (PTSD), and other mental health issues among teenagers.
- The threat of gun violence contributes to an underlying sense of insecurity and fear when attending social or recreational events and school and when moving about their community. Due to the ever-present fear of violence, parents now frequently advise their teens to be aware of their surroundings, to look for a safe exit at large gatherings, and to stay in contact by cell phone.
- In 2023, there were more than three hundred active shooter incidents and warnings at K–12 schools in the United States. This record-high number has prompted most schools to implement

strict safety measures, including active shooter drills, enhanced security protocols, and designated escape routes and shelter-in-place locations.

- According to the Gun Violence Archive, there were 648 mass shootings (four or more people killed) in the United States in 2022.[9] This shocking number has remained consistent for the past few years. For American teenagers, the news about a mass shooting is now nearly an everyday occurrence that has contributed to their anxiety and fear for their own safety.

In communities where real-life gun violence is common, adolescents may develop PTSD, trauma, anxiety, depression, hypervigilance, and increased aggressive behavior. The constant threat of being a victim of gun violence can cause teens to be constantly on edge and fearful, which can also interfere with their ability to focus, learn at school, and participate in normal social activities.

Expert opinions from psychologists and law enforcement personnel, as well as data regarding gun violence, advise parents, educators, and other caregivers to monitor and, when possible, limit their children's exposure to violent media content.

It's important for parents and their teens to have open discussions about the differences between fictional and real-life gun violence and its consequences. In movies and video games, a character may be shot, punched in the face repeatedly, kicked in the stomach, and thrown violently onto the ground and then get back up with hardly a scratch. In real life, just one punch in the face would land most people in the emergency room.

One highly respected and credible source regarding the effects of violent media on adolescents is Common Sense Media, a nonprofit organization that provides a range of educational resources and advocacy to families in support of safe media and technology use for children and young people.[10]

Common Sense Media offers extensive reviews and age-appropriate ratings for films, video games, books, TV shows, apps, podcasts, and websites to help parents make smart, informed decisions about the content their children consume. Reviews evaluate content for educational value, violence, sex, language, consumerism, and positive messaging.

Common Sense Media offers practical advice and tips on how to help children evaluate and manage healthy media consumption. The organization also publishes guides and reports for parents, educators, and government policymakers. Its advocacy work helps legislators develop regulations and other safeguards that protect privacy online and mitigate the impact of digital advertising targeted at young people.

It's important to acknowledge that the impact of violence in media on teen behavior is a complex and nuanced issue. Every teen is different and will relate differently to the media they consume. Other factors certainly play important roles in teen behavior, including the stability of the family, personal mental health, environment, culture, and emotional intelligence.

## THE GREAT POLITICAL DIVIDE

The current divide in American politics is nothing new. Ironically, Americans have been divided since our country's founding. Few people realize that the Revolutionary War was not only a war with Britain but also a civil war. The number of Americans who identified as Loyalists represented about 20 percent of the population. Many of the Loyalists fought alongside the British.

There have always been diametrically opposing viewpoints, with each side attempting to impose its ideas on the rest of the nation.

The emergence of a two-party system was the natural outcome of this divide. Most of the time, the two sides compromise.

But not always.

The Civil War, which is estimated to have claimed the lives of around 750,000 people (about 2.5 percent of the population at the time), was the period of greatest political instability in American history. The war shaped the trajectory of America to this day. Many of the same opposing viewpoints comprise the frequently rancorous political discord that is evident now.

When adults are counseling teens to learn to cooperate, to be kind and compassionate, and to empathize with others who are different, they often see adult politicians and pundits behaving in the opposite manner—lashing out at political opponents, lying, spreading misinformation, and grasping for power.

Children and adolescents model the attitudes and behaviors of the adults around them. This behavior is not only confusing to them, but it also sends mixed messages about what is appropriate and what is not.

Parents rely upon gaining the respect of their teens so that they may guide them mindfully and set a solid foundation for their future success. Parents can help teach their teens that no matter what one's political feelings are, it is important to treat those with opposing views with respect.

The GAIN principles can be a guide:

- Let's be grateful that we have a (generally) functional political system. Looking at other countries around the world helps us appreciate the way things are here in the United States, even during turbulent political election cycles.
- We benefit from accepting others even when we disagree or when they behave poorly. Sadly, violence seems to be embedded in human nature, and there are always examples elsewhere in the world and even here at home. We cannot change how others act—we will find greater peace through acceptance.
- We can exercise our intention to be present, nonviolent, compassionate, and patient with ourselves and others.
- We can rewire our brains to be nonjudgmental, or at least less judgmental. We can learn to be more forgiving and understanding in a neutral manner with respect to others, the world, and, eventually, even ourselves.

It is helpful to examine our own behavior periodically. Have we been respectful in discussing or arguing with those embracing political ideals with which we disagree? Are we setting an example for teens that we can be proud of as parents? Rather than forcing our political views on our teens, are we encouraging them to examine the issues, search for the truth, and think for themselves?

Are we being mindful?

## CLIMATE CHANGE AND ECO-ANXIETY

Few issues are more critical than climate change and the environment, which point to existential threats to our planet. We are all aware of the dangers and potentially catastrophic consequences of a progressively warming planet. Teens are paying close attention and rightfully wonder whether the planet will be habitable for their children and grandchildren.

Scientists have reached a consensus on the drivers of climate change. Thousands of scientific studies show that it is caused primarily by burning fossil fuels, deforestation, and pollution.

Key indicators of the present status of climate degradation include:

- Increased carbon dioxide levels—The $CO_2$ levels in the atmosphere have increased from 280 parts per million prior to the beginning of the Industrial Revolution around 1760 to 420 parts per million today. This is the highest level of $CO_2$ in the atmosphere in at least six hundred thousand to eight hundred thousand years.[11] Carbon dioxide emissions have increased by more than 60 percent since 1990, setting a record of about thirty-six billion tons in 2021.[12] Higher $CO_2$ levels have been linked to the rise in global temperatures. Since oceans absorb about 30 percent of $CO_2$ emissions in the atmosphere, they have become more acidic, causing serious harm to marine life and coral reefs.
- Increasing global temperatures—2023 saw record global temperatures nearly every month, making it the hottest year on record since humans began taking reliable measurements. The temperature increases worldwide compared to historic levels neared 1.5 degrees Celsius, an important statistic, because the Paris Climate Agreement set this figure as its long-term limit before a potentially catastrophic climate change would occur.[13]
- Rising sea levels—Globally, sea levels have risen steadily since 1900, primarily caused by warming seawater and melting ice. During the past 125 years, sea levels have risen 20 centimeters (nearly 8 inches). If the trend continues unabated, it will have catastrophic effects on the earth, especially coastal and low-lying areas.

- Extreme weather—In recent decades, the frequency and intensity of extreme weather events—wildfires, hurricanes, heat waves, and floods—have increased. The United States has experienced millions of acres of wildfires in the past few years. Devastating wildfires also ravaged Australia, Canada, Spain, Greece, Chile, Portugal, Italy, Russia, Turkey, and Brazil. Record-breaking heat-baked hot spots in the United States in 2021 and 2024 experienced temperatures exceeding 49 degrees Celsius (120 degrees Fahrenheit). Europe suffered some of its hottest months on record. The intensity and frequency of hurricanes have increased in recent years due to warming oceans. The 2020 Atlantic hurricane season was the most active on record. The 2022 monsoon in Pakistan led to unprecedented flooding, submerging a third of the country underwater, causing seventeen hundred deaths and impacting thirty-three million people. The temperature above the Arctic Circle reached 100 degrees Fahrenheit for the first time in recorded history in 2020.[14]
- Pollution—First, the good news. The Clean Air Act, initially enacted in 1963, has resulted in significant progress in reducing harmful pollutants in the air. Major air pollutants have decreased by as much as 88 percent.[15] Progress has been made cleaning up lakes and rivers. The government is tackling the cleanup of more than thirteen hundred toxic waste sites. The Environmental Protection Agency is working on regulations to address water pollution from agricultural runoff and industrial wastewater. Work is underway to reduce chemical contamination in drinking water, such as PFAS (per- and polyfluoroalkyl substances) and microplastics. But although the United States has made significant progress in mitigating pollution, it is still a problem, especially worldwide. Globally, most of the 368 million metric tons of plastic produced ends up in landfills, lakes, rivers, and oceans. It's estimated that the average American ingests microplastic particles equivalent to a credit card every week. In the Pacific Ocean, plastic debris has accumulated in a large patch estimated to cover an area of approximately 620,000 square miles in size, about twice the size of Texas.

Most teens in America have experienced one or more extreme weather conditions in recent years. Teens know climate change is happening. They are also aware of adverse changes in the ecosystem—they hear adults talking about rising sea levels. They see Instagram, TikTok posts, and YouTube videos pointing out all the toxic ingredients in the food they eat. They don't know if their water is safe to drink. And they wonder how these things will affect them personally.

Unfortunately, the actions taken by governments and activist organizations around the world appear to be largely ineffective in slowing or reversing the causes of climate change. Many teens are very worried about the future of the planet—frequent news reports on climate change and environmental destruction are dramatic enough to heighten their anxiety.

Fifty years ago, none of these concerns weighed on the minds of teenagers.

Teenagers can get involved in mitigating climate change and protecting the planet from further degradation. Encouraging teenagers to do so may help them develop a sense of purpose regarding the environment. For example, teens can help reduce waste and unnecessary consumption. Teens can choose reusable rather than single-use plastic and paper products, recycle and reuse materials, and compost organic waste. Most communities sponsor volunteer cleanup events. In many communities, groups of people, including many teens, devote a weekend day to cleaning up discarded waste and trash washed up from the ocean; this may contribute to community service requirements imposed by many high schools. Teens can be reminded to be mindful when buying products, choosing items with minimal packaging, purchasing secondhand instead of new, and supporting brands that practice sustainable manufacturing.

Teens can help raise eco-awareness. Teenagers play a critical role in helping protect and repair the planet. Many teens have a natural desire to make a difference. Teenagers are talented at organizing events, with perhaps a little support from adults. They can organize recycling drives and cleanup events at parks or beaches, participate in tree planting, support wildlife conservation projects to protect endangered species, and help with the restoration of habitats. Organizations like One Tree Planted and Arbor Day Foundation offer teens a chance to get involved and see the results of their efforts by planting hundreds of thousands of trees. Teens can advocate for stronger environmental policies with government officials, write to publications expressing their desire for "green" laws, and raise awareness of environmental issues on social media, at school, and in peer groups. Some teens have started podcasts or created YouTube videos to discuss ecological issues.

International organizations like Fridays for Future (https://fridaysforfuture.org/) provide teens with an activist forum for protesting the lack of action by governments to address the climate crisis. This organization was formed in 2018 after a group of young activists led by fifteen-year-old Greta Thunberg sat in front of the Swedish parliament for three weeks to protest the lack of action to address climate change. Thunberg's posts on Instagram and Twitter quickly went viral. Teens also can make an impact on the planet by supporting local farmers, choosing organic produce, reducing food waste, and trying to reduce their energy usage. Awareness of environmental dangers and taking steps to support eco-friendly practices are signs that your teen is being mindful.

Intention and involvement are key aspects of mindfulness. Sometimes teens feel overwhelmed by thoughts of global warming and other disturbing realities and retreat into their smartphones or video games. But when they see forests growing in part because of their actions, they generate less waste. When they feel their government representatives have heard them, their self-confidence and self-worth increase. Intentions and involvement create skills, reduce fears, and demonstrate what is possible, all of which benefit teens greatly.

The Latin phrase "carpe diem" (seize the day), coined by the Roman poet Horace, has been interpreted over the years to mean being present and taking action to get the most out of life, to make things happen. When parents, teachers, coaches, and others who influence teens during these important formative years encourage and support teenagers to seize the day, it can create positive repercussions that last a lifetime.

## DRUGS, ALCOHOL, AND SMOKING

By their senior year in high school, about one in three teens report having an alcoholic drink in the past month.[16] Worse, binge drinking (five or more consecutive drinks) was reported by nearly one in six twelfth graders in 2023. Though overall alcohol use by teens has declined during the past decade, it remains a significant problem. The reported statistics of teenagers dying due to alcohol-related causes don't represent a high percentage of teens, but if you are the loved one of the thirty-five hundred teens who died because of excessive drinking, the pain lives with you for a lifetime.

These depressing statistics don't include teenage drivers who drink and drive. The National Highway Traffic and Safety Administration reported that in 2020, 2,738 people died due to accidents involving a teenage driver.[17] Thousands more were injured. And the cost of these accidents is in the billions of dollars. Drinking and driving can follow a teen for the remainder of their life.

Background checks are easier to do and more thorough than ever before, and the impact of a single DUI can be profound. A tech executive in Silicon Valley was arrested for driving while under the influence of alcohol twenty years ago after a party, a one-off incident for him. He was only a light social drinker. But the DUI he was issued has been on his record ever since, despite his efforts to have it expunged. Although it hasn't impeded his success in business, it is something he always must explain during interviews with prospective new employers.

Teens are famously oblivious to the future consequences of their actions, but a solid grounding in mindfulness supports emotional intelligence, which in turn provides teens with the critical thinking needed to make smart decisions about alcohol and drugs.

To teens who first begin to experiment with alcohol and drugs, it's a sign of maturity, of feeling "adult." This is nothing new. But the potential consequences for today's teens can be much more serious than for previous generations. Drugs are perhaps even easier for teens to acquire than alcohol—and they are far more dangerous.

Of the many drugs now easily available to teenagers, marijuana is by far the most commonplace. Nearly every high school and college student knows someone who can sell them pot. The National Institute on Drug Abuse reported in 2023 that slightly more than one in five high school seniors had used marijuana in the past month.[18] For new and young users of marijuana, the effects can most greatly impair their cognitive abilities, judgment, and motor skills. The Centers for Disease Control and Prevention (CDC) estimates that 13 percent of teens involved in fatal crashes tested positive for marijuana. Many teens who drive under the influence of marijuana also have consumed alcoholic beverages, which increases their risk of being in an accident.

Parents who use these drugs themselves may have more difficulty protecting teens from the worst consequences of alcohol and drugs. Their use gives tacit approval to their teens. It's hypocritical to advise teens to stay away from these substances and then go on a binge drinking session—something more than one in four adults engaged in during the past month, according to the CDC. Likewise, the one in eighteen adults who drink every day won't likely convince their teens to abstain.

More than one in ten adults smoked marijuana during the past month. Although marijuana may be a benign and minimally risky drug for adults to use and, in some cases, a therapeutic treatment for pain or anxiety, teenagers are far less able to use the drug responsibly and safely. In addition, pot is now (unpredictably) stronger than ever and may be laced with fentanyl or other very dangerous substances.

The drugs that teenagers are exposed to now are more dangerous than at any time previously. Opioids (drugs such as oxycodone, hydrocodone, and fentanyl) are highly addictive and led to more than eighty thousand overdose deaths in 2023, according to the CDC.[19] Fentanyl is a potent synthetic opioid that is seventy-five to one hundred times more potent than morphine and is linked to many of these deaths. In some cases, teens have been given a pill that they thought was a relatively safe dose of a drug like Ecstasy (MDMA, Molly) but died because it was laced with fentanyl.

In 2023, Julia, a seventeen-year-old girl from Lilburn, Georgia, died after taking what she thought was Percocet, a common prescription opioid-containing painkiller. She purchased it from someone who was aware of the fentanyl content but sold them to her anyway. Julia was found dead by her mother shortly after ingesting the pill.

Christopher, a seventeen-year-old from La Porte, Texas, unknowingly took a fentanyl-laced pill and immediately fell into a coma. He died after a week in the intensive care unit, just one day before his eighteenth birthday.

Sienna, who was also about to celebrate her eighteenth birthday, accidentally took a pill laced with fentanyl and died in Austin, Texas, in 2024, one among hundreds of other unsuspecting teenagers who have died in recent years from fentanyl overdoses.

As any parent knows, the death of a child for any reason is heartbreaking, but especially one from a potentially avoidable cause. Many will be unable to forgive themselves, thinking that they could have done something to prevent the tragedy. The guilt can be crushing.

One of the primary responsibilities of parents is to keep their kids safe. In today's world, that isn't easy. It's crucial to have honest conversations with your teens about the dangers of illegal drugs and for them to be aware of any drugs sold on the street. Besides the dangers to their health, teens need to know that purchasing and using illegal drugs can lead to serious legal consequences. Although possession of a small amount of prescription opioids without a prescription may be a misdemeanor in most jurisdictions, it can result in fines, probation, mandatory drug counseling, and up to one year in jail. Fentanyl is classified as a Schedule II controlled substance. It is illegal to buy, possess, or distribute fentanyl outside legitimate medical channels. Simple possession of fentanyl is a felony punishable by imprisonment ranging from one to several years. Distribution or trafficking of fentanyl can result in lengthy prison sentences of twenty years or more. And if someone dies after purchasing fentanyl illegally, the seller can face manslaughter or murder charges.

Opioids aren't the only drugs that endanger teens. Methamphetamine is a highly addictive stimulant that can cause serious mental and physical health issues. "Meth," as it's commonly known, can cause severe anxiety, paranoia, violent behavior, hallucinations, and brain damage. Long-term users may lose their teeth ("meth mouth") or experience damage to their skin and organs. Smoking meth can lead to serious lung issues, including chronic lung diseases. Meth can cause liver damage, including hepatitis and cirrhosis. Over time, the use of meth accelerates aging—users often look decades older than their actual age.

Two other dangerous drugs, cocaine and heroin, seem to be declining in popularity among teenagers. This good news is tempered by the fact that hundreds are still harmed by them every year. Both drugs are highly addictive. Both drugs kill people. Cocaine is a powerful stimulant that may cause heart problems and neurological damage. Heroin is highly addictive and causes serious effects on physical health. There were approximately fourteen thousand overdose deaths from heroin in 2023.

Other drugs teens are exposed to include benzodiazepines like Xanax and Valium, stimulants such as Adderall or Ritalin (sometimes legally prescribed to teens for ADHD), hallucinogens such as LSD and psilocybin ("magic mushrooms"), and Ecstasy, a popular party drug.

Compared to the risks associated with these other drugs, smoking and its addictive ingredient, nicotine, seem to pose less of an immediate risk. Cigarette smoking has declined significantly every decade since the 1960s due to effective public health campaigns and greater awareness of the health effects, including a greater risk of cancer and heart disease. Still, the CDC estimated in 2023 that approximately one in nine adults smokes cigarettes.

Teens often erroneously believe that vaping, the inhaling of aerosolized chemicals in e-cigarettes, is somehow safer than regular cigarettes. E-cigarettes are frequently marketed to teenagers by flavoring the chemical concoctions. Vaping can cause serious health problems, including serious lung damage, bronchitis, heart disease, heavy metal toxicity, poor oral health, and nicotine poisoning. E-cigarettes containing THC, the psychoactive ingredient in marijuana, have been linked to lung damage in teens. Vaping may also lead to a lifetime of smoking, with serious health effects.

Knowing the dangers of addictive substances is the first step in educating your teen about them. You can provide well-informed advice and support to help them make intelligent decisions when they are inevitably faced with decisions about whether to use illegal drugs.

Open and honest communication is crucial. Maintaining a close and open relationship with parents is one of the most important influences for children, including teens. When parents are supportive and nurturing, teens make better decisions. Starting at an early age helps, even well before children are at significant risk of experimenting with alcohol and drugs. Starting when kids are in elementary school is not too early. It is not uncommon for children as young as twelve to try alcohol and marijuana. About half of children this age have obtained and tried prescription pain relievers for nonmedical purposes.[20] The earlier parents talk to their children about drugs and alcohol, the greater the chances that their behavior will be positively impacted. Having an open dialogue allows parents to establish clear rules regarding what they expect from their kids.

Parents will have to decide exactly how honest they choose to be with their children when it comes to discussing drugs and alcohol. Many parents, of course, experimented with drugs and/or alcohol during their teenage years. Many teens, of course, will ask their parents about their use.

Here are three possible ways parents might respond:

- Be less than truthful and tell their teen that they never used drugs and waited until they were of legal age to drink alcohol.
- Redirect the conversation back to the teen; for example, "We are not talking about what I did at your age; we are talking about what's happening with you."
- Err on the side of authenticity in the relationship and be open about the experience.

Parents should make a decision regarding these very important discussions after carefully considering the teen's maturity level and how they may use the information. Full disclosure may strengthen the bond and trust in the parent-child relationship. According to the Substance Abuse and Mental Health Services Administration, "If you talk to your kids directly and honestly, they are more likely to respect your rules and advice about alcohol and drug use."[21]

On the other hand, in some cases, teens may use this information to justify their substance use; for example, "You said that you were out drinking when you were my age, so what's the big deal?" Deciding how much information to disclose to a teen is a very personal and pivotal decision on the part of parents. There is some data to support that parents discussing their own drug use with their children can be detrimental.[22]

Whatever the parents decide, consistency in the message and establishing boundaries and expectations is vital.

Stress and anxiety contribute to teen use of drugs and alcohol. By embracing, modeling, and teaching them mindfulness practices, such as the GAIN practice, parents can help ameliorate these root causes. This can be a vital component of a multipronged approach to mitigating substance abuse in adolescents.

There are excellent resources available online to help parents decide how to approach this challenging issue.[23]

It's important to set clear expectations and boundaries. Your teen needs to know what your family's stance on drug use is, and parents must set firm, consistent rules regarding substance use, especially illegal drugs. In many cases, your teen will (perhaps secretly) welcome these boundaries; they want to know how they should behave. It is important to emphasize the serious legal and health-related consequences that these substances can cause: addiction, impaired judgment, health issues, and that being registered in the law enforcement and legal system can wreck their lives.

For parents, leading a mindful life and setting a good example is the best way to influence their teens, who will absorb sound values and good judgment by osmosis. Teens are more likely to follow our actions than our words. We can express our gratitude for them and the other riches in our lives, model acceptance of things we don't like but cannot change, demonstrate how having intention and making a plan can result in success, and be more nonjudgmental ourselves—they are watching.

By doing these things you may find that you will not only raise a responsible, loving, compassionate adult, you may become a better person yourself.

## Chapter Three

### *Bottom Line*

- Discuss peer pressure your teen may be experiencing, especially at school.
- Reinforce to your teen the importance of living up to their ideals and values, helping them to build the inner strength that enables them to refuse to participate when pressured by friends to use drugs.
- Be vigilant and aware of the signs of drug use, including changes in behavior, poor academic performance, or a new group of friends.
- Stay active in your teen's life without being overbearing or intrusive—encourage your teen to follow their interests and attend their sports events and show enthusiasm for their participation in extracurricular activities.
- Be present when your teen most needs your support.
- Intervene early if you suspect that your teen is using drugs—don't procrastinate hoping the issue will resolve on its own.
- Seek professional help if necessary.
- Never give up on your teen—they may someday thank you for saving their life!

# PART II

*Parenting Strategies*

FOUR

# THE ROLE OF PARENTS AND PARENTING

No one will argue with the notion that the preteen and teenage years are among the most challenging years of one's life. Adolescents face the challenges of establishing their personal identity while reaching biological and sexual maturity. They are discovering how to have healthy and intimate sexual relationships while establishing a sense of independence and autonomy in society.[1] Meanwhile, they must also handle changing perceptions of their body and status among their peers. They contend with intense social media pressures at a formative time in their development. They are encouraged to become involved in an array of extracurricular activities while they deal with expectations regarding college and career. The time pressures on them are sometimes overwhelming. Teens are expected to manage their mounting stress and regulate their emotions during this period of biological, social, and psychological growth and change.

How can their parents help adolescents cope with all these daunting challenges? Parents have their own fears and anxieties as they watch their teens venture into the world and its hazards. Parents must contend with letting them go and granting them the freedom they need to grow and bond with their peers while keeping them safe. Conflict with their young adult children seems inevitable.

The relationships between parents and their teenagers are of paramount importance. Given the myriad stressors teens face, their development may bump up against some of their parents' concerns, such as a teenager searching for identity and autonomy staying out later than a parent feels comfortable with. Let's see how these challenges may play out through a not-so-imaginary vignette.

Mr. and Mrs. Apple enter the consulting room with their fourteen-year-old son, Mario, begrudgingly trailing behind. They sit on separate couches while Mario sits across the room in the armchair, plopping down with a sigh, arms crossed and gazing down. He would rather not be there.

In a prior meeting, Mario's parents revealed that they are entering therapy because the conflict in their household has become intolerable. Their intimacy has gradually dissolved as Mario has been at the forefront of their marriage since he was born. They are having a difficult time connecting with Mario. Mrs. Apple complains about a palpable feeling of emptiness in their home. Even when they are all physically present, they gravitate toward their respective rooms and activities and keep to themselves.

Mr. Apple has started working longer hours at his job as an investment banker. The increasing hours and commitment to his career earn him more income, and he reassures himself that this benefits the family. Mr. Apple admits that he spends more time at the office to avoid coming home to a stressful household. Mrs. Apple left her career as a nurse even as she was becoming a "rising star" in the department. She gave up the gratification of being recognized for her work and put her career on hold to focus on caring for Mario. She feels that this sacrifice was never acknowledged by Mr. Apple. She is frustrated that despite her efforts to be more present at home, she has observed increasingly poor behavior from Mario. "He never comes home when he is supposed to, and when he is home, he just locks himself in the room playing those stupid video games!"

At school, Mario earns lower grades than he once did. Mr. and Mrs. Apple receive complaints from teachers about the decreasing quality of Mario's work and his disengagement. They learn that he often fails to finish his work; when he does, it seems half-hearted and completed minimally.

Mario rarely spends quality time with his parents. The family cannot easily recall the last time they did anything together. There seems to be nothing to talk about. Mario would rather play video games, though he knows that his parents consider this a waste of time that will not help him get into college. He would rather connect with his friends online while he games. Mario says that his friends understand him and don't pressure him about his grades, and he can relax around them. In short, they "get him."

The Apple family communicates poorly and too infrequently. As we soon see, communication between parents exhibits an air of criticism and contempt. In addition, each parent tends to point the finger at the other for their marital and parenting troubles. They blame each other. According to relationship expert Dr. John Gottman, this style of communicating can predict the failure of a marriage and the failure of this family in staying together.[2]

In a therapy session, Mrs. Apple, looking intensely at Mr. Apple, declared, "If only you would come home from work sooner and pay more attention to what is going on in this family, I know that things would not be this bad."

Mr. Apple is quick to shoot back, "Someone has to keep working and earn money to pay these bills!" His body tenses up as he looks to his therapist for support. "It's been long enough since she has worked; you would think she could get back to it already!"

Their interactions are laden with contempt, criticism, and judgment. Mr. Apple resents Mrs. Apple for not working. She resents him for not helping at home more. Mr. Apple describes the tremendous stress and pressure he feels as the sole breadwinner for the family.

With the presence of contempt, criticism, and defensive responses, the GAIN elements are missing. There has been no expression of gratitude among the family members. They do not acknowledge the good things they all do contribute to the family. They resist rather than accept each other's apparent flaws, and this magnifies their hostility and unhappiness. They make little or no effort to change their circumstances. They judge each other harshly. They are stuck in a negative cycle.

Given the communication styles they utilize, it is no surprise that Mr. and Mrs. Apple have grown apart. The distance between them has contributed to a divide and inconsistencies in their parenting. They point fingers at each other when things go wrong. Each blames the other and assumes they handle things the right way. Mario has become aware of this split—he learned that if he goes to mom, he is likely to get a "yes" on a sleepover; if he goes to dad, he will likely get a "no." Dad says, "Homework first, then play," whereas Mrs. Apple thinks it is important for Mario to have time to decompress when he comes home from school. Mrs. Apple has become more flexible with Mario due to Mr. Apple's absence. She is tired and feels guilty. Mr. Apple has become convinced that her lack of boundaries with Mario causes his poor grades and his feeling entitled to do whatever he wants.

The Apples do their best to keep their interpersonal conflicts from Mario, but they feel shame because they are not very effective at this. After their arguments, they observe Mario acting more distant and reserved. Teens usually know more about what is going on than adults realize. They are keen observers.

It is stressful and potentially traumatizing for youth to observe conflicts between their caregivers. Dr. John Gottman and his coauthors write, "It hardly matters whether a couple is married, separated, or divorced; when a mother and father display hostility and contempt for each other, their children suffer."[3] This is critically important and reinforces Gottman's notion that contempt must be eliminated from relationships.

Criticism, contempt, defensiveness, and stonewalling represent Gottman's "Four Horsemen of the Apocalypse."[4] The Four Horsemen are unhealthy forms of communication that can predict relationship failure. Criticism is highly problematic in love relationships—it can be very stressful and even traumatizing for children to observe. Contempt is the strongest predictor of relationship failure. Criticism and contempt are made apparent through verbal communications such as "you-ing," blaming, name-calling, and nonverbal communication such as eye-rolling, scoffing, or mimicking. Criticism and contempt are pathways to defensiveness and stonewalling, which damage the relationship and family. As these elements of the Four Horsemen come into play, Mr. and Mrs. Apple become "flooded." Characterized by increased heart rate and a surge of stress hormones during an argument, flooding is an acute stress response. When we are flooded, the emotional side of our brain takes over, suppressing the logical side. Hopes for a productive discussion slip away. We say things we don't mean; we bring up issues from the past; we stop listening; and we repeat ourselves. This happens at times to nearly all of us when the Four Horsemen ride in.

The good news is that the right kind of therapy can help create change in this family's dynamics (see table 4.1). Just as we, as individuals, can rewire our brains through *intention* thanks to our

**Table 4.1.** The Antidote to the "Four Horsemen"

| HORSEMAN | DESCRIPTION | ANTIDOTE | DESCRIPTION |
|---|---|---|---|
| Criticism | "You" statements that are blaming in nature or that point the finger at the other. | Soft start-up | Initiating conversation with "I" statements in which neutral, non-blaming descriptions of behaviors are used and positive needs are expressed. |
| Contempt | A more serious form of criticism in which insults and/or name-calling is utilized; one partner feels morally superior to the other. | Short-term strategy: focus on sharing one's own thoughts and feelings; long-term: share fondness and admiration | When communicating with your partner, focus on your own thoughts and feelings and do not make statements about your partner. This may include "putting words in their mouth" or mind reading. Offering one's partner specific statements about what we admire about them and gratitude for them fits in naturally here as well. |
| Defensiveness | The natural response to criticism, defensiveness involves trying to fend off perceived attacks from the partner and can involve counterattacks. | Taking responsibility, even partially, for one's role in a situation. | As partners we must be willing to take ownership for how we contribute to conflicts, since it is likely that we each play some role in what develops in a relationship. By naming our role and taking ownership and apologizing, we can contribute to important repair work after a conflict. |
| Stonewalling | This occurs when someone is physiologically flooded and overwhelmed by emotions and distress. It is the natural outcome of contempt over time. We can operationalize this physiologically by looking at a heart rate somewhere around one hundred beats per minute. | Physiological self-soothing | This is actively engaging in some form of stress management or relaxation exercise. When one or both members of the couple becomes overwhelmed, pause the interaction and make an appointment to resume the conversation at least twenty or thirty minutes later. In the meantime, each is responsible for calming themselves down and preparing to reenter the dialogue with more empathy, understanding, and compassion. |

*Source:* Adapted from John Gottman and Nan Silver, *The Seven Principles for Making Marriage Work: A Practical Guide from the Country's Foremost Relationship Expert* (San Jose, CA: Harmony Press, 2015).

neuroplasticity, the relationships between family members can be guided toward mutual gratitude, tolerance (acceptance), intention to treat each other with loving-kindness, and nonjudgment. The key ingredient is intention—the family must have the desire and motivation to grow and change. Of course, the family and therapist must develop a strong therapeutic relationship that opens trust and provides fertile ground for therapeutic change.

During therapy, the family is redirected from harsh, judgmental expressions of contempt and criticism. The seeds of positivity in the family are introduced by highlighting some of the good qualities that each member brings to the table. They are encouraged to become aware of each other's inherent worthiness and the irreplaceable specialness that each of them provides as a member of the family. In keeping with the Gottman method, "fondness and admiration," the antidotes to contempt, are emphasized. This is an important area of intervention that we learn about later in this chapter.

During family therapy, the couple is seated so that they can make eye contact with each other. As Mr. and Mrs. Apple begin to tell their story, the great difficulties they have faced over the years and their effects on Mario become apparent. Mrs. Apple's father had died several years ago. He was a powerful elder in the family to whom Mario looked up and with whom he shared a bond. Mario began to cry at the memorial service, and his parents did not know what to do to console him. Young and confused, he may not have had the language abilities at the time to verbally express his feelings about this traumatic loss. Since this loss, Mario appeared less happy and less interested in certain activities. Mr. Apple's absence from the home compounded Mario's grief and may have led to Mario developing an anxious and/or avoidant attachment pattern. Anxious attachment may be associated with an increased fear of rejection, abandonment, and withdrawal,[5] whereas avoidant attachment can be linked with mistrust, withdrawal behaviors, and avoidance of deeper intimacy.

What kind of interventions would be most productive for this family? A key area for intervention in psychotherapy is addressing the family members' abilities to regulate their emotions. Emotions are felt and lived in the physical body, the vehicle through which we interact in this world through sensory experience. A key area to attend to in psychotherapy is one's stress response. When we are under physical, emotional, or psychological threat, our bodies mobilize the "fight or flight" or "fight-flight-freeze" response, which results in a surge of adrenaline in our bodies. This may be an adaptive and necessary alarm signal that can save our lives. Like any alarm system, however, it can become dysregulated and either go off unnecessarily or fail to turn off when the threat has passed. Even with someone we love, we may become flooded with adrenaline during a disagreement. Our negativity bias comes into play. Mindfulness and other aspects of the GAIN model can be highly effective in regulating this acute stress response or flooding.

We begin with slow, deep breathing—this activates the relaxation response via the parasympathetic nervous system. Our heart rate slows, and we can feel the adrenaline in our bodies begin to dissipate. We notice the air flowing in through our nose as our chest fills. We pause, then we effortlessly allow the air to leave our bodies. We bring our attention to our gratitude for our loved ones and the joy they have brought us. We are grateful to have them in our lives. We acknowledge the pain we sometimes feel—we suffer from bouts of anger, negativity, and impatience. We recognize that we are not perfect. We transition to our intention, our ability to rewire our brains by taking baby steps in the direction of loving-kindness, letting go of our negativity bias, and returning our attention to the present moment, the only moment we truly ever experience. We feel ourselves letting go of judgments as we picture the Earth as seen from space—it is neither good nor bad. It simply is as it is. Turning our attention toward ourselves, we recognize that we are neither good nor bad. We simply are exactly as we are. As we return our attention to the breath, we feel bathed in peace, in presence. We are then in a much-improved condition to communicate with our partner or child.

This GAIN meditation may take as little as a minute or two. It serves to open our hearts and allows the stress response to dissipate. As our heart rate and breathing rate slow, we can feel the veil that covers our rational thinking fade away. We can then return to the embrace of our loving relationships. The GAIN method is always accessible, just as our breath is. It can be accessed at any time, such as when we recognize our adrenaline surging during a disagreement.

As underscored in table 4.1, the long-term strategy for overcoming contempt and improving family relationships is the expression of fondness and admiration.[6] This represents a philosophical mindset shift toward highlighting qualities in our partners and children that we admire. From the GAIN perspective, this is about offering expressions of gratitude, acceptance, and openheartedness and a nonjudgmental and compassionate stance toward oneself and others. This compassionate stance requires intention and can be developed through the GAIN process as well as compassion-focused meditations in which we recall positive memories and experiences that we have shared with our spouse and children. These memories and fond recollections are to be shared and recounted in family gatherings.

We can learn to view and experience our family life as a safe and sacred space to which all family members can retreat daily from everyday life challenges and stressors. Another way to connect to these positive feelings is through guided imagery. Guided imagery is a simple practice of taking a few moments to sit comfortably and quiet your thoughts through deep breathing. When we feel settled through mind, body, and emotions, we can invite into our awareness a memory of a time when we were having a beautiful moment together as a family. We can focus on this memory using our five senses. We may think of experiences in nature, on vacations, or within the home. What is it like to immerse ourselves in this memory? Can we again experience the feelings that we had in that moment bubble back up? If so, let us allow ourselves the time and space to savor these positive feelings; let them carry us into our next interaction with our partner or child. When we are ready, we can release this practice and notice the difference in how we feel.

Let's consider the parenting styles of Mr. and Mrs. Apple against this background. Mrs. Apple has adopted a permissive style of parenting. Mrs. Apple is not placing enough demands on Mario. Mr. Apple, on the other hand, is withdrawn, uninvolved, and neglectful. He is not present and does not provide appropriate and responsive parenting to Mario. These two styles of parenting have negative consequences for Mario. With respect to a permissive style, Mario may have difficulty regulating his emotions and making good decisions later in development. For example, Mario may be more at risk when it comes to decisions regarding drugs and alcohol. Mr. Apple's uninvolved style may leave Mario susceptible to poor self-confidence and low self-esteem and vulnerable to seeking out an inappropriate proxy figure to replace the neglectful parent.

Healthy parenting, on the other hand, utilizes an authoritative style. Authoritative parents provide clear expectations for their children, who are then held accountable to those standards.[7] These parents provide a rationale for their points of view and their child's perspectives are given respectful consideration. Authoritative parenting is associated with the most positive interpersonal, behavioral, and intrapersonal outcomes. Interpersonally, these children may demonstrate friendliness, cooperation, cheer, and vigor. Intrapersonally, they may experience more self-reliance and self-esteem. Behaviorally, they may be more curious, self-controlled, and achievement driven. More specifically, in a study of socially vulnerable adolescents, youth who reported increased connection to their parents reported less depression, suicidal ideation, non-suicidal self-injury, and conduct problems, and stronger self-esteem and healthier use of free time.[8]

Mario's parents must shift toward a more authoritative style. They must also heal the family's attachment wounding through increased compassionate presence, bonding activities, and healthy communication.

Psychologists recognize the importance of early attachment relationships. Understanding the impact of one's early experiences on current relationships is critical. We do this by completing the necessary psychological and spiritual work to heal developmental trauma and other forms of attachment wounding. It is through a healthy early attachment relationship with our primary caregivers that we feel safe to adventure out into and master our environment.[9] Therefore, it is the formation of healthy attachment to caregivers that enables children to utilize the caregiver as a "secure base." The secure base is the safe and reliable connection to the adult caregiver to whom the child can turn for protection and support when the child feels vulnerable or under threat. The sense of safety and trust provided within the structure of the family nucleus is a wellspring from which healthy development can flow. It is also worth mentioning that establishing a community of support beyond the immediate family is vital as well. Socially vulnerable youth who reported greater connection to their school noted lower depression, suicidal ideation, social anxiety, and sexual activity and greater self-esteem and more productive use of free time.[10] The researchers also stated in their sample of socially vulnerable youth that community connectedness was linked with less social anxiety but more sexual activity, and no relationship was found between peer connectedness and youth adjustment.

Going back to the Apple family, parental conflict and poor communication disrupted the formation of healthy attachments and created an unsafe emotional environment in the home.

The good news is that things can change. Like our individual brains, the family has its own version of plasticity. The Apple family *can* eliminate the Four Horsemen and generate empathy, compassion, and validation as key operating principles in their relationships with each other.

Through therapy and everyday effort at home, the Apple family gradually realized that their relationship with each other played a central role in their ability to live with fears and anxieties. Indeed, supportive family relationships buffer against stress, promote healthy behaviors, and enhance self-esteem and well-being. Members naturally feel safe within the context of supportive family relationships. Therefore, enhancing relationships and building a sense of safety is a critical intervention area.

To create emotional safety in family relationships, family members need to communicate positive feelings and love to each other and show empathy, acceptance, and validation of each other.[11] Empathy is one's ability to see the world through another's eyes and identify what the other is feeling. Compassion is an extension of empathy toward heartfelt action to help the other. Validation means letting our partner or children know that their emotions are meaningful to us, that their experience makes sense to us, and that they are accepted, heard, and understood. This takes not only insight but also practice.

Effective communication skills that encompass empathy and validation are often missing in relationships. This is not due to negative intentions in most cases but rather due to the family's lack of training in communicating in this manner. Things are further complicated by the poor modeling handed down from prior generations, psychological scarring from prior experiences, the immense stress everyone is under, and the emotional triggering that happens in family relationships. These stressors make us vulnerable to empathy and compassion breakdowns.[12] Our brain pathways linked to threat can be rewired when one is engaged in compassion; unfortunately, they are reinforced when in a state of self-criticism. Research has shown that cultivating compassion is related to an increased parasympathetic response, characterized by an increase in heart rate variability, a sign of a healthy, well-functioning heart and nervous system. As discussed in the next chapter, compassion training can be transformative and could be included in the Apple family's therapy.

The Apple family can work in therapy toward developing healthier attachment relationships, compassion, and empathy toward each other. This is a process of recognizing existing patterns that have not worked with each other, and it is an innate human drive to be interconnected and seek secure relationships.

Indeed, we all strive to establish a "secure" attachment. In the book *The Power of Showing Up: How Parental Presence Shapes Who Our Kids Become and How Their Brains Get Wired*, Dr. Siegel and Dr. Bryson suggest that developing secure attachment involves the four S's.[13]

First, caregivers/parents must help kids feel *safe*. This means helping children feel protected and sheltered from harm.

Second, children need to be *seen* by adults. They need to know their parents care about them and pay attention to them.

Third, children need to be *soothed*. This is the experience of being present with our children when they are in a moment of suffering.

Fourth, children need to feel *secure*. Siegel suggests that when the first three elements—safe, seen, and soothed—are in place, the youth develops the awareness that they can trust their parents to predictably help them feel at home in the world and then learn to help themselves feel safe, seen, and soothed.

The key takeaway regarding establishing secure attachment is consistently being present for our children.

To be present for our children, it is critical for parents to do their psychological work to move toward healing and integration of their own past attachment wounding. Examples include psychotherapy, community engagement, self-care, exercise, and meditation. The GAIN practice is one example. As we learn every time we travel on an airplane, we must place the oxygen mask on ourselves first before we can help others.

When one achieves healthy attachment despite adverse life experiences, they have successfully earned secure adult attachment.[14] Secure attachment is embodied by adults who value relationships and demonstrate flexibility and objectivity when speaking about attachment-related issues. These are "coherent narratives" about their life history that describe how they have come to understand their life experiences. These narratives are created during development in school-age children and reinforced in teens. They are the product of having a secure attachment to caregivers.

The journey for Mario and his parents involves healing work for all family members individually and a shared commitment to healing between family members. Part of the healing process for attachment wounding is for each of the individual family members to work on establishing a coherent narrative about their past with the help of a skilled therapist. An attuned therapist effectively mirrors a client's experiences through empathy and validation. The client can then achieve deeper insight into their physical, emotional, and psychological responses. Through insight comes the *A* in GAIN: acceptance. As the therapist demonstrates nonjudgment, the individual may begin to let go of their self-judgment. They can then begin to make objective sense of their experiences. "Reflection, when repeated, also allows the client to savor, revisit, and so further integrate the complex emotional experience."[15] Through a therapeutic alliance with the therapist, the individual practices acceptance of their own experiences and may begin to generate more effective ways of being in relationships with oneself and others. The therapist aids the individual in learning skills to modulate intense emotional reactions that lead to flooding. Learning to notice and regulate the breath and to practice GAIN elements may be invaluable. Acceptance in the context of the family allows for each member to feel safe and seen.

A skilled therapist may assist the client, couple, or family in slowing down their emotional responses to stress so that closer and more intimate contact can be made with emotional experience. Part of this slowing-down process also allows for relationship repairs to be made through effective communication strategies.

Effective communication skills, such as the soft startup, can be effective for the Apple family in overcoming problematic communication styles. The core of this approach is for one family member to name the what and the why of the emotions they are experiencing in a neutral, objective, and nonjudgmental manner. They then specify their recipe to fulfill their needs. The Apples will learn how to summarize what they hear each other say accurately and to meet each other with empathy, validation, and compassion.

The Apple family will work toward establishing a culture change with an improved expression of gratitude, acceptance, positive intentions, and nonjudgment of each other and, ultimately, of themselves. The GAIN elements remedy the family members' miscommunications and destructive emotional responses. These everyday expressions of gratitude and appreciation serve to "rewire" the negativity that has accrued between family members over time. The Gottman method utilizes the motto "small things often"; likewise, the GAIN method is best embraced by practicing for three to five minutes each morning. When simple, positive acts are done consistently over time, they tend to lead toward the bigger changes we seek. This is consistent with the GAIN approach, wherein baby steps are taken daily—we learn in small increments by practicing regularly.

The therapist will work with Mario and each of the parents separately to reinforce their engagement in fun, stress-free, noncompetitive activities to strengthen their bonds. The family will commit to practicing these activities at least weekly, for example, for fifteen minutes or more. It will be essential for the parents to have a strong interpersonal relationship to effect behavioral change for Mario. As they make increased demands on Mario toward positive behaviors, they can leverage their trust and rapport with him as a mechanism for change.

## PARENTAL STRESS: AN ADVISORY FROM THE SURGEON GENERAL

In August 2024, the US surgeon general, Dr. Vivek Murthy, issued an advisory in response to the growing problem of stress among parents.[16] The advisory highlights the contributors to the profound stress that many parents currently experience and how this adversely affects not only their mental health but that of their children. There is a positive feedback loop at play—parental anxiety and stress adversely affect their kids, and childhood/teen challenges create worsening parental anxiety and stress.

The statistics reported are impressive. Almost half of parents say they are so stressed that they cannot function most days—they are completely overwhelmed. This is double the prevalence of severe stress among adults without children. The key drivers for parents' unprecedented levels of stress include:

- rising childcare costs, groceries, and health care
- increasing work hours
- worry about children struggling with anxiety and depression
- worry about their children's safety—being bullied, shot, kidnapped, or abducted or having problems with drugs and alcohol
- increasing pressure and expectations for their children to excel in and outside school

Social isolation and loneliness are on the rise, especially among single parents. Sleep deprivation, time scarcity, and helping children—especially teens—manage amid very challenging times exacerbate parental anxiety and depression.

The surgeon general's advisory makes several recommendations:

- Employers should provide expanded maternal, paternal, medical, and sick leave benefits, and mental well-being checks should be incorporated into primary care.
- Parents and caregivers should prioritize stress relievers like exercise, adequate sleep, and recreational activities.

- Parents should also nurture relationships with other parents, caregivers, or supportive friends, obtain insurance coverage for themselves and their families, and seek mental health care when needed.

"While parents and caregivers bear the primary responsibility for raising children, society as a whole must see itself as sharing in this responsibility—and shaping policy, programs, and individual behavior accordingly," the advisory said.

Mindfulness meditation practice will not solve all these problems, of course. However, mindfulness practices can reduce stress, improve sleep, and enhance communication and bonding with children and teenagers. Deep, slow, deliberate breathing exercises and focus on gratitude, acceptance, intention, and nonjudgment help ease the self-propagating cycle of stress, anxiety, and poor sleep—which leads to more stress and anxiety. Even a simple gratitude practice can help reduce signs of depression. We sincerely hope that the tools provided in this book help initiate and strengthen your ability to succeed in dealing with the multiplicity of stressors facing parents today.

## *Bottom Line*

- The GAIN elements may be applied to individual as well as family therapy to build trust and reinforce positive behavior changes.
- Changes in adult attachment and parenting styles can facilitate significant improvements over time.
- The key principles described in this chapter can be reinforced by a skilled therapist and practiced by each family member individually and together by taking small steps every day.
- Parental self-care is essential to address stress and anxiety—for the benefit of both parents and their teens.

FIVE

# CULTIVATING COMPASSION, FORGIVENESS, AND EMPATHY

Forgiveness is the decision, through *intention*, to let go of resentment-based emotions, thoughts, and behaviors. These negative responses are quite common among teens, who often feel teased, disrespected, and bullied. Forgiveness means that we develop positive regard for the offender. This may be manifest as compassion for the other person. Forgiveness does not equate with forgetting, excusing the harm, or condoning bad behavior. It does not mean that we deny our feelings.

The past will never change, and wishing it was different keeps us stuck there. Remaining chronically angry, vengeful, and hostile causes chronic stress. It interferes with our ability to be happy and adversely affects our sleep as well as our cardiovascular and immune systems. Resentment keeps us mired in the past, controlled by the person, entity, or situation that created our suffering. Using our intention, we can let go of resentment and anger. Letting go of grudges and bitterness builds self-esteem and healthier relationships.

Forgiveness is a path to reduced anxiety, stress, hostility, blood pressure, and symptoms of depression. Letting go of negative emotions promotes longevity.[1]

Let's decide to improve our forgiveness "skills" and those of our teens through simple practice and repetition.

Over the past twenty years or so, there has been increasing interest in the health benefits of forgiveness, as it helps reduce negative thoughts and emotions arising from interpersonal conflict. The well-being that results from forgiveness can reduce health risk behaviors that often originate during the teenage years, including smoking, vaping, and recreational alcohol and drug use. Forgiveness can also lead to improvements in learning and education, which are so vital for success during adolescence and beyond.

Forgiveness and compassion go together. Compassion is generally defined as a recognition of suffering and a desire to help. The Dalai Lama said, "If you want others to be happy, practice compassion. If you want to be happy, practice compassion." Compassion means that we notice the pain of others and then ask ourselves whether there is anything we can do to help. People who volunteer for hospice and work with the dying are compassionate, and people who patiently teach children to read have a similar kind of benevolence. Compassion can be practiced at home when someone you love is struggling, and you listen, observe, and see how you can help.

Dr. Fred Luskin is an expert on forgiveness and compassion. He says that great compassion may emerge during forgiveness training. A mother who had lost a son to violence was struggling with anger and bitterness. When she learned that other mothers in Dr. Luskin's training group had endured similar horrific experiences, deep compassion arose within her, freeing her from her emotional prison. Dr. Luskin has seen divorced people release some of their bitterness as they learned to feel for others experiencing a bad marriage. One of the qualities that makes forgiveness possible is cultivating compassion toward those who are suffering, including ourselves.

In a classic social psychology study, sixty-seven students from the Princeton Theological Seminary were recruited and given personality questionnaires.[2] They were told they would give a brief talk in a nearby room. One group was asked to give a short talk about the types of jobs for seminary graduates, and those in the other group were asked to talk about the Good Samaritan parable. On the way to give their talks, all of the participants would encounter a man lying in a doorway, coughing and doubled over.

The participants were all given one of the following three instructions:

1. "Oh, you're late. They were expecting you a few minutes ago. We'd better get moving."

2. "The assistant is ready for you, so please go right over."
3. "It'll be a few minutes before they're ready for you, but you might as well head on over."

This created three conditions: high, medium, and low "hurry." Here is the breakdown of the percentages of students who offered help:

- Low hurry: 63 percent
- Medium hurry: 45 percent
- High hurry: 10 percent

Of those students who had been asked to discuss the Good Samaritan parable, 53 percent gave aid. Of those asked to talk about careers for seminarians, only 29 percent helped the man in the doorway. These results reveal that subtle circumstantial elements have a significant effect on behavior. When we are in a rush, we are less likely to help others—and ourselves. We are more compassionate when we are not rushing. In addition, our frame of mind affects our ability to be kind and helpful to others.

Research has repeatedly demonstrated the power of mindfulness and compassion training. One study assessed people in a crowded waiting room to see if anyone would give up their seat to someone on crutches.[3] The number of participants who gave up their place was surprisingly low before mindfulness training. After a three-week training course using a mobile app, compassionate responses were assessed by whether participants gave up their seats to allow the uncomfortable person with crutches to sit, thereby relieving their pain. The percentage of compassionate people rose significantly. Research also shows that compassion arises in present-moment awareness, particularly in the presence of others' suffering, without reflexive response or judgment.

In another study utilizing a comparable model, participants were randomly assigned to an eight-week course in one of two nondenominational meditation groups, one of which focused on mindfulness and the other on compassion, or a control group.[4] After the course, individual participants were led to a waiting area containing three chairs, two of which were occupied, and the participant sat in the third. A person wearing a large walking boot, using crutches, and apparently in pain entered the waiting area. Compassion was assessed by whether participants gave up their seats to allow the person on crutches to sit. Those who had received mindfulness or compassion training gave up their seats more frequently than those in the control group. This study suggests that mindfulness and compassion meditation training enhance compassionate behavior; that is, it can be learned. Both forms of meditation enhanced a prosocial response among the participants. In fact, both forms increased the odds of acting to relieve another person's pain fivefold—quite a significant effect!

Several studies have shown that even two weeks of training can cultivate compassion and improve personal well-being.[5] Compassion training increases altruistic behavior by strengthening neural mechanisms that support understanding others' states, greater frontoparietal executive function, and activation of positive emotion systems. This is yet another example of neuroplasticity—we *can* rewire our brains!

When we practice compassion, we experience reduced stress hormone release and more positive social behavior, affect, and empathy. Once again, we see a positive feedback loop at play—kindness improves our physical and psychological health, increasing our capacity to be compassionate. Let's use our power of intention to become more compassionate, including seeking appropriate training.

We can be kind to ourselves or self-compassionate whenever we struggle, fail, or face loss or difficult change. Self-compassion, however, may be very difficult for us to learn. Teachers see how many straight-A students are hard on themselves. Many bright, accomplished teens do not know how to go easy on themselves when they get a B, when they don't get an internship, or when they are rejected in love. Having self-compassion means directing kindness to ourselves and being gentle toward our own suffering. The good news is that we all have the capacity to shift from self-attack to self-kindness when we are taught how to do it.

It is important to recognize and teach our teens that no one is perfect, that everyone has weaknesses, and to stop singling themselves out for condemnation.[6] Many teachers have seen anxious students confess to their peers that they are afraid of failure. They push themselves very hard to achieve. They want to meet the high expectations of their parents, teachers, and peers.

How can teens learn self-compassion? They can practice compassion and gentleness on *themselves*.

Self-compassion is expressed in many religions and philosophies. Buddhism, for example, emphasizes the interconnectedness of all beings—there is no distinction between us and others. If we are compassionate toward others, it follows that we should be compassionate to ourselves. We should treat ourselves with the same kindness, support, and understanding during a painful time that we would manifest with a good friend.

Self-kindness means that we respond to our own imperfections, mistakes, and apparent failures with gentleness, care, and compassion, as opposed to criticism that generates shame and regret. We understand that missteps are a part of life—we are all flawed. We can learn to embrace a balanced awareness of our own pain and suffering. This process involves *acceptance* of ourselves as well as others and *nonjudgment* of ourselves. We can learn to open our hearts and see ourselves exactly as we are, without judgments of good or bad.

One strategy for cultivating self-compassion is to learn to be our own good friend.[7] We can practice speaking to ourselves the way that we would talk to someone we love. We are more likely to be supportive, to put things in perspective, to be less harsh, and to see things as temporary setbacks rather than permanent failures. We can practice kind speech and empathy toward ourselves. For example, teens learning compassion in a group setting might be asked how they would treat a good friend faced with an emotionally challenging situation, such as not being invited to a party at a classmate's home or failing to make the cheerleading team. Small groups of teens in the class are tasked with coming up with how they would approach this friend and what they would say. Then the teens are asked to imagine themselves in the same situation and what they would tell themselves. The larger group then meets to discuss their small group findings. With adults performing the same exercise, nearly 80 percent report treating their friends significantly kindlier than they treat themselves.[8] This exercise teaches teens that it only makes sense to treat themselves as well as they would treat their friends.

As a normal component of growth and development, teens are especially disposed to be highly self-evaluative. In some cases, this leads to self-criticism and low self-esteem. Increased introspection can lead adolescents to feel highly self-conscious, inadequate, and alone in their plight. They may feel as though they are being continually observed and judged, as though they have an imaginary audience. Many adults feel the same way, and these feelings commonly become ingrained during the teenage years. Mindfulness and compassion training in high school may be at least as important as algebra and calculus for most students. Many teens will never utilize their math education as adults, whereas mindfulness and compassion, including self-compassion, are essential to our happiness throughout life.

When someone has hurt us, forgiveness can feel impossible. Of all the religious and moral virtues, forgiveness is the most challenging. Recognizing that everyone suffers and that goodwill is beneficial is one thing. It is quite another to accept the fact that people can do awful things without guilt or remorse and that the innocent can pay the price.

Forgiveness may not happen overnight. Grief is a normal response to loss and difficulty. Grief brings waves of intense emotions, including anger, sadness, denial, regret, and anxiety. It is normal and healthy to be upset when awful things happen. The brain needs to integrate a new reality, and it struggles to adjust. Healthy people grieve their losses and make peace with their vulnerability. By accepting and observing our thoughts and feelings rather than resisting them, our upset can mellow into wisdom, empathy, and peace of mind.

Both compassion and forgiveness reduce conflict and help us navigate a complicated world without becoming bitter, hostile, and isolated. Compassion and forgiveness are innate skills that emerge with practice. Knowing that you have the emotional intelligence required to handle many of life's problems reduces fear and builds confidence.

Empathy is related to compassion—they are both ways of connecting with others. Empathy involves understanding and feeling what another person is experiencing. If a teen's friend is sad, they, too, may feel sadness. Compassion involves identifying and feeling what the friend feels, accepting it, and having the desire to take action to help alleviate it. With both compassion and empathy, there is kindness and support.

Empathy and prosocial thinking and behavior play a key role in social and emotional development in young people. Research demonstrates that these traits are linked to positive emotional and psychological adjustment—increased self-esteem, mental health, and happiness, as well as higher academic achievement and cognitive performance among children and adolescents.[9] Evidence indicates that empathy and prosocial responses lead to more positive interpersonal relationships and less antisocial behavior.[10]

Teens believe that both parents and peers play important roles in shaping their ability to be compassionate and empathetic. They report being influenced by modeling and encouragement from their parents and other family members.

What barriers do teens identify in embracing prosocial thoughts and behavior? Many feel that others may regard compassion and empathy as weaknesses, and they may resist showing empathy to avoid negative judgment; that is, to avoid appearing weak. Boys seem to be more influenced by this notion than girls.[11] The prevailing culture of intense competition in high school and the pressure to excel as individuals promotes self-interest over positive feelings toward others. Some teens feel that lack of guidance limits their ability to forgive and embrace compassion and empathy.

A common misconception is that self-compassion may decrease motivation or interpersonal responsibility—this has been shown not to be the case.[12]

The perception of these impediments to forgiveness, compassion, and empathy underscores the very important role of parents and other family members. Adults can have a big influence on teens' prosocial development. In the process, they can help their teens have more confidence and self-esteem, form better interpersonal relationships, and perform better in school.

Our teens are watching us—and they don't miss much. We can capitalize on this and teach them forgiveness and compassion *by example*.

When we have a vocal disagreement with our spouse that turns nasty, our kids are absorbing this. Parents can teach them a lot by apologizing to one another—in front of their children. We can ask each other for forgiveness—in front of our children. This speaks volumes to them about how to ask for and give forgiveness in relationships. They are much more likely to embody this with their friends and, later, with their spouses and children.

Of equal importance is apologizing to our children when we have lost our patience and raised our voices with them. This can mean a great deal to them, and they may remember such occasions for the rest of their lives. Some of us had such experiences with our own parents in which they spoke to us too severely and even "lost it." If they later apologized and asked our forgiveness, we may have always remembered it.

Can teens learn to be more forgiving and compassionate through programs in and out of school? Are forgiveness "interventions" or "forgiveness therapy" effective in reducing depression and chronic stress while promoting positive emotions? Indeed, there is high-quality evidence that such therapy can be successful.

One method designed to promote empathy, positive emotions, and forgiveness in adolescents is the Hero program.[13] Hero is a self-administered program accessed from the internet. To join the program, adolescents must generate a username and choose an avatar or a virtual identity that represents them within the application. The program is guided by a sensei who accompanies the adolescent throughout the application and presents the activities to be carried out through text and audio instruction, using the student's native language in a neutral accent. The program is structured in five linked modules for promoting empathy (understanding someone else's emotional state), gratitude (being aware of having received some type of personal benefit from someone), positive emotions (emotional experiences in which pleasure or well-being predominate), forgiveness (transforming negative thoughts, emotions, and behaviors toward an offender into positive, prosocial thoughts), and, finally, prosociality (voluntary behavior aimed at helping another person, such as a stranger, friend, or family member). Empathy, gratitude, positive emotions, and forgiveness were chosen to be used in the program because they can be taught and because empirical evidence shows their predictive effects on prosociality.

The program is presented as an adventure that consists of a trip to five islands. The adolescent participates in the different phases in a sequential, predetermined way by visiting the island of empathy, the island of gratitude, the island of positive emotions, the island of forgiveness, and the island of prosocial behavior. The stay on each of the islands coincides with an intervention session, which lasts approximately thirty to forty minutes. After arriving on an island, the adolescent watches one episode of an educational video that deals with the behavior to be stimulated and then performs a series of activities. The videos narrate different conflictive situations in the daily lives of four adolescents (two females and two males). The conflict is resolved in each episode by exercising the socioemotional variable corresponding to the island visited. The videos offer a brief explanation of this variable and conclude with three brief suggestions from sensei with exercises to stimulate it. The two or three activities that the adolescents then carry out are different on each island; some are playful, whereas others are reflective or relaxing.

A study of the use of Hero by more than one thousand participants between the ages of twelve and fifteen years found that the program was effective in promoting prosocial behavior toward strangers, friends, and family members. Females presented higher levels of prosociality toward the three targets (strangers, friends, and family) than males. Adolescents who participated in the program experienced higher levels of serenity, joy, and satisfaction than the adolescents in the control group. The Hero program was effective in promoting attitudes of forgiveness against an aggressor. Girls had fewer negative emotions and more positive emotions toward an aggressor than boys.

Another intervention for developing forgiveness is the REACH model.[14] REACH is an acronym for a five-step forgiveness approach. First, participants *recall* the hurt. Next, they develop *empathy* for the offender. Participants then consider forgiveness as an *altruistic* gift for the offender. Next, they make a *commitment* to forgive. Finally, they *hold* onto forgiveness in times of difficulty. Like other forgiveness interventions, REACH defines forgiveness and emphasizes its potential benefits as well as encouraging the development of empathy for the offender.

Empathy has been used as a synonym for compassion, referring to the ability to understand and share the emotions and feelings of others.[15] Empathy contributes to prosocial behavior, including actions undertaken to benefit others. Empathy and prosocial behavior are important interpersonal skills that may provide the foundation for wider moral principles, such as care, justice, and altruism.[16] These characteristics are linked to enhanced emotional and social development, including improved self-esteem, mental health, and better academic achievement among children and adolescents. Empathy facilitates social development and positive interpersonal relationships, which are vital for teens.

Unfortunately, research suggests that the level of empathy and prosocial behavior among teens seem to be declining.[17] One factor may be the effects of social media. Many teens find it easy to "be mean" and bully others on social media, given the anonymity involved, among other factors. The sheer volume of messages and tweets may lead to desensitization. The role of parents and parenting cannot be overstated (see chapter 4). Teens take many cues from us adults—when we demonstrate forgiveness and compassion and reinforce these behaviors in them, they respond positively. Teens are certainly also influenced by their friends, whom they often emulate.

Practical methods we can learn that help us become happier and more accepting of ourselves include a daily mindfulness practice. This practice may be a short three- to five-minute meditation focusing on self-compassion or the GAIN meditation. Daily practice provides tools for dealing with especially difficult moments that arise intermittently. Examples of these tools include the "How would I treat a good friend" exercise or self-soothing touch (for example, by putting a hand over the heart, perhaps combined with silently saying the phrase, "May I be kind to myself in this moment").

We humans have a *negativity* bias—we tend to remember and embrace our unpleasant thoughts and experiences and forget the positive ones. Accordingly, when we feel that we have been treated unfairly, disrespected, or bullied, we hang on to those memories. We dwell on the past in maladaptive or destructive ways. Although it is adaptive to ponder our past mistakes to the extent that we learn from them and savor past experiences with loved ones, dwelling on the past beyond these thoughts brings shame and regret. We beat ourselves up—we are our own harshest critics and judges. This book's themes include our negativity bias and obsession with the past and future. Happiness is in the present moment, so why don't we spend more time being present?

By focusing on our *gratitude*, the *G* in GAIN, we shift our attention toward the positive and away from the negative. We appreciate the good in our lives, including our spouses, children, other family members, and partners. We recognize the beauty of the light filtering through the treetops, the smell of freshly baked bread, and the warm water cascading over us in the shower. We experience an unlimited number of miracles if our senses are open. Being grateful for the positive elements in our lives paves the way for greater forgiveness, compassion, and empathy.

Certainly, our world is not all joy and wonder. There is pain and suffering within and all around us. Life during the COVID-19 pandemic brought this into focus. Many of us have been ill, lost loved ones, and experienced sorrow due to the global anguish related to the pandemic. To deal with pain and suffering without being constantly sad, we must discern what we can and cannot change. We must accept those elements that we cannot alter. *Acceptance*, the *A* in GAIN, means bringing the pain closer and closer until we merge with it and know we can live with it forever. When we open our hearts to the pain, it lessens.

Jon Kabat-Zinn described mindfulness as bringing our attention or awareness to the present moment on purpose, without judgment. The "on purpose" part means that we use our power of intention. The *I* in GAIN represents *intention*. We acknowledge our negativity bias and our obsession with the past and future. The good news is that our brains can change, even as adults. Our brains have the magic quality of neuroplasticity. We retain neuroplasticity even when we are forty, fifty, sixty, or seventy years old. Using our purposefulness or intention, we can "rewire" our brains. Much more on this later in the book.

The *N* in GAIN is for *nonjudgment*. By the time we are adults, we have become used to making critical assessments of everything in our world. We tend to label things as good or bad, too hot or too cold. We often judge others negatively—and we judge ourselves most critically. This is due in large part to our negativity bias. We feel self-conscious, unworthy, inferior. We notice that others may brag or bully—these actions are generally initiated to cover up feelings of inadequacy or negative self-judgment. These constant judgments use a lot of mental energy—they exhaust us!

To forgive and feel compassion, we can embrace the GAIN method and share this with our teens. First, we can experience our gratitude for the good in our lives—our family and friends, our relative health and wealth (compared to so many other less fortunate people around the world), and the opportunities with which we are blessed. We can open our hearts to the pain and suffering we experience, including being mistreated, cheated, or bullied. These experiences hurt us. The good news, though, is that we can route our intention to the present moment rather than ruminate over the hurt we have felt in the past. We can think of three good things that we experienced today (more on this later). We can learn to see the world exactly as it is instead of making judgments about it as good or bad. We can see others the same way—not as evil or bad, but simply as human beings. These processes are easy to practice.

Of course, it takes time to change the way we think. The best way is to take baby steps but to do so frequently and regularly—daily. We can start our day with a short GAIN meditation, which is discussed in detail later in the book. We can also help our teens incorporate these principles into their daily lives.

## Bottom Line

- Forgiveness and compassion are part of our nature but are often latent. Teens are often especially unforgiving and critical of *themselves*.
- Training in forgiveness and compassion can bring out these intrinsic qualities in all of us. Even short courses in these areas can have a powerful, positive impact on the way we think.

- Mindfulness training with an emphasis on forgiveness and compassion, including self-compassion, may be highly beneficial during adolescence.
- Parents and teachers can help teens be more forgiving and compassionate by embracing these ideals themselves, as well as by sharing even small insights at dinner and other shared moments with the family.

# SIX

# MINDFULNESS

## WHAT IS MINDFULNESS?

Mindfulness, as defined by Jon Kabat-Zinn, is "awareness that arises through paying attention, on purpose, in the present moment, non-judgmentally."[1] Paying attention to the present moment seems intuitive—are we not prone to doing this all the time? Unfortunately, we are not! Two issues with which all of us struggle are (1) our negativity bias, whereby we tend to remember our negative experiences and forget the positive ones, and (2) our obsession with dwelling on the past and the future. We are continually rehashing the events of yesterday, last month, and years past. Combined with our negativity bias, this often causes us feelings of shame, embarrassment, self-criticism—and depression. Similarly, our thoughts about the future are often veiled in negativity—we imagine the worst things that may come to be and become fearful and anxious.

Happiness, in fact, resides in the *present moment*, as Dr. Kabat-Zinn reminds us. When we think of our happiest moments, it becomes clear that we were *present*. As we walked among the tall trees in the forest and looked skyward through the glistening canopy of leaves, marveling at the majesty and timelessness of these giants, we were not thinking about what happened yesterday or the list of things we need to do when we get home. Likewise, with the experience of sharing an intimate moment with a loved one—we were right there, right then.

It is adaptive to review what has happened—to an extent. We want to learn from our mistakes. We enjoy savoring loving times with family and friends. These are examples of adaptive thoughts. Unfortunately, we tend to overdo it and get stuck replaying unpleasant memories. We ruminate over something we said or did—or perhaps failed to say or do. We beat ourselves up. We judge ourselves negatively—we are certainly our own harshest critics. These maladaptive thoughts play repeatedly, reinforcing patterns of neural firing and connecting that bring us discomfort and sadness. Our negativity and ruminations are clearly maladaptive. Teens are especially proficient at this process of rumination.

Maybe it was once adaptive to obsess about the future—to be very wary of what might happen next. Could a predator or foe lurk just beyond our vision field? Obsessing over what has yet to happen, combined with our negativity bias, leads to fear and anxiety—the latter being one of the most prevalent maladies of our time. Perhaps "catastrophizing" thoughts represented an evolutionary advantage for our forebears—planning for every possible disaster meant living longer. In modern times, however, most of us no longer need to be quite so distracted and wary; it is unlikely that disaster awaits us outside the front door. Although learning from our past mistakes and planning for good times ahead may be adaptive, we no longer need to become overwrought about the worst thing that may be about to transpire.

Our teens are especially prone to worrying about what is yet to come. Will I get into a good college? Will I be invited to the prom? Will people at my new school like me?

Although our brains seem to be hardwired to dwell on the past and future and rarely enjoy the only moment we truly experience—the present one—there is some good news. Our minds can be modified to let go of negativity as well as our past- and future-mindedness. We all have brains with a quality called "neuroplasticity." Our brain cells communicate with each other at their connections, or synapses. The pathways and synapses in our brains can be reorganized to form more positive and present thought processes. We can do this through *intention* (the *I* in GAIN), ideally with a daily practice of purposeful focus on the present moment; that is, mindfulness.

As a state of awareness, mindfulness means paying deliberate attention to present-moment experience without judgment and with compassion. All of us practice mindfulness at times, and we generally experience peace, happiness, and joy at these times. Wouldn't it be great if we could exist in a state of mindfulness more of the time? Thanks to neuroplasticity, mindfulness can be further developed through practice, which promotes enhanced psychological health.[2]

The mindfulness-based stress reduction (MBSR) program is an eight-week course that was developed in the 1970s by Jon Kabat-Zinn at the University of Massachusetts Medical Center to treat depression and stress for those suffering from chronic illness.[3] MBSR uses a combination of mindfulness meditation, body awareness, yoga, and exploration of patterns of behavior, thinking, feeling, and action. The course became very popular a few years after its inception and remains even more so today. Why? The simple answer is that chronic stress has become a national epidemic.

Stress is associated with increased adrenaline (epinephrine) in our bodies—this causes an increase in our heart rate and blood pressure and adverse effects on our heart and blood vessels. The hormone cortisol is also elevated during stress, causing a rise in our blood sugar and suppression of our immune system. Acute stress, or the fight-or-flight response (also called the fight, flight, or freeze response), may be adaptive. For example, when we hear the splash of a toddler falling into the swimming pool at an outdoor party, the acute stress we experience heightens our senses. The adrenaline release helps us mobilize quickly to jump into the pool and rescue the child.

Chronic stress, on the other hand, is almost always maladaptive. It wreaks havoc with our hormones, cardiovascular system, and immune system and induces changes in our chromosomes akin to those seen as we age.[4] Chronic stress makes us biologically older! We can visualize this if we look at our telomeres.

Telomeres are tiny caps at the ends of our chromosomes.[5] They protect the tips of our chromosomes, much like the plastic tips on our shoelaces protect and prevent them from fraying. Every time our cells divide, our telomeres shorten. Telomere length can be restored by an enzyme called telomerase, but chronic stress and the incumbent chemical changes it induces on our bodies deplete our supply of telomerase. Telomeres naturally shorten with age; chronic stress exacerbates the shortening process. This may begin even in early childhood.

Exposure to stressful early life events, such as neglect, abuse, and exposure to violence during childhood, appears to set into motion persistent mechanisms that cause accelerated shortening of telomeres throughout life. These processes can escalate during adolescence. This is why it is so important that we impart to our teens the tools to deal with acute stress and mitigate or prevent chronic stress.

It is OK to experience acute stress, even if it is simply in response to *thoughts* rather than actual threats. The key is to have *resilience*—the ability to quickly neutralize the physiologic and hormonal changes that arise due to acute stress so that the adverse changes do not become long-lasting and pose dangers to our physical and mental health. This is especially important in teenagers, who are establishing lifelong patterns of interacting with their environment and their own bodies and minds.

As discussed in chapter 3, there are many causes of chronic stress among teenagers, including academic and other high-performance expectations, negative thoughts and beliefs about themselves, worries about physical appearance, and conflicts with friends. These may be compounded by family problems, such as parental divorce or separation, a family member with an illness, and family financial challenges. There may be gang involvement or neighborhood violence.

Chronic stress impairs the executive function of our brains, which reduces our ability to resist impulses. It is not hard to imagine that this is of particular concern for adolescents, since they have impaired executive function compared to adults at baseline. Chronic stress can increase the reward responsiveness of our brains, too. If teens are already predisposed to addiction, they can become addicted to unhealthy foods. For example, they may crave so-called comfort foods, which are high in sugar and/or fat. There is a growing prevalence of obesity in our teens, which exacerbates issues with body image and self-esteem (more on this later). Chronic stress may also increase craving for and addiction to recreational drugs. Chronic stress causes sleep impairment. It is not hard to appreciate the positive feedback loop at play—chronic stress leads to an unhealthy diet and disrupted sleep, which leads to fatigue, which leads to lack of exercise and increased desire for unhealthy comfort foods, poor attention span in school, and increased academic pressure stemming from poor grades, all of which cause more stress!

Mindfulness can be a great tool for breaking these maladaptive cycles and for building resilience. It is an antidote to chronic stress. Mindfulness can help teens begin to rewire their brains away from the negativity on which they often dwell. It can also neutralize their tendency to ruminate over the past, often leading to depression and to overthinking the future, creating fear and anxiety.

Mindfulness encourages us to slow down and notice our present-moment experience. Mindful awareness is not complicated. In fact, it is a distinctly uncomplicated process. It can involve the simple act of noticing our breath and sensations in the body and observing what is happening around us. Mindfulness also teaches us to let go of negative and unhelpful thoughts, helping us rewire our brains toward being more positive. In our daily lives, there are plenty of opportunities to practice. We can go outside and see the sunset, feel the softness of our pet's fur, taste that flavorful slice of pizza, smell the fragrances of the flowers in the air, and really listen and take in the music that we love! As adults, we can encourage our teens to engage in these very simple activities—largely by doing them ourselves (yes, they are watching us) and participating regularly with our teenagers.

Mindfulness practice facilitates the relaxation response, our body's way of turning off the stress response. As the relaxation response kicks in, our breathing slows and deepens, our muscles relax, and our blood pressure decreases.[6] Not all mindfulness methods work for everyone, so it is helpful to try several of them and see what works best. Practices can be simple, such as closing your eyes and deepening the breathing into your abdomen. Focusing on slowly breathing in through the nose, perhaps to a count of three, pausing for a count of three, then slowly and deliberately exhaling to a count of four activates the parasympathetic nervous system through the vagus nerve. This is our "unconscious" nervous system that keeps the sympathetic, fight-or-flight response in check.[7] Practicing this even for brief periods of time allows your body and mind to relax; then, you can try adding focus on a single word or "mantra." You can choose a word that helps you feel relaxed or even just repeat, silently to yourself, "Relax."

Self-awareness is required to know when we need to relax. This self-awareness includes focusing on how one's thoughts and feelings may generate behaviors in response to everyday events. Mindfulness is like a magnifying glass that amplifies our ability to accurately label thoughts and feelings and thus increase opportunities to choose healthier behaviors. Self-awareness or self-knowledge allows us to respond appropriately in the face of life's stresses. Mindfulness by itself can increase self-awareness. However, when a teen is wrestling with problematic negative self-talk, mood symptoms, and maladaptive behavior, psychotherapy may be necessary. Cognitive behavior therapy (CBT) is one such psychotherapy approach that complements mindfulness.

The CBT model describes the bilateral relationship between one's thoughts, emotions, behaviors, physiology, and environmental domains.

During a life experience or situation, our thoughts contribute to emotional and physiological responses. An emotional response is what we feel; these feelings reside in our bodies and are linked with physiological responses; for example, physical sensations. We tune in to our emotional experience as a critical step toward developing psychologically. Dr. Paul Ekman, who researches emotions, suggests that we all have six basic emotions: anger, surprise, disgust, enjoyment, fear, and sadness.[8] These feelings trigger behaviors, the actions we take.

Distorted thoughts lead to biased beliefs and undesired emotional and physiologic responses, especially in adolescents. According to CBT theory, a common metaphor for our biased way of seeing the world involves sunglasses.[9] Just as when we look through sunglasses with a particular tint that colors our world, our beliefs filter our view of ourselves, others, the world, and the past, present, and future. We judge others, the world, and ourselves through lenses colored with our biases rather than seeing things as they truly are. Due to our negativity bias, these automatic judgments can be overly unfavorable. CBT may be very useful for three standard core belief systems: (1) catastrophizing, (2) negativism, (3) and resistance. Teens may manifest each of these.

The catastrophizer expects and fears the worst possible outcomes. Consider Mike, who, as a high school junior, already has experienced a few relationship breakups. Mike has developed a fear about his current relationship and believes that it is only a matter of time before his partner breaks it off with him. Therefore, he finds himself becoming tense when his girlfriend voices any sort of complaint. Through CBT therapy, Mike develops a new belief pattern that recognizes that not all complaints will result in a breakup. It can be healthy when a partner voices complaints. These complaints can then be worked on and addressed to strengthen the relationship and increase Mike's self-confidence.

Most of us are negative at times. However, when negativity is excessive and chronic, it can have a profound impact. Negative thoughts are commonly directed toward oneself and may be reflected in statements such as "I am a failure," "I am unlikeable," or "I am unlovable." Consider Bridget, whose parents are concerned about the absolute and damaging statements she makes about herself, such as "I am bad." She also feels that she does not deserve the love and kindness her parents genuinely feel for her. More severe cases of overly negative core belief systems about oneself may be associated with a range of self-harmful behaviors. A therapist can help address this faulty belief system and work with Bridget on developing new thought patterns. Bridget will learn skills for dealing with challenging emotions so that they do not lead to problematic and dangerous behaviors.

The externalizer or deflector points the finger at others and is blaming. The deflector assumes that others intentionally act against them and do not like them. Tomas often finds himself in classroom disputes with peers. Tomas has developed contempt toward his classmates. He overtly lets others know just how smart he is. Tomas often speaks out of turn in class and answers questions before anyone else has a chance to. He has a hard time understanding why classmates snub him in the hallways. Tomas deflects taking any responsibility for this and just assumes they are "idiots and jerks." Tomas does not see that his contempt and sense of superiority puts off his classmates. Tomas can develop social skills in therapy and increase awareness about his behavior, contributing to how others view him. He will learn that by easing off in class, giving others a turn, and becoming more supportive, he can develop friendships.

What are teens' common thinking mistakes?

The thinking mistakes or cognitive distortions that teens typically experience are described below. Cognitive distortions and other problematic thoughts can become automatic and are therefore referred to as automatic negative thoughts (ANTs). Such ANTs occur just below awareness and are a manifestation of deeper negative core beliefs. Core beliefs differ from ANTs in that core beliefs tend to be very short, absolute statements about oneself, others, and the world; for example, "I am bad," "Others are mean," and "The world is a sucky place." Between the deeper level of core beliefs and the more salient level of thoughts are assumptions. Assumptions typically follow an if-then format. For instance, at a party, Mike sees a girl he thinks is attractive. He thinks to himself, "If I talk to that girl, then I will say something stupid; she will reject me, and others will laugh at me." We can surmise that Mike will not talk to this girl. Thus, ANTs, negative assumptions, and core beliefs shrink one's world and willingness to try new things. It is vital to help teens become aware of their automatic thoughts, assumptions, and core beliefs since these influence teens' ideations and behaviors.[10]

Here are nine "thinking traps" that are commonly observed in adolescents:[11]

*Extreme thinking.* Someone may be "all good" or "all bad." There is not much room or flexibility to recognize that most people have some good and some not-so-good.

*Overgeneralizing.* This occurs when someone thinks that because one negative thing happened, it will continue to happen. An example of this would be, "We lost the first game in the series. Therefore, we will continue to lose the others." You can likely see how this is not the best mindset to win a series.

*Mental filtering/discounting the positives.* This involves overemphasizing negatives at the expense of considering and focusing on the positive. For example, Michelle complimented Brian. Brian interpreted this compliment as "she is just being nice" rather than accepting it in a positive way.

*Jumping to negative conclusions.* One of the most common thinking traps, it involves either negative mind reading—that is, assuming others are thinking negatively about you—or negative fortune telling, such as predicting negative outcomes in the future without any data to support this. For example, Samuel predicts that his date with Barry won't go well because they never do!

*Magnification/minimization.* Due to our inherent negativity bias, we all have a tendency at times to amplify negatives and reduce the importance of positives. Mary shot five for eight beyond the three-point arc in her last basketball game. Mary can only think about those three shots she missed rather than allow herself to feel good about the five she hit. This can be problematic when she gets back on the floor in the next game because her mindset is oriented toward failure rather than success.

*Shoulds/musts/ought tos.* Another prevalent thinking error, this is a form of self-criticism or criticism toward others. Directed inwardly, someone might have a narrative that "I should be smarter at math," "I should only get A's," "I ought to get into every college I apply to," and so on. These distortions can also fuel anger. "They should know better than to cut me off in the intersection."

*Emotional reasoning.* This is faulty thinking in which one makes conclusions that they believe are facts based on emotions alone. "I feel like such a loser. Therefore, I am one."

*Labeling.* Put simply, this is name-calling oneself or others. "I am such a moron." "He is so not cool!"

*Personalization and blame.* At times we may accept too much blame for things that are not our fault. This can also be applied to others—blaming others unfairly and not taking one's own share of the responsibility for a problem. Sometimes children or teenagers blame themselves for their parents' divorce. They may blame a teacher for getting a bad grade when, in fact, they did not take the time to prepare for the exam.

The above nine thinking mistakes play a role in generating and sustaining mental states such as depression, anxiety, and, in some cases, post-traumatic stress. Mindfulness training and therapy can challenge these thinking errors to generate alternative and more balanced thoughts.

What do these nine thinking mistakes have to do with mindfulness, and how can mindfulness help transform how teens think?

Mindfulness is a comprehensive practice that can help us change our thought processes at all levels. Mindfulness practice puts us in contact with the present moment by focusing on breath, body, emotions, cognition, and the intuitive, existential, and spiritual domains. Mindfulness practice can be directed toward transforming our thoughts, thereby directing teens' "thinking traps" and emotional functioning in a positive direction. Mindfulness practice accomplishes this by directing our attention to what we are experiencing in the present moment and encouraging a more compassionate stance on what we notice.

Some great news: mindfulness classes have been in schools for years now. What course could be more important? Mindfulness means being aware of what is happening *right now*. If teens can be truly focused on what is being taught in math, history, or English class *right now*, they are poised to learn. Therefore, mindfulness provides the basis for learning all subjects taught in school. The alternative is having one's mind wander during class—lapsing into our natural tendency to ruminate over something said or done yesterday or last week or considering the list of possibilities that may transpire tomorrow or next week. Our brains can focus on only one thought at a time, contrary to the popular belief that we can "multitask" effectively. Learning to be mindful also means gaining skills to set one's mind on intention, including the commitment to make the most out of each lesson in school to optimize true learning. Finally, mindfulness means stopping judgments—letting go of the notion that the material being taught is "boring," that the teacher's style is "bad," and that the student at the next desk is "smarter" than me.

An example of a successful program for teaching mindfulness to teens is "Peace in Schools." Peace in Schools started out as an afterschool mindfulness program offered to a few local schools by its founder, Caverly Morgan, in Portland, Oregon. In 2014, a high school principal concerned about high rates of teen suicide was blown away by the impact of the program. When he asked Caverly, "How do I get this to more teens?" She replied, "Put us during the school day." So he partnered with Peace in Schools to launch Mindful Studies—the nation's first for-credit semester-long mindfulness class in a public high school.

Mindful Studies is an in-depth, research-backed elective course for tenth through twelfth graders. Like any other subject, the class is fully integrated into the school day. In Mindful Studies, teens explore different mindfulness tools and learn important life skills, like how to deal with stress, anxiety, and self-doubt.

Mindful Studies is not an independent study course; the learning and transformation that takes place happen in a community context. Students sit in a circle, and every lesson begins with a brief mindful minute, inviting each teen to welcome whatever experience they are having. Through mindfulness and meditation, students learn to bring awareness to their thoughts and to practice directing their attention. It is through directing their attention that many students experience a feeling of empowerment and expand their capacity to be with thoughts and emotions as they arise. Mindfulness exercises are followed by thoughtful community conversations that allow students to hear and learn from each other's experiences. Through the class, teens support each other in living authentically and seeing possibility in life and in themselves.

What's also significant about this class is that mindfulness serves as a backdrop for further inquiry rather than an ending point. The cultivated practice of mindfulness assists teens in asking important questions within a supportive group, questions like: "Who am I?" "How can I have hope?" and "How do I belong?"

According to surveys administered to students taking the class, their participation resulted in the following benefits:

- 79 percent of teens reported increased acceptance of others and themselves
- 94 percent of teens reported an increased ability to relax and diminished anxiety
- 93 percent of teens reported feeling generally more present and aware
- 73 percent of teens reported greater compassion for themselves and others

Below are some quotes from teens after completing the course:

- "Mindfulness class changed my life for the better. It's helped me accept and honor myself. I learned that it's okay to be me."
- "This class has helped me realize the value of living and has helped me enjoy many of the moments I experience. I feel more appreciative of my friends and family."
- "I've realized that stress will be a constant in my life, but we follow where we put our attention. I'm learning and practicing living with stress and worry and still finding peace during times of stress."

Other organizations, such as Pure Edge, have expanded mindfulness programming to include delivery and research of health and wellness curriculums beyond students to include educators, school staff, and districtwide personnel. According to the Pure Edge website, they have been studying the impacts of their programming since 2011. One of their published studies examined a school-based yoga program among urban high school students. The study, a randomized controlled trial, indicated that students who participated in more than forty-nine yoga sessions earned a significantly higher mean GPA.[12] One of the authors of this book, Dr. Rettger, was a Stanford University research team member studying the impacts of Pure Edge's curriculum on children. A key finding of this research was that a school-based health and mindfulness curriculum led to improvements in objectively measured sleep over a two-year period.[13]

A variety of mindfulness guides or practices can be found online and elsewhere. One example is called RAIN (which coincidentally rhymes with GAIN!).[14]

*R* stands for relaxing into a meditative state, taking a pause in the face of challenging emotion, and *recognizing* what is happening now.

Report to yourself on your experience concerning:

- What you are thinking
- What you are feeling (one word—name the emotion)
- What you are experiencing physically and physiologically (heart rate, physical sensation, shallow breathing, butterflies in the stomach, etc.)

- What your desires are in terms of behavior (Do I want to run away, avoid, suppress, or alter consciousness through drugs or alcohol?)

*A* represents *accepting* and *allowing* our present-moment experience. Rather than turn away or avoid, we breathe and let ourselves simply feel this experience.

*I* means that we *inquire* gently within ourselves and hold a conversation with ourselves about what our emotions may be offering. Just as physical pain alerts our brain to something significant happening, emotional pain also points out that something important, meaningful, and substantial is happening. We can learn from this moment. We take time to sit in meditative awareness and allow our experience to simply be.

*N* reminds us to practice self-*nourishing* and *non-identification* with whatever this experience is, knowing that this moment, like all other moments, will pass. Self-nourishment is an act of being compassionate with oneself. What phrases can we offer to ourselves that bring a message of acceptance, peacefulness, and gratitude? Again, we can treat ourselves like our own best friend.[15] What does receiving this type of best-friend kindness feel like? We can also offer ourselves a gentle, healing touch, such as a hand on the heart, to help soothe ourselves in times of distress.[16]

When we conclude the practice of RAIN, we release the meditation, open our eyes, and observe any changes we have experienced. We might ask ourselves, "Do I feel any calmer? More relaxed? More centered?" Journaling about our experiences before moving back into our day is beneficial.

RAIN bears similarities to GAIN. They are both simple to learn and utilize. They both can be practiced in just a few minutes while sitting in a comfortable chair, on a mat on the floor, or even while walking along the road or hallway. Through practice, we can make progress with baby steps, little by little. There is no such thing as failure! After a few months of regular practice, we will look back and notice how much calmer and more optimistic we feel. We are gradually rewiring our brains to a more positive, present awareness.

## Bottom Line

- Teenage and adult brains are vulnerable to negativity bias and the inability to be "present." The good news is that our brains have neuroplasticity—we can literally rewire our brains through the deliberate practice of mindfulness.
- Teens face stressors related to academics, relationships with their peers and family members, performance demands, self-image, and other factors. Excessive access to social media may exacerbate this stress. These triggers of the acute stress response may lead to chronic stress without resilience—the ability to neutralize the body's responses so they do not become chronic. Mindfulness practice can help teens become resilient and neutralize the acute stress response so that chronic stress is minimized.
- Chronic stress causes adverse changes in our cardiovascular and immune systems, diet and exercise habits, and sleep, and even induces changes in our bodies akin to aging.
- Mindfulness study in schools is an important innovation in teaching mindfulness to all grade levels.
- RAIN and GAIN are relatively simple practices that can help teens rewire their brains away from their inherent negativity bias and obsession with the past and future toward more positive thought patterns and behaviors. We adults can help them embrace these practices by demonstrating them and participating with our teens.

# PART III

*The GAIN Method*

SEVEN

# GRATITUDE

Why is gratitude so important?
Gratitude is essential to our well-being and central to our experience of happiness. It is possible to be happy and poor, happy and blind, and even happy with chronic pain. On the other hand, it does not seem possible for a person to be happy and ungrateful. Gratitude is the foundation of happiness. That is why the GAIN method begins with the letter *G* for gratitude!

Most of us have much for which to be grateful. We have loved ones—family and friends—in our lives. In general, most of us live in a relatively safe place compared to others in the world. We have access to food. We have running water and electricity. In fact, it is rather miraculous that we can shower and experience warm water cascading over our bodies almost any time we want. Imagine the infrastructure and technology by virtue of which we can enjoy modern amenities such as warm showers, refrigeration, automobiles, airplanes, and streaming music. Although many of us cannot claim perfect health, most systems in our bodies are functioning rather remarkably. So why are we not more grateful for these blessings?

Our brains are wired in ways that tend to interfere with our ability to be more grateful—and happy. We are programmed to have a *negativity bias*—we tend to remember the negative and forget or marginalize our positive experiences. We are wary of the world around us. The neural networks that represent how our brains are wired developed over long periods to augment our ability to survive. Survival trumps happiness in the Darwinian sense. Consider our forebears, early Homo sapiens living in caves 150,000 years ago, gathered around a fire, keeping our families warm and safe. It behooved them to consider that there might be a saber-toothed tiger lurking outside the mouth of their dwelling. They kept their spears at hand. Preparedness to defend themselves against such enemies helped keep them alive. The acute stress response was readily triggered by the threats they constantly faced. If they were wary of these threats and prepared themselves accordingly, they tended to live longer and have more offspring. The genes that coded this wary and even fearful mindset propagated in the population.

Fast forward to today—we rarely benefit from continuously imagining that danger lurks nearby. Yet we are endowed with these neuronal connections that became the basis for such patterns of thinking. We have the tendency to consider the world around us in a rather negative manner. We constantly judge the world around us, including others who pose little or no threat. Unfortunately, given the ways in which our brains are now wired, we judge ourselves most harshly.

Teens are especially predisposed to negative self-judgment:

"I am fat—my body is gross."
"My skin is awful."
"I have an ugly face."
"I am not as smart as my friends."

The tween and teen stage of development is characterized by significant physical, emotional, and cognitive transformation during which their exaggerated self-awareness is called "adolescent egocentrism."[1] Adolescents are highly focused on themselves and often very self-conscious. Combined with a negativity bias, they can be highly insecure and self-critical. This way of thinking may dominate their consciousness, making it difficult to focus on gratitude.

The good news: their brains (and ours) are malleable and can be rewired to be more positive and self-assured with our help. By helping them learn gratitude, we can help them think in a more positive way and improve their self-confidence.

Most cultures, philosophies, and religions embrace the power of gratitude. Gratitude is central to Christian, Buddhist, Muslim, Jewish, Baha'i, and Hindu spiritual traditions. Worship with gratitude expressed to God is common to these religions, and the concept permeates religious teachings and traditions. Being grateful for the bounties provided by God is an essential part of Judaism worship and manifests in many psalms and prayers. There is great emphasis on gratitude for acts of human kindness and sacrifice. Martin Luther cited gratitude as fundamental to Christian thinking, and gratitude is still considered "the heart of the gospel."

The Quran references gratitude, and Islam makes expressing thanks to God a daily ritual. The call to prayer reminds believers to thank God five times daily for His goodness. Abiding in a state of gratitude is central to the purpose of fasting during the month of Ramadan.

The Buddha taught that every human birth deserves gratitude. Gratitude helps develop *ksanti* (or *kshanti*), meaning patience, forbearance, and forgiveness.[2] Appreciation for the gifts of life is integrated into most Buddhist mindfulness practices.

Thanksgiving services were routine in what became the Commonwealth of Virginia as early as 1607. The Thanksgiving tradition became "official" in the United States with a proclamation by George Washington in 1789 to celebrate the bounties and blessings of the past year. A common practice before enjoying a Thanksgiving feast is to have each person at the table express their gratitude.

In psychology, gratitude may be considered a "trait involving a life orientation towards noticing and appreciating the positive in life."[3] A growing body of evidence underscores that more grateful people have higher levels of well-being, greater sense of control over their environment, more personal growth and purpose in life, and enhanced self-acceptance.

Interventions involving the practice of appreciation typically result in people feeling happier.

We tend to get caught up thinking about things that go wrong and take good things and people for granted daily. We often overlook the beauty around us, a kind word or gesture from a friend or stranger, the warm sun on our skin on a cool day. Again, this is our negativity bias at work. We can begin to rewire our brains to be more positive and grateful by practicing "Three Good Things." This simply involves writing down three things that we noticed during the day that went well or brought us happiness—we can do this as we prepare for bed at night. Studies have shown that the Three Good

Things practice reduces stress and depression and improves our sleep and overall happiness. Even thinking about three good things in the evening reinforces our gratitude and improves our sleep and overall outlook. This requires no time—we can do this as we prepare to sleep at night.

Let's look at a few studies that demonstrate this apparent cause-and-effect relationship.

In one study, health care workers completed the Three Good Things practice for fifteen days and were evaluated at one, six, and twelve months afterward using the Maslach Burnout Inventory.[4] They exhibited significant improvements from baseline in emotional exhaustion, depression symptoms, and happiness at one month, six months and twelve months, and in work-life balance at one month and six months. The findings were similar in another study by the same investigators in which health care workers received daily links for fifteen days to submit three responses to the prompts "What went well today?" and "What was your role in making it happen?" Well-being improvements endured at all follow-up time points (one month, six months, and twelve months).[5]

The impact of a gratitude-related writing intervention on hope and happiness has been tested.[6] Participants were randomly assigned to write about either gratefully remembering a past hope that had been fulfilled or a control condition. The "grateful remembering" condition prompted significant increases in hope and happiness, underscoring that grateful remembering is a practice that can bolster satisfaction and positive expectations.

The longer-term effects of gratitude were tested in a study wherein three groups of participants were asked to write a few sentences each week focusing on specific topics. One group wrote about things they were grateful for, the second group wrote about things that irritated or displeased them, and the third group wrote about events that had affected them positively or negatively. After ten weeks, those who wrote about gratitude were more optimistic, felt better about their lives, exercised more, and had fewer visits to physicians than those who focused on sources of aggravation. Cultivating gratitude involves *intention*. Fortunately, it is not that difficult!

Being grateful can make us happier, improve our relationships, and reduce the incidence and magnitude of depression and post-traumatic stress disorder. Gratitude practice is associated with not only our psychological well-being but also our physical health.

Gratitude practice shows up in our cells and our heart rhythm! Telomeres, the caps at the end of each strand of DNA, protect our chromosomes and affect how quickly our cells age. Telomeres naturally shorten as we get older. Being optimistic, mindful, and grateful is associated with the preservation of telomere length.[7] A gratitude journaling intervention in seventy asymptomatic heart failure patients improved heart rate variability (a sign of a healthier heart) and reduced inflammation.[8]

One theory supporting the positive effects of gratitude on health is the "broaden-and-build theory of positive emotions."[9] This theory hypothesizes that positive emotions such as gratitude contribute to the development of long-term physical, psychological, social, and intellectual resources. These factors are mutually self-sustaining—the more grateful we are, the better our mood and physical health, the more we socialize and participate in self-care, the more grateful we become, and so on.

On the other hand, negative thinking begets negative thinking. Psychologists have long known that the more we think about or ruminate on a negative thought, the more entrenched it becomes. Negative and traumatic thoughts tend to "loop"—they play themselves over and over until we intentionally interrupt the pattern. The more these negative thoughts loop, the stronger these neural pathways become, and the more difficult it becomes to stop them. This is why thoughts that cause depression, anxiety, panic, obsessions, and compulsions can become so difficult to combat.

Even for teens, these patterns of negative thinking do not develop overnight—they take years, going back, in many cases, to early childhood. Therefore, morphing these negative circuits into more positive ones in teens will take time. If things are moving in the right direction, there is cause for optimism. We rewire our brains in small increments. Let's use our power of intention to think positively, one baby step at a time.

We can rewire our brains to be more grateful and, therefore, healthy in mind, body, and spirit because our brains possess the amazing quality of *neuroplasticity*. Neuroplasticity is the brain's ability to reorganize its neural pathways in response to environmental changes. Remarkably, we can take advantage of this property to alter the brain's molecular structure in ways that make us healthier—and *happier*. One way of doing this is by having thoughts of gratitude and expressing them.

Imaging of areas of the brain associated with the expression of gratitude light up when we gather with friends and family and experience connection.[10] Other areas of the brain associated with stress relief are also set into motion. Practicing gratitude on a regular basis activates the neuroplasticity of networks involved in happiness and social bonding. Once again, a positive feedback loop is involved here—thoughts of gratitude beget more thoughts of gratitude and improved mood, socialization, relaxation—and happiness itself.

Wouldn't our teens benefit from activating such neural pathways and improving the abilities of their developing brains to wire for greater interest in socializing, stress relief, gratitude, and happiness?

How can we teach our teens to be more grateful? Simply lecturing them on the value of gratitude will likely result in eye-rolling and arm-crossing—that is, resistance. Teens tend to respond more favorably when they are guided in figuring things out for themselves. This is part of the approach embraced by the Youth Gratitude Project (YGP), launched by the Greater Good Science Center (https://ggsc.berkeley.edu/).

The YGP curriculum incorporates three key processes:

1. Exploring identity: Students can explore their character strengths (e.g., honesty, curiosity, perseverance, humility). Students take an online assessment of their virtues and, working in groups, create posters that display these traits.
2. Capitalizing on strengths: Rather than focusing on perceived deficits, a gratitude curriculum builds on the students' positive attributes. Students are encouraged to take pride in the posters they

have created. Teachers utilize students' strengths to encourage peer relationships in the classroom.
3. Building positive relationships: Students leverage their strengths to connect with others in and outside of school. They acknowledge each other's positive attributes by leaving encouraging sticky notes on each other's posters; for example, thanking them for their help with the assignments.

Gratitude cannot simply be imposed on teens, especially those who have serious problems with their home life, health, abuse, neglect, or poverty. Teens who do not receive ample support from their parents and other adults in their lives may have difficulty embracing gratitude. It may be all we can do to listen with empathy and sensitivity while acknowledging their feelings. Curricula like the YGP emphasize their character strengths, identity, and positive peer relationships and have the potential to serve as a starting point for building positive experiences of gratitude in school. Parents can amplify these lessons by exhibiting gratitude in their own lives—our teens certainly take cues from us!

When left untended, hurt manifests as anger, resentment, hatred, or other negative emotions that block the experience of gratitude, love, and other blessings. When teens harbor these toxic emotions long term, there are damaging consequences, such as closing off from love, isolating themselves, or manifesting disease in the body. Preoccupation with negative emotions or negative thoughts drains meaning, joy, and satisfaction from life.

We *can* rewire our neuroplastic brains. Our thoughts influence our epigenetics, the expression of our genes. Our thoughts help create proteins that tell our genes what to do. These proteins can turn some genes on and others off or make them less active. Positive thoughts of gratitude can lead to more positive thoughts and even changes in the body. Making gratitude an ingrained habit will rewire our brains for the better. Gratitude is a powerful antidote to depression, despair, regret, and resentment. Gratitude is the gateway to deeper states of understanding, love, and compassion.

## Bottom Line

- Keep a gratitude journal. Make it a habit to write down three things for which you are grateful every day. You can do this with your children! If they are not willing to participate, you can relate your entries with them at the dinner table or bedtime. If you are not a journaler, simply think of three things that went well during the day as you prepare for bed—be grateful for those three things.
- Count your blessings. Take time to reflect on your life and recall the blessings you have received. You could appreciate your eyesight, hearing, and the ability to walk. You may be grateful for having vibrant health, a thriving career, or the financial abundance to buy a beautiful home, travel across the globe, or donate to your favorite charity. Again, share this with your teens during dinner or a car ride.
- Express your appreciation in the presence of your teenager. Think about the people who have positively impacted your life. That could include your family for their support, your team for the excellence they deliver to your clients, or your gardener, who maintains a thriving garden while you focus on other things. Write a thank-you note and send it or (even better) deliver it in person. Do this at least once a month. Write one to yourself occasionally!

# EIGHT
# ACCEPTANCE

We decide that we cannot instantaneously change these things at this moment, so we open ourselves to the sensations and thoughts they may bring. We become the observer of our thoughts. We let go of the resistance, which associates incremental suffering with these uninvited feelings.

We may still feel pain, but by letting go of our resistance, the suffering is diminished:

$$\text{Suffering} = \text{Pain} \times \text{Resistance}$$
$$\text{or}$$
$$\text{Suffering} = \text{Pain} \div \text{Acceptance}$$

We can increase our acceptance and thereby lessen our suffering, even if the pain remains (for now).

Acceptance is within all of us, but it has been veiled by years of "resistance training" (unfortunately, not the good kind practiced in the gym).

Accordingly, we must apply our intention to rewiring the brain and unveiling this essential ingredient to happiness. This requires a commitment followed by regular practice. Every time you practice acceptance, you create and strengthen healthy neural pathways in your brain. The good news is that this gets easier over time as we rewire our brains.

Of course, we should not accept everything that bothers us. We must discriminate between what we can change and what is beyond our ability to improve. We do not have the time or power to change everything that seems wrong with ourselves or the world. We may devote ourselves to improving the environment or our relationships at work and elect to volunteer to deliver food to the homeless in our communities. We cannot, however, make everything at work perfect or even perhaps pleasant, just as we cannot feed all of those who are hungry. So we explore what we might change to the best of our abilities and commit to accepting the rest.

Acceptance does not mean apathy, passivity, or disavowing responsibility. Quite the opposite, in fact—we actively *practice* acceptance with caring and integrity. Acceptance does not mean being resigned to a particular way forever. Through acceptance, we may learn that, over time, some issues gradually move from the unchangeable to the changeable, and we can redirect our efforts to effect improvements around and within us.

Acceptance can be practiced in all areas of life—our current experience or reality, others' beliefs or ideas, appearance, emotions, health, and past and present thoughts, for example.

One of the more commonly quoted expressions of the importance of acceptance is the Serenity Prayer. The Serenity Prayer teaches us that wisdom is knowing what to accept and what to change. Having the wisdom to discern the difference between things we can change and things we cannot change is essential for peace of mind: "God grant me the serenity to accept the things I cannot change; courage to change the things I can; and the wisdom to know the difference."[1]

We do not necessarily endorse what we accept in these areas. Rather, we recognize that although we cannot change the nature of this moment, we can decrease suffering and pain by lowering our resistance to that we cannot change right now; that is, through acceptance.

Deepak Chopra sums it up poignantly in his meditation on "The Law of Least Effort":

> I will practice acceptance. Today I will accept people, situations, circumstances, and events as they occur. I will know that this moment is as it should be because the whole universe is as it should be. I will not struggle against the whole universe by struggling against this moment. My acceptance is total and complete. I accept things as they are now, not as I wish.[2]

Acceptance is especially important for teenagers, as their innate tendency is to dwell on negative thoughts and feelings. How can teens learn to practice acceptance? There are programs designed to teach acceptance. Both parents and teens may benefit greatly from engaging in acceptance and commitment therapy.

## ACCEPTANCE AND COMMITMENT THERAPY FOR TEENS

Acceptance and commitment therapy (ACT) teaches teens (1) to accept that they, like the rest of us, have a negativity bias, and (2) through commitment or *intention*, they can learn to enjoy their lives despite the negativity we all experience. ACT may provide teens with the tools they need to acknowledge their feelings of depression and anxiety and then learn to cope and move beyond them.

Note that ACT embraces two of the four domains of the GAIN practice—acceptance and intention. Both are essential to our happiness. Framed by gratitude and nonjudgment, these pillars form a complete mindfulness meditation practice that can greatly help teens and adults. We can model these principles for our children and students by embracing them ourselves.

ACT bears some resemblance to cognitive behavior therapy (CBT). CBT helps us identify our negative thoughts and feelings and then begin to guide them in a positive direction through self-help practices. CBT targets our core beliefs, dysfunctional assumptions, and automatic negative thoughts.[3] ACT also involves observing our negative thoughts—and acknowledging their validity so we can work through and past them.

For example, consider a teen starting a new school in a new community after her family relocated over the summer. With CBT, she would be advised to stop negative feelings by picturing a stop sign when she imagined that nobody would like her at the school. She would learn to replace the pessimistic thoughts that can lead to feeling isolated with the positive self-talk that she will make good friends.

With ACT, on the other hand, she would be instructed to first focus on and acknowledge the negative thoughts and then formulate strategies to befriend other students by taking an interest in their lives, by being kind, and so forth. She might say to herself, "No wonder I am anxious—being the new kid at school is stressful! I am likable and will move through these feelings quickly."

In other words, ACT teaches us that we all have a negativity bias, and thoughts of depression and anxiety are common to everyone. They are part of being human. They don't need to be "fixed." Rather, we can acknowledge our tendency to fixate on the future, assume the worst outcomes, ruminate over the past, and feel regret and shame. Acknowledgment is a big first step. We can then learn to live with these thoughts and emotions. The simple act of acknowledgment limits the negativity. We gradually rewire the negative patterns of thought and create new, more optimistic, and pragmatic neural networks. This is our brain's neuroplasticity at work.

ACT teaches us that the full range of thoughts and emotions, both positive and negative, are intrinsic to the human experience. This is how our brains are wired. They have evolved this way over tens and even hundreds of thousands of years. In some ways, negativity and wariness evolved to augment survival. Today, however, we do not generally benefit from our negativity bias—we are not commonly facing actual threats to our safety. One way of thinking about how our brains developed to be the way they are is that evolution favors *survival*—but not *happiness*. The good news is that our brains have the magical quality of neuroplasticity, and we can change how we think for the better—if we have a plan. This book's common theme is our ability to rewire our neuroplastic brains through the practice of gratitude, acceptance, intention, and nonjudgment.

ACT, like CBT, can be utilized to help treat depression, anxiety, eating disorders, substance abuse, obsessive-compulsive disorder, and other maladies common among teenagers. It is utilized by many therapists to treat these and other conditions, and success may occur even among those with major depressive disorder.[4] We also can utilize ACT to help our less severely afflicted teens in their daily lives. Through our behavior and interactions with our teens, we can reinforce the four *A*'s of ACT: *acknowledge, allow, accommodate,* and *appreciate.*

Suppose, for example, we are hosting a family holiday gathering one evening. There is a cousin, William, whom our teen considers very annoying. First, we acknowledge that William appears to be very egotistical and snobby. We then discuss why William behaves the way he does; maybe he is insecure and boasts to hide his insecurities. We discuss allowing this during the gathering rather than letting it get under our skin—how to observe without reacting. By accommodating the behavior without becoming upset, we might enjoy other aspects of William's personality—his jokes *are* pretty funny. We can even appreciate him in some ways. We may even find him likable once we get past the apparently negative aspects of his personality.

Acceptance is essential to the mental well-being of teenagers. They benefit greatly from learning to accept others and the world around them. Perhaps most challenging of all is *self-acceptance*. Learning to accept themselves means acknowledging their emotions without self-judgment—no easy task considering the physical, emotional, and cognitive developmental changes teens experience as they transition from childhood. Self-acceptance promotes resilience, regulation of rapidly changing emotions, and acquisition of coping skills needed to deal with the myriad of challenges they face, as described in previous chapters of this book.

Self-acceptance improves teens' self-esteem and, therefore, their overall mental and emotional health. It means they can embrace their own unique qualities, both strong and weak, with less judgment of and comparison to others. Celebrating their own identity and individuality promotes greater self-confidence in their abilities and helps negate the need to conform to peer pressure and societal expectations.

Acceptance means learning that we all make mistakes, have limitations, and may fail. When teens are OK with this, they are more prone to engage in self-exploration, self-expression, and personal growth and become more independent.

If we accept our own apparent weaknesses and mental and physical limitations, we are better equipped to drop negative judgments of others. This leads to the ability to foster healthier relationships. Teens who practice self-acceptance are more likely to empathize with others and form mutually supportive relationships. They can better resolve conflicts with their peers, teachers, and family members.

Embracing acceptance can be integrated into a broader mindfulness practice. Combined with the interrelated domains of gratitude, intention, and nonjudgment—that is, the GAIN practice—acceptance encourages teens to be more aware of the present moment and to let go of negative ruminations of the past and anxiety over the future. These domains are mutually self-reinforcing—being more present leads to greater appreciation or gratitude for the blessings in life. Gratitude helps us accept the elements in life we otherwise find unpleasant. When we feel grateful and accepting, we feel better about ourselves and are more confident and less judgmental of others and ourselves. We develop a more positive outlook on life. Our overall mental health improves. These processes are vital for our teens.

All of this leads to some effective strategies for helping our teens improve their sense of well-being:

- Encourage self-reflection on strengths and accomplishments but also on limitations. Emphasize that we are all limited—this is part of our human condition. We all have self-doubt, negativity at times, and even a degree of depression. We can learn to accept and even embrace our limitations.
- Help teens set realistic goals without being self-defeating.
- Promote self-care—making sleep, exercise, and nutrition priorities.
- Encourage independent thinking and decision making—while also being available to provide advice and counseling.
- Foster creativity and self-expression, including exploration of their interests and passions.
- Help teens celebrate their individuality as well as the diversity and uniqueness of others.

Of course, we cannot simply verbalize to our teens the essentials of acceptance, mindfulness, ACT, and other constructive ways of looking at others and ourselves and expect teens to listen. If we want to help our teens cope, we must model and embrace mindfulness practices ourselves. Our teens are watching us—and they don't miss much!

## Bottom Line

- When teens experience pain, help them discern whether it comes from a source they can change or not. If not, they *can* learn to accept it.
- Acceptance is essential to teens' self-confidence, independence, and positive development.
- Combined with gratitude, intention, and nonjudgment, acceptance is a pillar of happiness for teens—and for the rest of us.
- Therapy, such as ACT, can help teens cope with the myriad challenges they face during this crucial developmental stage.

# NINE
# INTENTION

Jon Kabat-Zinn is one of the fathers of what we call mindfulness and the founder of the Center for Mindfulness in Medicine. His definition of mindfulness—"the awareness that arises through paying attention, on purpose, in the present, nonjudgmentally"[1]—in the western world could be reframed as, "Happiness arises through paying attention, *on purpose*, in the present moment, nonjudgmentally." Or "Good relationships are built by paying attention, *on purpose*, in the present moment, nonjudgmentally." Or "I will be a better parent by paying attention, *on purpose*, in the present moment, nonjudgmentally with my children."

So much of what is truly good in our lives arises through paying attention, on purpose, in the present moment, nonjudgmentally. One of the key elements is purposefulness. The simple act of asking ourselves the question, "What is my intention?" is an act of mindfulness, bringing our attention to the present moment *on purpose*. We would be well served by posing this question to ourselves as we start each day and repeatedly throughout the day.

Setting a clear intention activates the prefrontal cortex, the brain's "corporate headquarters," thus establishing neural networks that facilitate success. Being clear about your intention will help you achieve your goals. Imagine that you are driving across the country without a clear intention. Will you ever arrive at your destination? How can you arrive at an unspecified location? Or, if you keep changing your mind about your destination, navigating all the detours will take much longer than necessary. It may be fun occasionally to simply drive without a goal. After all, "wherever you go, there you are." However, there are many times when arriving promptly is important. Otherwise, you may arrive after the wedding or birthday celebration has already taken place and your friends and family have departed. Or you may miss another eagerly anticipated experience.

What about the difference between intentions and goals? A goal is simply a desired outcome. It is future oriented. "Goal setting" is a valuable skill that helps us stay on track and get things done. Although goals move us toward what we think we want, they often take us out of the moment and create a feeling that what we have isn't enough. A general sense of "edginess" can blanket a goal-oriented life. Continual striving toward future goals diminishes the value of the present moment and displaces our attention from right here and right now. As the present moment is the power point, goal setting can feel disempowering.

Living our *intentions*, on the other hand, is much different than merely being goal oriented. Being intentional allows us to focus on how we want to be in this moment, independent of whether we are moving toward our goals. Allowing intentions to guide our moment-to-moment focus means that we are living our values and what matters most to us. Set positive intentions—how you want to show up or what immediate outcome you desire, rather than negative intentions—what outcomes you don't want or how you don't want to be. Being affirmative increases the chances of desirable responses.

Focusing on your intentions does not mean giving up your goals or desire for achievement. By partnering your goals with your intentions, you can savor the journey. After all, living is a *process*—there is no destination!

To summarize the distinction between goals and intentions:

- Goals are focused on the future. Intentions are in the present moment.
- Goals are a destination or specific achievement. Intentions are lived each day, independent of reaching the goal or destination.
- Goals are external achievements. Intentions are your inner relationships with yourself and others.[2]

The area around Stanford has some wonderful biking routes. Riding to the top of Skyline Boulevard is a challenging but thoroughly enjoyable trek. The scenery is gorgeous along any of the several routes to the summit. There are inspiring views of the countryside. Once at the top, the views are even more spectacular. A goal for undertaking this ride might be to see the Pacific Ocean. At the same time, one might set their intention on breathing with each rotation of the pedals on the climb, taking in the views on the less strenuous portions—breathing in sync with the movement of the wheels while experiencing the miracle of the body's muscles operating in harmony. Let's say the fog rolls in just before reaching the top, as it often does in this coastal range. One may reach the summit only to find the view obliterated by the fog. Although the goal of seeing the Pacific Ocean was not achieved, there need not be disappointment. The intention was fulfilled, and the ride was thoroughly enjoyable during each moment of the ascent. Having returned home afterward, one feels empowered and happy despite not having achieved the goal of seeing the ocean.

To use another physical fitness example, let's say we are at the gym, and our goal is to complete twelve repetitions on the bench press. We intend to maintain excellent form, keeping our spine neutral and our elbows elevated. Our intention is to breathe out slowly while pushing the bar away from our body and to breathe in deeply while returning the bar to our chest. Breathe in, breathe out, repeat. We remind ourselves to go through these steps until our muscles are fatigued but not in pain. We want to avoid injury. It turns out that we experience fatigue with the tenth rep and decided to stop short of twelve reps, which had been our goal. We are not disappointed that we did not perform twelve reps. Instead, we are satisfied that our intention guided us during the exercise—we attended to our posture and breathing and set the bar down when it was appropriate. We are content!

The same applies to a multitude of other activities. The goal might be to finish a book tonight, whereas the intention may be to enjoy every page. The goal may be to visit three countries abroad in the coming year; the intention may be to make the most of each trip while there. The intention may be actuated satisfactorily even if the goal is not met.

We can consider measures of intention in how we achieve and maintain good health.[3] "Behavioral intention" in this context refers to factors that influence our health habits—the stronger our intention to perform a healthy behavior, the more likely we are to succeed in sticking to healthy ways of eating, sleeping, and exercising.[4] With respect to our diet, we might eat less meat and consume more fruits and vegetables *today*. We can incorporate this intention into our daily mindfulness practice. Similarly, we may be committed to improving our sleep hygiene—our intention might be to go to bed at the same time and awaken at the same time every day, or to put the laptop away at least an hour before bedtime, or to forego an afternoon cup of coffee. It may extend to exercise, with a plan for a vigorous, daily, two-mile walk with your dog.

For teenagers, behavioral intent can be well applied to sleep, exercise, and nutrition, as well as quitting smoking and recreational substance use, weight management, and improved school performance by adhering to better study habits. Parents can reinforce these behavioral intentions during the drive to school, at the dinner table, or during commercials while watching television with the family.

One of the central tenets of this book is that we are more likely to succeed living according to our intentions if we take small bites or "baby steps." This applies especially to teens, who may expect immediate results. After all, they are growing up in the point-and-click internet world of computer games. They will benefit from lots of positive reinforcement with the notion that progress is often made in small, incremental steps. We often give up if we try to do too much too soon. This principle is one of the bases of "time preference," or the tendency to place a higher subjective value on rewards received immediately rather than those obtained in the future, which often leads to choosing a smaller, immediate reward instead of a larger reward down the road. Besides being more immediate (and *present*), people generally take smaller steps when their intention is focused on short-term results.

Practicing good health behaviors often involves immediate sacrifices—such as giving up favorite foods—to gain benefits that may not occur until far into the future. This is why we may struggle to focus on long-term goals, such as eating healthily and remaining physically active. We may be more successful if we encourage our teens (and ourselves) to pay attention to *today*, *tomorrow*, or *this week*. Eat one less piece of candy today, meditate for three minutes this morning, and take the stairs every day this week. Frequent feedback from an "accountability partner" may be very helpful. To help our teens create and reinforce healthy habits, we can suggest small rewards; for example, the reward of a special purchase upon meeting a particular health-related goal.[5]

Some argue that regularly providing rewards for completing tasks or behaving in a certain way may cause more harm than good. Although parents and teachers may implement reward and incentive systems at home and in school, an analysis of articles published prior to 2000 concluded that younger children are more focused on the reward than the actual task and lose interest when the reward is not offered.[6] More recent studies are mixed. Using praise and stickers as rewards can be very effective in encouraging children to try new foods that are healthy.[7] It may be that offering rewards to unmotivated teens may help get them on the right track to healthier exercise, dietary, and study habits. Conversely, extrinsic rewards may undermine intrinsic motivation for highly motivated teens, whereas "autonomous self-regulated learning" leads to better results.[8]

Giving teens regular feedback regarding their performance in relation to their predetermined goal, their past performance, or the performance of others can help to ensure that intentions translate into desired behaviors. Health and wellness applications, such as Fitbit or MyFitnessPal, incorporate this strategy by allowing comparison of daily step counts to previous days or to those of "friends" in a person's network, as well as to personal goals set by the user. Once we set our intention to achieve a practical short-term goal, reaching that goal makes us feel good, and we are more likely to succeed with the next little goal. Once again, success begets success!

Intention setting is valuable in establishing a mindfulness practice for teens and adults. First, we can set our intention on committing five minutes a day to mindfulness meditation. During our meditation, we can focus in part on the content of our intention, as we do in the GAIN practice. A central theme in this book is that our brains are wired to be negative and to wander to the past and future—not to be aware of the present moment. Through mindfulness practice, we can begin to rewire our brains to be more positive and present. We can spend a minute during our mindfulness meditation focusing on our present experience—the sensation of the pressure of the chair or floor against our body, the tingling in the soles of our feet, the sound of an airplane passing in the distance, the movement of air through our nose as we breathe slowly and deeply. We can also reaffirm our intention to be more grateful and optimistic when we are feeling depressed—we can spend a few moments of appreciation for our friends and loved ones, our relative health, and the good fortune to have a roof over our heads and access to good food.

To set your intention, sink into your heart and discover what you truly want. You will feel excited and inspired when you reach what is important and essential to you. You can separate your sincere desires from your list of things you "should" do. What people truly desire sparks joy, energy, and engagement, whereas what people think that they *should* do often evokes feelings of stress, anxiety, and even depression. The list of "shoulds" emanates from a *judgment* about how things should be. When you set your intention, pause and listen to your heart. Tune into your emotions and witness what you deeply feel. If you feel energized, that is the right direction. If you feel dread, that is the wrong direction. Listening to your heart will guide you in the right direction. Discussing and modeling this with your teens will do them a world of good.

## Bottom Line

- Set your intention for the day every morning—it is an essential part of the GAIN meditation described later in the book.
- Actualize your intentions by taking small bites or baby steps—this sets you up for success, and success makes you happier and more committed to embracing the next intention.
- Remind yourself that intention is all about the *process*—there is no *destination*.
- Discuss and model these concepts with your teen.

# TEN

# NONJUDGMENT

As Eckhart Tolle reminds us, nonjudgment is interwoven with acceptance. If we simply accept things, we see that no judgment is required. Judgment also describes how we value everything we see and hear as good or bad, too tall or short, too quiet or too noisy. We are prone to categorizing and naming everything. These workings of the mind also constitute judgments. Judgment is so ingrained in our thoughts and feelings that it seems impossible to eliminate at first consideration. Even dictionaries seem unable to get by without this word—the root word, "judgment," partly defines "judgmental" and "nonjudgmental."[1]

Nonjudgment is an essential ingredient in mindfulness. Jon Kabat-Zinn defines mindfulness as "awareness that arises through paying attention, on purpose, in the present moment, nonjudgmentally."[2] We can cultivate mindfulness by paying close attention to our experience right now, in this moment, while letting go of judgment. "This moment" changes continuously, but we can flow with this understanding. As we relax into this moment, we can try briefly to avoid getting caught up in our ideas, opinions, likes, and dislikes. Then we can see things as they truly are, as opposed to how we perceive them through the lens of our point of view.

The first step in this process is becoming aware of the continuous stream of judging, labeling, valuing, categorizing, and reacting to what we encounter. Our initial response to hearing, seeing, feeling, and tasting is to name it: *that sounds awful . . . looks beautiful . . . feels soft . . . tastes bitter*. If we decide to take a step back and pay attention to the labeling done continuously by our thinking self, our mind, we will experience the judgments we continually make. Things do not *have* to be good or bad. We do not *have* to categorize all our thoughts, arranging them into neat little packets. Letting go of our judgment of everything we encounter takes practice. Just as with focusing on our gratitude, acceptance, and intention, we can commit to taking baby steps. We can try this for a few minutes every morning.

This all-too-human habit of reducing and categorizing our experiences is deeply ingrained in our thinking processes based on years of practice. We react automatically without even noticing. Judgments fill our minds, blocking our ability to see clearly and objectively. We fail to appreciate the full spectrum of colors around us, having donned colored eyeglasses that alter our entire field of view. Always making judgments not only robs us of the fullness of life's pleasures, but it is also exhausting! Our minds bounce from one critical condemnation to the next without rest. As Jon Kabat-Zinn suggests, "If you doubt this description of your mind, just observe how much you are preoccupied with liking and disliking during, say, any given ten-minute period as you go about your day."[3]

As with gratitude, acceptance, and intention, it takes practice to rewire our critical minds to be less judgmental. First, we must identify these automatic judgments. Then we can pause and ask ourselves, "Do I really *need* to label this experience as good or bad, something I like or dislike?" We can recognize that this process is tiring, sapping our energy. It prevents us from seeing the totality in front of us. It reinforces our fears and anxieties, holding us hostage.

Once we identify the brain's tiring compulsion to judge everyone and everything, we can begin to curb this habit. For example, you could suspend judgment of the first person you see each morning about whom you begin to form judgmental thoughts. Maybe the driver in the next lane changes lanes in front of you without using their turn signal. You could practice this again in the afternoon, or the first time you smell cigarette smoke on the jacket of the person in front of you at the grocery checkout.

On the other hand, when we find ourselves categorizing people we meet and putting them into little boxes labeled "good" or "bad," we do not have to stop ourselves every time. *Baby steps.* Simply being aware that we are doing this is a positive development. Slowly but surely, we will realize how silly and unnecessary this is. We will begin to truly embrace the differences in our colleagues, coworkers, relatives, and everyone else. We will find joy in this—after all, what a boring world it would be if everyone were like us. At least as importantly, we will acknowledge that we are imperfect, and others who may judge us may do so with a measure of disdain. We will likely realize that these judgments are counterproductive in the process of sinking into happiness.

We all tend toward negative thoughts and are inherently judgmental to varying degrees. This is especially true of teenagers. One of the main causes of stress in teens is negative thoughts and judgments about themselves. Rapid changes in their biology and emotional constitution, as well as interaction with peers and society, predispose them to be self-conscious. Given their negativity bias, they become self-critical. Teens also tend to be sensitive to perceived judgment by others; they often experience feelings of rejection by their friends, peers, and adults in their lives. Sensitivity to rejection has been associated with problems having healthy relationships, anxiety, and depression.[4]

The good news is that mindfulness-based interventions, especially those focused on nonjudgment, may decrease teens' adverse sensitivity to rejection.[5] Teens can learn to let go of judgments, especially negative ones of others and themselves. Mindfulness training teaches nonreactivity to one's experience—this reduces automatic, reflexive feelings of rejection and encourages more adaptive responses. We do not resist judgmental feelings—we simply become observers of these thoughts and emotions and learn to detach from negative interpretations.

Several studies have zeroed in on the role of mindfulness and nonjudgment training in adolescents and young adults. College students who were less likely to be judgmental had less tendency to have feelings of rejection.[6] Undergraduate students reported that mindfulness practice, including nonjudgment, was associated with less "negative affectivity," including emotional lability, anxiety, and insecurity.[7]

The combination of negativity bias and overthinking the past leads to "rumination" in teens. Rumination is the obsessive dwelling on negative thoughts—repeatedly. Unwanted, often disturbing thoughts crop up repeatedly. Rumination is maladaptive—it can cause significant emotional and psychological distress. It has been associated with anxiety and eating disorders, obsessive-compulsive disorder, depression, and substance abuse. Adolescents learning nonreactivity and nonjudgment through mindfulness training are less likely to suffer from rumination.[8]

Adolescents often use drugs and alcohol to cope with stress, particularly those who have experienced stress during childhood, such as growing up in a low-income family. So-called stress-related substance abuse highlights the need to identify and implement coping resources in these teens. A study explored whether mindfulness skills, including nonjudgment, might buffer against stress-related substance use among teenagers.[9] The population studied was a group of 212 diverse adolescents regarding gender and race. Interestingly, the results of the study suggest that nonjudgment and acceptance may be protective against stress-related substance abuse in girls but not boys. In a study of undergraduate students with problematic alcohol use, mindfulness skills, including nonjudgment, were associated with decreased anxiety.[10]

Teens are often focused on their bodies—again, their negativity bias leads them to form negative judgments regarding their body size and shape. There is good news here as well—mindfulness-based training emphasizing nonjudgment and neutral observation and acceptance can decrease unhealthy feelings, including shame, pertaining to physical attributes.[11]

Many teenagers are perfectionists. It is generally good for young people to have high expectations for themselves. So perfectionism among teens is a good thing, right? It leads to high achievement in school, the arts, and sports. There is a dark side, however. Adolescent perfectionism may have adverse emotional and physical effects during adolescence and adulthood. Perfectionism may be associated with eating disorders, anxiety, anger, and depression.[12] It turns out that more than a quarter of teens are afflicted with "maladaptive perfectionism," the striving for unrealistic performance that ultimately causes anxiety and depression. The incidence is even higher among college students.[13] The COVID-19 pandemic magnified the prevalence of perfectionism.[14] Among teens, girls are more likely to be affected than boys.

Once again, there is good news—mindfulness training can greatly benefit teens who are perfectionists and highly self-judgmental.

Mindfulness, with a special focus on nonjudgment, may be especially effective in helping perfectionists deal with high stress levels. Nonjudgment mindfulness helps perfectionists recover from stress.[15]

Exposing teens to mindfulness training focusing on nonjudgment benefits them throughout their lives. Mindfulness training helps us to rewire our brains away from our negativity bias and distraction, even obsession, with the past and future. Mindfulness training helps us become more positive, optimistic, and present. Studies have shown that learning nonjudgment during the teen years may help adults deal with stressful circumstances. A study in women with breast cancer revealed that those with mindfulness skills of nonjudgment and nonreactivity to inner experience were better able to deal with stress, depressive symptoms, fatigue, and sleep disturbance and experienced improved quality of life. This was especially true among women with greater exposure to childhood adversity.

Let's help our teens learn mindfulness now and reap the benefits for the rest of their lives!

How can parents and other adults help teens become less judgmental? First, they can embrace nonjudgment as part of their own mindfulness practice. We cannot expect our teens to listen to us and do what we suggest if we do not "walk the walk" and demonstrate positive and pragmatic habits ourselves. We can model nonjudgmental behavior. We can demonstrate our own respect for diversity, our willingness to listen to others (especially our teens) without forming judgments, and our empathy toward others. We can openly discuss stereotypes and biases and how these lead us to make unfair judgments. Let's identify common misconceptions and substitute facts and our own experiences that counteract such erroneous beliefs.

Every person is unique—let's discourage comparisons to others and labeling people as good or bad. Let's discuss various cultures, beliefs, and points of view with our teens. Let's expose teenagers to diverse art, music, literature, and experiences. We can encourage open, nonjudgmental communication by allowing our teens to express their thoughts, fears, and opinions without fear of judgment. Let's model empathy toward others in the family, including ourselves.

Let's practice the art of listening with our teens and encourage them to do likewise. Active listening requires being fully present and without judgment.

We are our own harshest critics. We judge ourselves through a veil of negativity much of the time. For many of us, this is perhaps the most significant barrier to finding peace and happiness. As we learn to let go of the reductionist approach of assessing others and the world, we still may tend toward self-criticism. Too often, we rehash our mistakes, obsessing about what we might have done differently to achieve a better result. We might try a cognitive behavioral approach—pretending to be talking to a friend whom we would not judge. Consider how reassuring and empathetic you would be with a friend. Why not treat yourself the same way? There is a certain undeniable logic to this thought experiment. It is helpful for many of us to practice this way of thinking. As with all other aspects of rewiring the brain, though, this will be a gradual process comprised of small steps.

A little less judgment, a little bit at a time; then breathe in, breathe out, and repeat.

## *Bottom Line*

- Help your teens become aware of how they categorize and make judgments when such thinking is not beneficial. They, like us, can learn to *discern* without judging.
- Release judgments as they arise. Start with the first person you encounter each morning as you head to work. You can then help teach this skill to your teens.
- Help your teens learn cognitive behavioral skills so they can be less self-judgmental. The next time their self-talk is especially harsh, they can pretend that they are talking to a dear friend. They will almost certainly be kinder to themselves.
- Teaching teens mindfulness with a focus on nonjudgment will help them for the rest of their lives.

# PART IV

*Putting It All Together*

## ELEVEN

# THE GAIN MEDITATION

Meditation is an ancient practice that is at least as relevant now as ever before. Most of us are under a tremendous amount of stress. We experience anger, are quick to react, and suffer fatigue from the ever-present strain. We are wired to obsess over the past, generating regret and shame, and the future, producing fear and anxiety. We spend too little time enjoying the present moment, which is the only moment we can ever truly experience! It is always *now*, and we are always *here*, yet we seem to be elsewhere, missing the beauty and fun—missing our lives! The good news is that we can rewire our brains—they remain malleable and ready to be redirected. Through meditation, our brains can be primed to refocus on the here and now. Meditation can help us experience our gratitude, accept the pain we feel, utilize our intention to point in the direction of happiness, and let go of our constant judgments. In other words, we can actualize GAIN through even a brief meditation. This is a very liberating discovery!

Many people believe that meditation occurs while sitting on the floor in a fixed (often uncomfortable) position for long periods while eliminating all thoughts. In fact, you can meditate in any position or situation. You can even meditate while walking or doing activities of daily life. Meditation does not require a certain body position or attaining a state without thoughts. There are no rules, in fact. Meditation can be a quiet contemplation enjoyed in any position of comfort. If we activate our intention to sit peacefully, accepting thoughts for what they are as they filter past—transient sensations, nothing more—we can sink into our hearts and allow a sense of peace to sink in.

It is OK to change positions or scratch an itch during meditation.

Meditation is not actually *doing* anything specific at all. It is more like *non-doing*.

Meditation has many forms. Meditation does not have any intrinsic connection to religion or philosophy. It can be practiced for a few minutes or for hours at a time. Several forms of meditation have become popular in our culture; for example, mantra-based, movement-based, and mindfulness meditation. Meditation can be contemplative, wherein we focus our thoughts on specific areas, as with the GAIN meditation, in which we focus on gratitude, acceptance, intention, and nonjudgment sequentially as we breathe deeply, slowly, and deliberately.

Spiritual meditation is practiced in Eastern religions, including Buddhism, Hinduism, and Taoism, as well as the Christian faith. Spiritual meditation may be based on the repeated internal pronouncement of a special word or "mantra." A mantra is a sacred utterance, a word or group of words that practitioners believe to have psychological and spiritual powers. The word *mantra* can be broken down into two parts: *man*, which means "mind," and *tra*, which means "transport" or "vehicle." Our mantra can be a source of energy for our intentions during meditation. Spiritual meditation can be practiced anywhere, including at home or in a place of worship. This practice is beneficial for those who thrive in silence and seek spiritual growth.

Movement meditation can be practiced while walking through the woods or the corridors of the workplace, while gardening, or during other activities. The rhythm of moving and focusing on the breath is centering, with or without a mantra. Movement meditation is good for those of us who find peace in body rhythms.

Mindfulness meditation originates from Buddhist teachings and is the most popular meditation method practiced in the West. With mindfulness meditation, we focus on the breath while allowing our thoughts to drift by—we do not resist them but rather witness them. We take note of our thoughts without judging them as good or bad. We are neutral observers. Mindfulness meditation can bring greater health, happiness, clarity, and well-being, even amid pain and suffering. It can soothe grief, self-judgment, and fear.

Jon Kabat-Zinn created an eight-week mindfulness-based stress reduction (MBSR) program at the University of Massachusetts in 1979, recruiting a group of chronically ill patients to participate.[1]

These patients were not responding well to conventional medical therapy. After his eight-week MBSR course, the participants enjoyed improved health and overall quality of life. Since then, MBSR and the mind-body connection have been gradually incorporated into mainstream medicine and beyond. Many studies performed over the past decades confirm that people can find a degree of peace within their minds and bodies through the practice of MBSR.

A 2010 study evaluated changes in brain gray matter concentration attributable to participation in an MBSR program.[2] MRI images from healthy, meditation-naive participants were obtained before and after participation in the eight-week program. The results suggest that MBSR training is associated with positive changes in gray matter concentration in brain regions involved in learning and memory processes, emotion regulation, self-referential processing, and perspective taking. In other words, the study identified anatomic changes, or neuroplasticity, induced by meditation that were associated with improvements in quality of life. This study added to information gleaned from several cross-sectional anatomical MRI studies demonstrating that experienced meditators exhibit a different gray matter shape and size, or morphometry, in multiple brain regions when compared to nonmeditating individuals.

Other studies using functional MRI (fMRI) have shown equally striking examples of neuroplasticity induced by mindfulness meditation. Subjects completing MBSR training have been shown by fMRI to have increased neuronal activity in the brain network associated with the "present moment" experience.[3] We can learn to be present more of the time through simple meditation, as opposed to being caught up in the constant chattering in our minds relating to maladaptive thoughts of the past (regret and shame) and future (fear and anxiety).

A popular form of meditation that focuses on increasing our capacity for forgiveness and connection to others, as well as self-acceptance, is the loving-kindness meditation.[4] As with other forms of meditation, we find a few minutes of quiet time, sit comfortably, close our eyes, and bring our attention to slowing our breathing. We may think of physical and emotional peace, gratitude, acceptance, intention, and nonjudgment.

Once we experience relaxation, we repeat a series of phrases silently to ourselves:

- May I be filled with loving-kindness.
- May I be safe.
- May I be healthy, peaceful, and strong.
- May I give and receive gratitude today.

This meditation may feel mechanical or awkward at times. It can also raise feelings contrary to loving-kindness—feelings of irritation or anger. If this happens, being patient and kind toward yourself is especially important, receiving whatever arises in a spirit of friendliness and kindness.

We then shift our attention to others in our lives—our partner, child, parent, or dear friend, and repeat:

- May you be filled with loving-kindness.
- May you be safe.
- May you be healthy, peaceful, and strong.
- May you give and receive gratitude today.

Practicing meditation reduces the adverse responses to psychological and physical stress. One study evaluated the size of blisters resulting from a laboratory-induced skin injury.[5] Blister size was smaller among subjects after MBSR training, and individuals who spent more time meditating showed a greater benefit than those who practiced less. In another study, people who meditated during light therapy treatment for psoriasis healed four times faster than those undergoing the treatment without meditation.[6]

Meditation appears to enhance emotional IQ (EQ) as well. MBSR training was delivered to a group of corporate employees who were stressed out.[7] Brain activity in areas in the prefrontal cortex known to be associated with the expression of emotions shifted, demonstrating that the meditators were handling emotions such as anxiety and frustration more effectively. Remarkably, those in the MBSR group mounted a brisker antibody response to the flu vaccine than did those who had not taken the course. The meditators with the most favorable shift in emotional reserve had the highest immune response.

Meditation can also reduce loneliness, itself a risk factor for mental and physical health problems. Adults ranging from age fifty-five to eighty-five showed a reduction in loneliness, a decrease in C-reactive protein (a marker of inflammation), and reduced expression of genes related to inflammation as measured by immune cells in the blood.[8] Inflammation and social isolation are both believed to be factors in the development of Alzheimer's disease, so meditation may be of benefit with respect to this disorder.

There are many impressive examples of how the power of meditation favorably influences our bodies and minds. Even better news is that meditation is easy. Start now and take baby steps forward.

The foundation of meditation is attention to the breath. Slow, deep breathing increases oxygen delivery to our tissues and optimizes ventilation-perfusion matching in our lungs—that is, it improves lung function. Both the signal intensity and duration of the firing of the pulmonary stretch receptors increase because of the increased expansion of the lungs from a deeper and longer inhalation relative to normal. This activates the vagus nerve, decreasing our heart rate and blood pressure, lowering stress hormone levels, and causing our muscles to be more relaxed.[9]

What more do we know about the science of meditation and how it might greatly benefit teens and their families? We know that meditation can increase blood flow to various regions in the brain associated with executive function, particularly the prefrontal cortex, cingulate gyrus, and hypothalamus. Practicing meditation and other "concentrative practices" activates a beneficial feedback loop involving these areas of the brain.[10] Meditation activates neuroplasticity—inducing structural and functional changes in these areas of the brain. For example, increased activation of the anterior cingulate gyrus has been identified in mindfulness meditators relative to nonmeditators.[11] This area of the brain is associated with focusing and directing attention and sorting out conflicting information. The prefrontal cortex is important for complex cognitive function—mindfulness also activates this region. Mindfulness meditation may decrease brain volume loss in the prefrontal and frontal cortex in older individuals, suggesting that it defends against neural degeneration with age.[12] Meditators have displayed increased brain volume in the prefrontal cortex, an area involved in executive function.[13]

What is executive function? The term encompasses mental processes based on the prefrontal and frontal lobes of the brain that enable us to focus our attention, plan, juggle multiple tasks, and make well-informed decisions. It helps us plan, solve problems, and "self-regulate." Executive function is critical for focusing attention, emotional regulation, forming successful relationships, and many other activities of daily living.[14] Executive function evolves rapidly during the teenage years. It is well known that teens often have difficulty paying attention, keeping their emotions in check, and making good decisions. They have immature executive function.

Consider the components of executive function for teens as they learn to drive. A driver needs to be able to quickly shift their attention between the road in front of them and the mirrors for their rear and side views. They must effectively inhibit any attention to distracting discussions between other passengers (and themselves). They also need the ability to update their working memory with revised directions in case their original route needs to be changed. How many parents are fearful about their teen's ability to drive a car without becoming distracted? Why not introduce routines into their lives that have been shown to improve executive function?

Meditation also causes alterations in important neurochemicals in the brain, including dopamine, serotonin, glutamate, gamma-aminobutyric acid (GABA), dimethyltryptamine (DMT), N-acetyl aspartyl glutamic acid (NAAG), and corticotropin-releasing hormone (CRH).[15] Evidence suggests that consistent training in meditation, for example, strengthens this brain circuitry and leads to an increased number of connections between neurons in the brain that secrete dopamine and, therefore, higher dopamine levels. This may further increase one's ability to focus their attention.

In other words, there appears to be a very favorable positive feedback loop in play here—meditation practice can augment important neurotransmitter levels, including dopamine, that facilitate an improved ability to pay attention and focus one's thoughts. Focused attention begets more focused attention. And there is more to the story of meditation and the physiology of the brain and the body, including its potential to help combat one of the deadly enemies of good health: inflammation.

There is a fascinating relationship between meditation and inflammation. Inflammation in the body contributes to the diseases of aging—cardiovascular disease, neurodegenerative diseases (e.g., Alzheimer's disease), metabolic syndrome (type 2 diabetes, obesity), and even cancer. Inflammation also has been associated with poor performance in tasks that require attention.[16] Mindfulness meditation training may lead to improvements in attention and focused thinking in part by reducing inflammation.[17]

Again, practicing meditation helps improve focused attention by strengthening selected circuits and chemical levels in the brain. These circuits and neurochemicals, including dopamine, play a role in reducing inflammation. Inflammation contributes to degenerative diseases of the brain as we age. Reducing inflammation likely helps stave off these degenerative changes, preserving our ability to focus our attention—and meditate!

Teens with a variety of challenges might especially benefit from mindfulness meditation training. Substance abuse has been associated with dysfunction in the prefrontal and frontal cortex and impaired executive functioning.[18] Mindfulness meditation also improves executive function and well-being in teens and preteens with ADHD.[19] Even brief mindfulness meditation sessions in school have been shown to improve mental health and well-being among teens and preteens.[20] Mindfulness meditation has been found to facilitate healthy brain development in adolescents involved in the juvenile justice system.[21] It makes good sense to consider how mindfulness meditation practice can be integrated into elementary, middle, and high schools—it might help mitigate or prevent the development of these conditions.

How much meditation do we and our teens need to reap these benefits? There is a famous saying, the origin of which is attributed to Zen Buddhism: "You should sit in meditation for twenty minutes every day—unless you are too busy. Then you should sit for an hour." The fact is that few of us have the patience to sit for that long. We resist doing so even if we believe it would be healthy for us to do so. So let's start with three to five minutes a day. This will begin the process of rewiring the brain. Our brains have become wired the way they are over hundreds of thousands of years—we will not see major change for the better in a day or a week. On the other hand, simply sitting for a short time every day can begin the process in remarkable ways. The more we practice mindfulness meditation, the better we will feel and the more we will commit to this new way of thinking and being. Let's explore one mindfulness meditation practice called the GAIN method.

## THE GAIN MEDITATION

Some of you have tried meditation and believe that you "failed." Others may be longtime meditators, possibly off and on during your adult life. Perhaps you have tried mantra-based meditation or MBSR. The mindfulness meditation theme of this book is a contemplative practice based on GAIN—gratitude, acceptance, intention, and nonjudgment, principles discussed in previous chapters. With GAIN meditation, there are no rules—no required body positions or equipment. Sit in a chair or on the floor. Get comfortable. If you become restless or uncomfortable in one spot, rearrange your body into a more comfortable pose. Add a pillow, yoga bench, or chair. Lie down if you prefer (though best not to fall asleep!). Scratch an itch if you like.

It is very common for busy people to say, "I do not have time to meditate," or "I tried meditation but could not keep thoughts out of my mind and therefore never felt as though I benefited." One of the foundations of GAIN meditation is that it does not require a significant time commitment. We can begin with a focus on our breathing, then move through GAIN in only three minutes. We can remind ourselves that there is no such thing as failure. We can add small exercises focusing on the GAIN principles throughout the day. These may take no additional time at all, since we can do them while walking the dog, making the bed, or preparing a meal.

Start by taking small bites, or baby steps, when beginning this practice of GAIN meditation. You can start with a three-minute session each morning. The important thing is to commit to doing so every day, so it becomes a habit. This practice sets the stage for the rest of your day, preparing you to be more present. It will be the foundation for practicing gratitude, acceptance, intention, and nonjudgment as the day unfolds. It is best to do the GAIN meditation first thing in the morning. Set the alarm clock three minutes earlier than usual. Setting your alarm reminds you that no massive change in routine is needed. Everyone can manage to get up three minutes earlier!

As with other forms of meditation, we begin by finding a relatively quiet place and sitting in a comfortable position on a chair, cushion, or floor. Again, there are no rules, no special way to sit. Close your eyes. Notice the shape of your body, its weight. Let yourself relax and become curious about your body seated here—the sensations, the touch, the connection with the floor or the chair. Relax any areas of tightness or tension. Just breathe.

Begin to pay attention to the breath entering your nostrils and passing through your throat into your belly. Notice the rise and fall of your belly and chest. Slow your breath a bit—this helps to bring awareness to it. It may be helpful to focus on the timing of the phases of your breathing—inhaling deeply through your nose to a silent count of three, holding your inhalation for three seconds, then slowly exhaling through your nose or mouth to a count of four.

Your breath is your center, and you can return to paying attention to it whenever useful. In the beginning, count the seconds for inhaling (three), holding (three), and exhaling (four). Notice the relaxation of your body as you breathe. You might do a "body scan" as you breathe deeply and slowly, noticing the release of any tension in your face, neck, chest, belly, pelvis, legs, and feet. Remain aware of your breath during all phases of the meditation.

Once you have developed a slow rhythm of breathing and letting go of muscle tension, begin noticing your gratitude. For example, "I am so grateful for my relative health (your health may not be perfect, but we can be grateful for the parts that are working well!), my friends, and my loving family. I am fortunate to have such a connected community at home and at work. Unlike many others in the world, I am grateful for having a roof over my head and good food to eat. I am grateful for having a home with running water and electricity. I am so fortunate."

Now that you feel grateful, gently transition to acceptance. Life is as full of suffering as it is of joy, and we need to embrace this rather than resist it. We all suffer, and we all have experiences that trigger sadness and pain. You can be mindful of this without judgment or resistance—as a neutral witness. You might quietly recognize the residual vibration of human suffering over the centuries, including wars and enslavement of people around the world and the loss of hope and freedom of entire populations. You might notice the destruction of habitats around the globe as humanity expands its domain. You may become aware of the pain you are experiencing in your own life and the blame and shame you heap upon yourself. As you breathe in the pain and suffering inherent to life itself, notice that you cannot change many of these problematic circumstances. You did not cause them, and you cannot fix them. You did not create violence in the world, famine, or environmental disasters. The understanding begins to permeate your awareness—the key is to accept that which you cannot change. Let it be. It simply is as it is. You begin to release your resistance to life's pain and suffering, to breathe it out as you slowly exhale. Relax as you breathe slowly, deeply, and deliberately, and let it be.

The next phase in GAIN meditation is to focus on your intention as you link this domain to your breathing. Start by noticing the pressure of the chair against your body, the tingling sensation in the soles of your feet, and the sound of a car or airplane passing by in the distance. Stay with this attention for five, ten, or fifteen seconds. Your mind may begin to wander after only a few seconds—simply bring your attention back to your sensations as you breathe deeply and deliberately. Then be aware of the in-breath as it brings with it the awareness that you have the ability and strength to decide how you want to think and act. You can choose happiness. You can remember three good things that happened yesterday and smile. You can gradually rewire your brain, aiming to be grateful, accepting, and without judgment. You can decide to treat others with kindness and respect, regardless of their apparent station in life or relationship to you. You can decide to eat more healthily, exercise regularly, and prioritize sleep. You are empowered to manage your own life as you see fit. You are blessed with the force of intention. Breathe in this new understanding, slowly inhaling, pausing, and exhaling.

You next turn to nonjudgment. You do not have to label everything as good or bad, worthwhile or useless. Instead, you can observe dispassionately, with benevolent indifference. As Krishnamurti said, "I do not mind what happens." You can cherish the way the world is as it is, choosing not to weigh the good against the bad and come to some arbitrary conclusion. Again, the world simply is as it is, in all its beauty and splendor. It will go on being that way regardless of your naming or judging it.

As we breathe deeply, slowly, and deliberately, we might picture an image of the earth suspended in space—perhaps one of the beautiful NASA images with which most of us are familiar. It is apparent that the earth is a lovely planet—yet it does not possess the qualities of goodness or badness. It is neither good nor bad. It is simply the planet that it is. No judgment. It is only logical to believe that we are neither good nor bad. We are simply who we are. As we breathe in and out, we acknowledge that "I am neither good nor bad. I simply am the person that I am. I simply am. I am." We link this understanding to our breath. "I am neither good nor bad. I simply am." We are rewiring our brains to let go of judgment. As we are our own most harsh critics, this practice of letting go of self-judgment is vital.

Return to your breath, slowly taking it in, holding it, and releasing it without effort. You notice that you feel good. Rest this way for as long as you want. Then, very gradually, open your eyes, resting in your refreshed awareness of gratitude, acceptance, intention, and nonjudgment. Now you are ready to head out into the world.

You might be surprised by how quickly the process of rewiring your brain begins. The next time you notice negative self-judgment, focus on deep, slow, and deliberate breathing. The experiences of gratitude, acceptance, intention, and nonjudgment will begin to appear. Zoom in on linking the "I am simply the person that I am" understanding with the breath. You are continuing the process of rewiring your brain toward a happier, more peaceful way of being.

As mindful meditation becomes part of your daily routine, consider sharing the practice with your teen. Start with just the breathing part, then introduce other elements you enjoy. Your teen may surprise you by accepting and embracing this as they, too, experience the benefits.

### Bottom Line

- Start with a three-minute GAIN meditation every morning.
- Set your alarm three minutes earlier than usual the night before—this solidifies your intention to do the practice.
- Get comfortable in a quiet, welcoming place.
- Begin with the breath—slow inhalation, pause, slower exhalation.
- While keeping attention on the breath, calmly focus on gratitude, then acceptance, then intention, then nonjudgment. Though this may seem a bit difficult at first, it will quickly become familiar and effortless.
- Open your eyes slowly.
- Promise yourself that you will do at least one brief exercise today; for example, "Today, I will be nonjudgmental of the first person I see." As the day progresses, you can do several other little gratitude, acceptance, intention, and nonjudgment practices.
- Share this practice with your teens!

## TWELVE

# EXTRACURRICULAR ACTIVITIES

During the COVID-19 pandemic, students were deprived not only of classroom learning experience. They also could not participate in most extracurricular activities, including sports, academic groups, clubs, and even volunteering in their local communities. They were deprived of the many benefits these activities have to offer. Fortunately, the option of virtual extracurriculars developed. Once the acute phase of the pandemic subsided, participation in in-person activities increased sharply. Current trends include increasing student involvement in STEM-related (science, technology, engineering, and math) extracurricular activities, including robotics clubs. Girls and minorities represent a growing segment of STEM participants.[1] Participation in esports, or organized video game competitions, has grown rapidly during the past several years.[2]

Participation in sports at the high school level declined in the years prior to the COVID-19 pandemic and bottomed out during the pandemic. Fortunately, it has rebounded dramatically with a sharp increase in participation during the 2022–2023 school year.[3] This is good news.

Why are extracurricular activities so important?

### COLLEGE APPLICATIONS: BUILDING A RESUME

As all high school juniors and seniors applying to college (and their parents) know, grades and test scores alone are insufficient to gain acceptance into the best schools. Admissions committees care about involvement in clubs, sports, theater, dance, and other engagement outside of the classroom. They want to learn about the person your teen is becoming, the skills they might bring to the college, and the level of commitment and hard work they demonstrate outside of academics. Accordingly, teens are increasingly pressured to engage in extracurricular activities as part of college application requirements.

Colleges want to know what makes applicants unique.

What are the best extracurricular activities for making an impression on college admissions committees? The ones that match your teen's passions and interests. High schools offer many programs, including sports teams, cheerleading, music (bands, orchestra, choir), school publications (yearbook, newsletters), student government, drama, debate, and chess.

Community activities may be attractive—they facilitate engagement in local directives, serving others meaningfully. Volunteering for a nonprofit allows one to demonstrate one's true values, level of commitment, and work ethic. If your teen is interested in animal welfare, volunteering at a local animal shelter demonstrates passion for helping animals and compassion for others.

Independent extracurricular activities include online courses, such as computer software coding, hosting an online podcast, or even starting a small business. Colleges want students with a passion for learning, ingenuity, and hard work.

Beyond being attractive to colleges, these extracurricular activities offer other benefits, such as learning new skills, meeting other students outside shared classes, and developing close relationships with other students and adults, including coaches and mentors.

## EXTRACURRICULARS CAN HELP TEENS BUILD CONFIDENCE AND SELF-ESTEEM

There are countless success stories wherein a student's engagement in one or more extracurricular activities facilitated tremendous growth, self-esteem, confidence—and perhaps acceptance into a college in which grades and test scores alone would not have permitted.

Angela participated in theater in middle school and as a high school freshman. Her love of dance led her to switch to cheerleading, or "cheer," by her sophomore year. Her presence on the cheer squad for varsity football and basketball made her more familiar and popular among her classmates. Her self-confidence grew. Her shyness gave way to a more extroverted persona. By her senior year, she was captain of the cheer team—her hard work and commitment had paid off in a multiplicity of ways. One was her newfound skill of time management—cheer practice was a two-and-a-half to three-hour daily commitment. She had to be efficient to complete her homework and maintain excellent grades. There was far less time for social media, for example—a positive side effect of her involvement in cheer.

Jackson was an avid jazz enthusiast and tenor sax player in middle and high school. He played in the school band and a jazz quartet. He became best friends with two of the others in the bands. They played on their own on weekends and attended local jazz performances on a regular basis. As seniors, they even recorded several tracks that were played on the local college radio station. They were featured on a podcast together. They wrote their own compositions. Their ability to work seamlessly with others as a team grew tremendously, as did their self-confidence. Once a bit socially awkward, Jackson became a magnetic and well-known personality at his high school. He was accepted at a first-tier college with a notable music program. He later majored in biology en route to medical school, but his love for jazz and music in general never waned.

As with Lily, Jackson's significant commitment to music had great benefits beyond enhancing his resume for college applications.

These included:

- forming close relationships with peers with common interests
- taking instruction from and being mentored by adult leaders
- learning how to work as a team in a collaborative manner with peers
- spending time with other students from a variety of backgrounds with diverse perspectives and life experiences
- increasing self-confidence and self-esteem
- learning greater time management skills—and *spending less time on social media*

Extracurricular activities are avenues for positive social and emotional development. They provide students with a sense of accomplishment and greater self-esteem. They may be an avenue to reduce stress and anxiety.

A bonus of extracurricular involvement may be the mindfulness skills your teen develops when coached and mentored accordingly. Let's consider sports participation as an example.

## SPORTS AND MINDFULNESS FOR TEENS

Participation in sports and other forms of physical activity helps promote positive development in several ways. At the middle and high school levels, team sports benefit from the extracurricular activities listed above—and perhaps others.

Involvement in sports offers a great opportunity to introduce mindfulness training. Mindfulness training contributes to a sense of well-being, decreases injury risk, and improves recovery from injury—and it is an invaluable tool in improving athletic performance.[4] As a bonus, children and teens involved in organized sports experience less anxiety and depression and tend to have less social inhibition and shyness.[5]

Mindfulness is distinct from other forms of mental training in sports, such as "psychological skills training" (PST). Among athletes, PST commonly includes goal setting, mental rehearsal, self-talk, and imagery.[6] PST focuses on modifying emotions and thoughts that may interfere with optimal performance in sports. Mindfulness, on the other hand, aims to change the athlete's *relationship* with their emotions and thoughts rather than the *content* of them. For example, nonjudgment is essential to mindfulness practices, such as the GAIN method. By embracing the GAIN practice, we learn that it is OK to have thoughts of self-doubt, as student-athletes commonly experience. Student-athletes tend to ruminate over past failures—by dropping the negative judgment associated with these thoughts, they are less likely to respond to their ideations in negative, maladaptive ways. Through mindfulness practice, we simply observe our negative thoughts rather than trying to resist them.

The impact of nonjudgment on well-being is well described in sports psychology literature and elsewhere.[7]

Burnout among athletes can occur as early as high school. Burnout is the emotional and physical exhaustion caused by chronic stress. High school students may quit sports activities due to burnout. This may leave them with a sense of failure and decreased self-esteem. Mindfulness practice may reduce burnout among student-athletes.[8]

Mindfulness practice offers several additional benefits that influence the student-athlete's athletic performance and quality of life. These include reduced pain, inflammation, anxiety, and depression (see chapter 6) and an improved ability to focus attention and enter a "flow state."[9] This is an adaptive mental state wherein athletes are completely immersed in the activity in which they are engaged. They are fully present without distraction. There is a sense of complete fluidity of body and mind. Cognitive and physical performance are enhanced—a soccer player in the flow state anticipates an opponent's next move and has optimized ball handling and shooting accuracy. The basketball player in flow effortlessly floats the ball through the basket without hitting the rim—nothing but net.

Coaches with mindfulness training can practice simple exercises with their students as part of daily training and before and during games. David Matthew Brown, founder of Underground Savages, has been counseling and coaching women's soccer and other athletes for more than fifteen years. He describes "mindset hacks" for athletes that incorporate mindfulness principles.[10]

A few favorites include the following:

- Visualize success by create a mental image of yourself succeeding at achieving a personal best race time, making a perfect basketball shot, or executing a flawless gymnastics routine.
- Rather than fixate on a goal or result, embrace the journey and the small victories along the way through *intention*. This is the *I* in GAIN (see chapter 9).
- Spend a few minutes just before practice or competition practicing mindfulness—for example, start with the breath and progress through the GAIN elements. This is one example of a pre-practice

ritual that can help calm nerves and facilitate getting "in the zone" or flow state. Repeat this simple process whenever negative thoughts creep in or during a time-out before a crucial moment in the game. As a team exercise, focus on slow, deep, deliberate breathing. Then link the breath to the experience of *gratitude* for the privilege of participating with the other team members today, *acceptance* of any imperfections in performance, *intention* of being fully focused on each moment of the game, and *nonjudgment* of team members and oneself.

Visualization can be powerful, especially when combined with slow, deep, deliberate breathing. Dr. Fred Luskin is a psychologist, author, and founder of the Stanford Forgiveness Project. He works closely with the Stanford women's basketball team. Coach Tara VanDerveer asked Dr. Luskin to meet with the team on a weekly basis to teach breathing exercises and meditation with guided visualizations. The latter often involved imagining what a successful practice looks like or thinking of warmth and affection toward a teammate. Team members refer to Dr. Luskin as "Stanford's happiness professor" and consider his role with the team as invaluable.[11]

## *Bottom Line*

- Extracurricular activities are vital for high school students' development and to demonstrate their well-roundedness and motivation for college. Starting in middle school gives students a head start!
- Extracurricular activities help teens build self-confidence and self-esteem.
- Extracurricular activities help teach teens teamwork and time management.
- Sports, in particular, offer the opportunity to learn mindfulness techniques that not only enhance performance but also provide skills that teens can use for the rest of their lives to reduce anxiety and depression—and improve the quality of their lives!

# CONCLUSION

In this book, we have reviewed the trials and travails of the teen years. Adolescence is a journey full of wonder, growth, new experiences, brain and body development, and unique challenges. Many of the difficulties that teens face nowadays are unlike any with which older generations had to contend. Some of the demanding elements are age-old, including biological changes referred to as puberty.

Consider the biological aspects of the teen's journey. Dramatic transformations in the body include growth spurts in height and weight, changes in the skin, voice, and speech, growth of body hair, and sexual development. Biological and social circumstances shape this process of puberty. Puberty involves a network of complex changes that includes neural and hormonal processes that occur over several years, affecting the physical development teens experience. Many of these developments begin to occur earlier in girls, typically between ten and fourteen years of age, whereas most boys mature between the ages of fourteen and seventeen. The changes may be rapid and may create awkwardness between boys and girls as the latter grow taller and more physically mature.

Personal relationships develop during these teenage years as well, and when teens become romantically involved, the discrepancy in physical development can be a source of stress and anxiety. Teens going through puberty can be very self-conscious, and this may have negative effects on their relationships with others, including peers and partners.

Adolescents need nurturing environments and support as they explore, learn, and experiment. Parents become important role models in many ways. Parents who embrace mindfulness practices are in a favorable position to provide a calming and reassuring influence. On the other hand, a disruptive family life makes adolescence even more challenging.

Adolescence does not begin with a "blank slate"—it is founded on earlier childhood experience. Parents' ability to positively influence their teens begins as early as the first year of life. Interestingly, puberty itself is influenced by childhood experiences and circumstances—it may occur earlier in response to stressors that include sexual and other physical abuse, absence of the father, obesity, and even environmental toxins, including chemicals in plastics, pesticides, and hair-care products.[1] Though these and other stressors predispose teens to depression and anxiety, they do not fully determine the course of the journey of adolescence, of course. When teens are provided with the best tools possible to be successful on their journey through adolescence, they can be remarkably resilient.

Socially, teens explore peer relationships as they establish autonomy from their family of origin. Later in adolescence, teens begin to develop complex social relationships and romantic interests, as well as higher-risk exploratory behaviors, including substance use. Teens may also seek to explore career options and establish some financial autonomy.[2]

Psychological and cognitive thinking become more sophisticated, moving from concrete to more advanced abstract thought. Adolescents also begin to develop morality and their sense of the political, philosophical, and religious/spiritual.[3] Teens' ways of thinking evolve dramatically as they undergo a rapid period of brain development. Adolescence is a crucial time when the brain experiences changes in executive functions such as memory processing, cognition, reasoning, focusing, decision making, and social skills.[4]

Given the biopsychosocial changes and transitions teens experience, it makes sense that they experience intense emotions, begin to explore their sexuality and social boundaries, express their identities and autonomy, and establish deeper relationships.

Teenagers are driven toward novel experiences that push them out of the comfortable nest of their childhood and provide them with new opportunities and the rewards their brains crave. The downside of novelty seeking can be underestimating the dangers associated with new behaviors, which can result in accidents, injuries, and other adverse outcomes.

Typically, being socially engaged contributes to positive psychological outcomes. However, being overly concerned about peer inputs and undervaluing adult inputs may leave teens at risk for poor decisions and choices. The positive is that there is a predictive link between close friendships in mid-adolescence and increases in feelings of self-worth. Healthy peer relationships decrease anxiety and depressive symptoms, which are common among teens.[5]

The increased emotional intensity experienced by teens can give life a lot of flavor and color. However, their decisions may be clouded by moodiness, impulsive actions, and reactivity and volatility.

The creative capacity of teens can open the door to innovative problem-solving approaches, keeping life fresh and fun. In pushing creative boundaries and exploring vulnerabilities, however, they may be susceptible to social pressures and toxic peer influence.

The neurotransmitter dopamine plays a vital role in generating the drive for reward in the teen brain. Dopamine release increases beginning in early adolescence. It tops off during middle adolescence and is associated with the teen drive toward novelty, excitement, and sensation-seeking behaviors, which can sometimes be a risky antidote to boredom. The neuropsychiatrist Daniel Siegel suggests that, compared to adults, a teen's baseline level of dopamine may be lower, but the dopamine response to life experiences may be higher. Therefore, the teen brain's dopamine response system can play an essential role in the development of addictive behaviors such as those linked with drugs and alcohol, but also those behaviors based on dysregulated technology use, social experiences, and extreme sports.

Teens may make risky decisions with serious consequences that they may not have considered. This is likely evident to parents who reflect on their own teenage years when they may have experimented with alcohol, tobacco, marijuana, psychedelics, and other risky behaviors, including unprotected sex, high-speed driving, or other extreme behaviors that may have had severe consequences. Adolescent mortality studies demonstrate that most deaths and morbidities during this developmental stage can be prevented.[6] The Centers for Disease Control and Prevention (CDC) reports that among fifteen to nineteen-year-olds, the leading causes of death include accidents, homicide, and suicide.

In the face of the COVID-19 crisis in 2021, the American Academy of Pediatrics (AAP) and several other associations concerned with the welfare of children and adolescents acknowledged the rise in mental health challenges that teens faced. They emphasized that children and their families across the United States had experienced tremendous adversity and disruption.[7] Ongoing problems such as inequities resulting from structural racism exacerbated the problem. By 2018, suicide was the second leading cause of death among youth ages ten to twenty-four. The pandemic made things even worse, with dramatic increases in emergency department visits for mental health emergencies, including suicide attempts. The joint AAP declaration pointed out that more than 140,000 children in the United States lost a primary and/or secondary caregiver during the peak years of the pandemic, with non-white youths disproportionately affected. They underscored the soaring rates of depression, anxiety, trauma, and loneliness too often leading to suicide.

In response to these conditions, the AAP-led consortium made a detailed declaration calling for the following:

- Increase federal funding dedicated to ensuring that all families and children, from infancy through adolescence, can access evidence-based mental health screening, diagnosis, and treatment to appropriately address their mental health needs, with particular emphasis on meeting the needs of under-resourced populations.
- Address regulatory challenges and improve access to technology to ensure continued availability of telemedicine to provide mental health care to all populations.
- Increase implementation and sustainable funding of effective models of school-based mental health care, including clinical strategies and models for payment.
- Accelerate the adoption of effective and financially sustainable integrated mental health care models, including clinical strategies and payment models, in primary care pediatrics.
- Strengthen emerging efforts to reduce the risk of suicide in children and adolescents through prevention programs in schools, primary care, and community settings.

- Address the ongoing challenges of the acute care needs of children and adolescents, including shortage of beds and emergency room boarding, by expanding access to step-down programs from inpatient units, short-stay stabilization units, and community-based response teams.
- Fully fund comprehensive, community-based systems of care that connect families in need of behavioral health services and support for their child with evidence-based interventions in their home, community, or school.
- Promote and pay for trauma-informed care services that support relational health and family resilience.
- Accelerate strategies to address longstanding workforce challenges in child mental health, including innovative training programs, loan repayment, and intensified efforts to recruit underrepresented populations into mental health professions, as well as attention to the impact that the public health crisis has had on the well-being of health professionals.
- Advance policies that ensure compliance with and enforcement of mental health parity laws.

Beyond the ongoing effects of COVID-19, today's teens must try to make sense of stressors rooted in global and national issues, environmental crises, school challenges, family challenges, friends, and so on. One does not have to think too hard to identify the numerous stressors teens face. There is ongoing global violence and war, gun violence in schools, social media pressure, academic performance, and the list goes on. Many of these stressors are environmental and interpersonal. They amplify teens' internal psychological battles.

The US surgeon general published an advisory reporting that we are experiencing a loneliness epidemic, with the largest group impacted being Gen Z youth aged sixteen to twenty-four.[8] Another report from the US surgeon general stated that even before the COVID-19 pandemic, mental health challenges led the way in causing disability and adverse life outcomes in young people.[9] Alarmingly, one statistic demonstrated that 49.4 percent of the 7.7 million children with a treatable mental health disorder in 2016 went untreated.[10] The CDC reports leading psychological disorders among children and teens include attention deficit hyperactivity disorder, anxiety, behavior problems, and depression.

Growing up in the digital age has included a dimension we parents and grandparents never imagined. The pros and cons of being so connected and "plugged in" via smartphones, tablets, and computers are profound. Indeed, social media offers a great mechanism for staying in touch with friends and family—and exposure to shaming, bullying, and entrapment by an endless stream of scammers.

The competition for college admission seems to be ever increasing, leading to anxiety and often unfavorable comparisons to classmates and friends.

Sexual identity issues have arisen in unimaginable ways. Pornography, so easily accessed on the internet, has influenced how teens view sexual relations—commonly in unhealthy ways.

The world is replete with anxiety-provoking realities. Given the unprecedented climate change affecting countless people around the globe, teens may well wonder whether there will be a viable planet for their children and grandchildren to inherit. War is nothing new—but with so many innocent civilians being killed in conflicts in the Middle East, Europe, and elsewhere, there is great sadness among our teenagers. The COVID-19 pandemic continues its deleterious effects on many of us, including teenagers.

There is also prevailing change regarding how we parent and teach our teens. The roles we parents and teachers assume are managed differently than they were even a generation ago. Parents are much more deeply involved in their children's lives today, and teachers must be more sensitive to how their students respond to challenges. Things are different nowadays.

Has the pendulum swung too far regarding our efforts to protect our children from potentially upsetting realities at home and in school? Is it OK to expose them—or allow them to be exposed—to a measured amount of discomfort?

We might be reminded of historical trends that resulted when parents began to avoid exposing their young children to substances that might trigger allergies. Peanut allergies, for example, were rare prior to the 1990s. During the next several decades, however, the prevalence of peanut allergies in the United States more than tripled.[11] Babies born in developing countries have a lower incidence of peanut allergies—but if their families move to a developed country, the likelihood that their children will develop peanut allergies increases.

A prevailing theory explaining this phenomenon, the "hygiene hypothesis," suggests that exposure to allergens, including peanuts and various germs, leads to immune systems that become better equipped to differentiate harmless from harmful substances. Evidence to support this hypothesis includes a lower incidence of allergies among children who grow up on farms or with pets. The LEAP (Learning Early about Peanut Allergy) study supports this concept. Researchers studied 640 infants under the age of one year who were at high risk of developing peanut allergies because they had other allergies or eczema, a known risk factor for peanut allergy. Half of these infants were fed snacks containing peanut products and the other half's parents were counseled to avoid all exposure to peanuts and peanut products. All the children were tested for peanut allergies at the age of five years. Remarkably, only 3 percent of children who were fed peanut products developed a peanut allergy, whereas the incidence of peanut allergy in the "avoidance" group of children was 17 percent![12]

"Extreme hygiene," the use of antibiotics when of questionable indication, and inadequate exposure to pets and outdoor play may predispose children to allergies. Under these conditions, the developing immune system overreacts to environmental substances that are not threatening.

In other words, being overprotective with respect to exposure to the environment may have seemingly paradoxical results.

Can we generalize this principle? By shielding our children from every possible risk, might we be training them to be overly fearful of situations that are not actually dangerous or risky at all? Are today's teens at risk of becoming "triggered" too easily? Are we hampering their ability to develop adult coping skills that they will need later? Should we teach our children that it is OK to fail and experience pain, that these are intrinsic experiences in life for all of us? Just as our muscles grow and strengthen when stressed, we benefit from mental challenges. Learning to accept pain that we cannot change lessens our suffering. A mathematical expression of this principle might be: suffering = pain/acceptance. When "acceptance"—the denominator—is large, "suffering" becomes small.

Rather than trying to shield our teens excessively from challenging experiences that may result in failure and discomfort, we can help teach them how to cope successfully with failure, stress, and pain in ways that will last a lifetime. That is the aim of this book.

## THE ROLE OF MINDFULNESS

Our brains are wired in ways that favor survival—but not happiness. We are wired to have a negativity bias—we remember and focus on the negative and forget and underemphasize the positive aspects of our lives. In addition, our brains are easily distracted—our thoughts tend to drift to the past or the future. If we simply close our eyes and try to pay attention to what we are currently experiencing—physical sensations, sounds—we have trouble remaining there for more than a few seconds. Instead, our attention goes to something we said or did yesterday or to the list of things we need to do later today or tomorrow. Combined with our negativity bias, our rumination of past events results in regret, shame, and depression; consideration of what the future holds brings fear and anxiety.

Teens are no exception. They are well skilled at resisting discomfort in their lives and judging the world, others, and, most notably, themselves in a negative manner. The resultant severe self-judgment and depression they experience are major factors in their lives. They are prone to lacking self-confidence and being self-critical. There is no limit to sources of anxiety in their lives—relationships with peers, body image, acceptance to college, and on and on.

Though not the sole driver for drug and alcohol use, the sadness and anxiety many teens experience may contribute to substance use. The results may be catastrophic.

Here is where mindfulness practice can be of great benefit. By embracing gratitude, acceptance, intention, and nonjudgment, for example, we can all find peace even in the face of physical discomfort and a world that so often does not seem to comport with our wants and needs. We can learn to focus on our breathing—slow, deep, and deliberate—and activate our parasympathetic nervous system to neutralize the stress response we experience frequently. We can model these vital tools for our children and students. They are watching us. When we appear calm in the face of all the stressful stimuli the world has to offer, we are paying attention.

Not only can we embrace mindfulness, but we can help teach it to our children. We can find the right times to discuss our gratitude for the comforts of daily life we enjoy and the love we share with friends and family. We can listen with our full attention as they express their worries and frustrations; we can guide them in acceptance of these inevitable aspects of life. Reminding them of all we must be grateful for is a key element in acceptance—the GAIN elements are tightly interwoven. We can help them to be purposeful in moving closer to acceptance and the peace it may bring. We can remind them that they are not alone—we are all wired in ways that may lead to sadness, depression, and self-doubt as well as fear and anxiety. Thankfully, our brains have the magic quality of neuroplasticity—if we stick to the plan, we can move in the direction of happiness. We can show our teens the way toward nonjudgment—the world is simply the realm that it is, neither good nor bad, and all of us are simply human beings, neither good nor bad.

## JOYS OF ADOLESCENCE

Despite the many serious challenges teens face, there are also significant joys and positives of the teenage years. In 2023, the *New York Times* asked a group of young people what they love about their adolescent years.[13]

Some of their responses:

- The best part about being a teenager is having fun and being with your friends.
- It's freedom and independence.
- It's not having to worry about paying bills or taking care of a family.
- It's getting to make mistakes.
- It's dreaming about the future.

Powerfully, the authors concluded that when asked if teens "could wave a magic wand and wish to be an adult," the teens resoundingly said "no." The teens interviewed in this article noted that they would rather not have burdens such as paying bills and taxes, worries about feeding the family, putting gas in the car, and the stresses of having a job.

It seems that a path toward strengthening parents' bonds with teens is to encourage them to enjoy this time in their lives, and parents may also take joy in their teens' joy.

Many teens feel good about themselves, are optimistic about the future, and hold dreams about what being an adult can be like. It provides us adults with a sense of relief that teens enjoy bright moments and joy during these years despite the many challenges presented them.

Our aim in writing this book is not to signal alarm but to instill hope that we can live happier lives despite the challenges we and our teens face. If we have a plan—that is, intention—we can continue to grow, transform, and embrace the present. We can create a brighter future for our teens and ourselves. We can model forgiveness, compassion, and empathy. We can learn to be more loving toward our teenagers, each other, and ourselves.

We hope that the central message of this book—that mindfulness practice can be adopted as an invaluable way of life for parents and teens—resonates with readers. We sincerely hope that this book serves as a useful resource for everyone caring for teens—parents, teachers, counselors, and school administrators.

We are grateful for the opportunity to contribute to helping our teens navigate the daunting process of growing into adulthood successfully.

# NOTES

## CHAPTER ONE

1. "Average Screen Time for Teenagers in 2024," Cosmo, February 14, 2024, https://cosmotogether.com/blogs/news/average-screen-time-for-teenagers-in-2024; Jonathan Rothwell, "Parenting Is the Key to Adolescent Mental Health," Gallup.com, November 30, 2023, https://www.gallup.com/analytics/610151/ifs-usa-parenting-research.aspx.

2. Maria T. Maza, Kara A. Fox, Seh-Joo Kwon, Jessica E. Flannery, Kristen A. Lindquist, Mitchell J. Prinstein, and Eva H. Telzer, "Association of Habitual Checking Behaviors on Social Media with Longitudinal Functional Brain Development," *JAMA Pediatrics* 177, no. 2 (2023): 160–67. doi:10.1001/jamapediatrics.2022.4924.

3. Jonathan Rothwell, "Parenting Mitigates Social Media–Linked Mental Health Issues," Gallup.com, October 27, 2023, https://news.gallup.com/poll/513248/parenting-mitigates-social-media-linked-mental-health-issues.aspx.

4. Petroc Taylor, "Percentage of Teenagers in the United States Who Have Access to a Smartphone at Home as of October 2023, by Gender," Statista, February 28, 2024, https://www.statista.com/statistics/256501/teen-cell-phone-and-smartphone-ownership-in-the-us-by-gender/.

5. Judy A. Beal, "Impact of Social Media on Adolescents," *MCN, American Journal of Maternal/Child Nursing* 47, no. 2 (March/April 2022): 108. doi:10.1097/NMC.0000000000000799.

6. US Department of Health and Human Services, "Surgeon General Issues New Advisory about Effects Social Media Use Has on Youth Mental Health," May 23, 2023, https://www.hhs.gov/about/news/2023/05/23/surgeon-general-issues-new-advisory-about-effects-social-media-use-has-youth-mental-health.html.

7. Sara Randazzo and Alyssa Lukpat, "Los Angeles School District Votes in Favor of Cellphone Ban," *Wall Street Journal*, June 18, 2024, https://www.wsj.com/us-news/education/los-angeles-school-district-votes-in-favor-of-cellphone-ban-667c1ff3.

8. Jocelyn Gecker, "Kids Are Using Phones in Class, Even When It's against the Rules. Should Schools Ban Them All Day?" AP News, February 27, 2024, https://apnews.com/article/school-cell-phone-ban-01fd6293a84a2e4e401708b15cb71d36.

9. Julie Jargon, "This School Took Away Smartphones. The Kids Don't Mind," *Wall Street Journal*, November 5, 2022, https://www.wsj.com/articles/this-school-took-away-smartphones-the-kids-dont-mind-11667614444.

10. https://www.overyondr.com/phone-free-schools

11. David Leonhardt, "Smartphones in Schools," *New York Times*, September 6, 2024, https://www.nytimes.com/2024/09/06/briefing/smartphones-in-schools.html.

12. https://teendriversource.research.chop.edu/

13. B. B. Kirley, K. L. Robison, A. H. Goodwin, K. J. Harmon, N. P. O'Brien, A. West, S. S. Harrell, L. Thomas, and K. Brookshire, "Young Drivers," in *Countermeasures That Work: A Highway Safety Countermeasure Guide for State Highway Safety Offices* (Washington, DC: National Highway Traffic Safety Administration, 2023), https://www.nhtsa.gov/book/countermeasures-that-work/young-drivers.

14. "Distracted Driving," US Centers for Disease Control and Prevention, May 16, 2024, https://www.cdc.gov/distracted-driving/about/index.html.

15. Renata Maria Silva Santos, Camila Guimaraes Mendes, Guilherme Yang Sen Bressani, G. Samara de Alcantara Ventura, Yago Jean de Almeida Nogueira, Débora Marques de Miranda, and Marco Aurélio Romano-Silva, "The Associations between Screen Time and Mental Health in Adolescents: A Systematic Review," *BMC Psychology* 11, no. 127 (April 20, 2023). doi:10.1186/s40359-023-01166-7.

16. *The Annual Bullying Survey 2017*, Ditch the Label, https://dtl-beta-website-assets.s3.amazonaws.com/ABS_2017_1_ae04a7734b.pdf.

17. J. W. Patchin and S. Hinduja, "Cyberbullying Facts," Cyberbullying Research Center, 2024, https://cyberbullying.org/facts.

18. Charisse L. Nixon, "Current Perspectives: The Impact of Cyberbullying on Adolescent Health," *Adolescent Health, Medicine, and Therapeutics* 5 (2014): 143–58. https://doi.org/10.2147/AHMT.S36456.

19. A. J. Skiera, "What Gen Z Thinks about Its Social Media and Smartphone Usage," The Harris Poll, September 10, 2024, https://theharrispoll.com/briefs/gen-z-social-media-smart-phones/.

20. P. M. Dennis, "Chills and Thrills: Does Radio Harm Our Children? The Controversy over Program Violence during the Age of Radio," *Journal of the History of the Behavioral Sciences* 34, no. 1 (winter 1998): 33–50.

21. Robby Soave, "People Have Been Panicking about New Media since before the Printing Press," *Reason: Free Minds and Free Markets*, November 2021, https://reason.com/2021/09/29/people-have-been-panicking-about-new-media-since-before-the-printing-press/.

22. Amy Orben, "The Sisyphean Cycle of Technology Panics," *Perspectives on Psychological Science* 15, no. 5 (September 2020): 1143–57.

23. Frank Furedi, "The Media's First Moral Panic," *History Today*, 65, no. 11 (October 2015).

24. Mary I. Preston, "Children's Reactions to Movie Horrors and Radio Crime," *Journal of Pediatrics* 19 (1941): 147–68.

25. *Television and Growing Up: The Impact of Television Violence* (Rockville, MD: National Institute of Mental Health, 1971), https://www.ojp.gov/ncjrs/virtual-library/abstracts/television-and-growing-impact-televised-violence.

26. S. L. Garrett, K. Burnell, E. L. Armstrong-Carter, M. J. Prinstein, and E. H. Telzer, "Linking Video Chatting, Phone Calling, Text Messaging, and Social Media with Peers to Adolescent Connectedness," *Journal of Research on Adolescence* 33, no. 4 (December 2023): 1222–34.

27. Blair Babida, "Hollow Flashlight," EEWeb, July 13, 2018, https://www.eeweb.com/hollow-flashlight/.

28. Google, "Empowering Kids to Be Safe, Confident Explorers of the Online World, Be Internet Awesome," August 2024, https://beinternetawesome.withgoogle.com/en_us.

29. "Ratings and Reviews Parents Trust," Common Sense Media, August 2024, https://www.commonsensemedia.org/.

## CHAPTER TWO

1. Craig B. Little and Andrea Rankin, "Why Do They Start It? Explaining Reported Early-Teen Sexual Activity," *Sociological Forum* 16 (2001): 703–29.

2. Lawrence B. Finer and Jesse M. Philbin, "Sexual Initiation, Contraceptive Use, and Pregnancy among Young Adolescents," *Pediatrics* 131, no. 5 (2013): 886–91, https://publications.aap.org/pediatrics/article-abstract/131/5/886/31308/Sexual-Initiation-Contraceptive-Use-and-Pregnancy.

3. M. J. K. Osterman, B. E. Hamilton, J. A. Martin, A. K. Driscoll, and C. P. Valenzuela, "Births: Final Data for 2020," *National Vital Statistics Reports* 70, no. 17 (2022).

4. "Sexually Transmitted Infections Workgroup," *Healthy People 2030*, January 9, 2025, https://odphp.health.gov/healthypeople/about/workgroups/sexually-transmitted-infections-workgroup.

5. J. L. Corcoran, P. Li, S. L. Davies, C. C. Knight, R. G. Lanzi, and S. L. Ladores, "Adolescent Chlamydia Rates by Region, Race, and Sex: Trends from 2013 to 2017," *Journal of Pediatric Health Care* 35, no. 2 (2021): 172–79. doi:10.1016/j.pedhc.2020.09.004.

6. I. H. Spicknall, E. W. Flagg, and E. A. Torrone, "Estimates of the Prevalence and Incidence of Genital Herpes, United States, 2018," *Sexually Transmitted Diseases* 48, no. 4 (April 1, 2021): 260–65.

7. L. Kann, T. McManus, W. A. Harris, S. L. Shanklin, K. H. Flint, B. Queen, R. Lowry, D. Chyen, L. Whittle, J. Thornton, C. Lim, D. Bradford, Y. Yamakawa, M. Leon, N. Brener, and K. A. Ethier, "Youth Risk Behavior Surveillance—United States, 2017," *Morbidity and Mortality Weekly Report Surveillance Summaries* 67, no. 8 (2018): 1–114.

8. "Pornography Statistics," Covenant Eyes, April 8, 2023, http://cvnteyes.co/1EV7964.

9. "How Many People Are on Porn Sites Right Now? (Hint: It's a Lot)," *Fight the New Drug*, 2023, https://fightthenewdrug.org/by-the-numbers-see-how-many-people-are-watching-porn-today/.

10. "New Report Reveals Truths about How Teens Engage with Pornography," Common Sense Media, January 10, 2023, https://www.commonsensemedia.org/press-releases/new-report-reveals-truths-about-how-teens-engage-with-pornography.

11. "New Report Reveals Truths about How Teens Engage with Pornography," Common Sense Media.

12. Ana J. Bridges, Robert Wosnitzer, Erica Scharrer, Chyng Sun, and Rachael Lieberman, "Aggression and Sexual Behavior in Best-Selling Pornography Videos: A Content Analysis Update" *Violence against Women* 16, no. 10 (October 2010): 1065–85.

13. Chyng Sun, Ana Bridges, Jennifer A. Johnson, and Matthew B. Ezzell, "Pornography and the Male Sexual Script: An Analysis of Consumption and Sexual Relations," *Archives of Sexual Behavior* 45, no. 4 (May 2016): 983–94.

14. Michael Leahy, *Porn University: What College Students Are Saying about Sex on Campus* (Northfield, VT: Northfield Publishing, 2009), 117–18.

15. Sheri Madigan, Ahn Ly, Christina L. Rash, Joris Van Ouytsel, and Jeff R. Temple, "Prevalence of Multiple Forms of Sexting Behavior among Youth," *JAMA Pediatrics* 172, no. 4 (April 2018): 327–35; Donald S. Strassberg, Deanna Cann, and Valeri Velarde, "Sexting by High School Students," *Archives of Sexual Behavior* 46, no. 6 (August 2017): 1667–72.

16. Wendy A. Walsh and Dafna Tener, "'If You Don't Send Me Five Other Pictures I Am Going to Post the Photo Online': A Qualitative Analysis of

Experiences of Survivors of Sextortion," *Journal of Child Sexual Abuse* 31, no. 4 (April 21, 2022): 447–65.

17. Aina M. Gasso, Katrin Mueller-Johnson, and Irene Montiel, "Sexting, Online Sexual Victimization, and Psychopathology Correlates by Sex: Depression, Anxiety, and Global Psychopathology," *International Journal of Environmental Research and Public Health* 17, no. 3 (February 6, 2020): 1018.

18. "2023 State of Deepfakes: Realities, Threats, and Impact," Security Hero, January 9, 2025, https://www.securityhero.io/state-of-deepfakes.

19. Alyson Orcena, Melissa Vallas, Shikha Verma, Ellen Bloch, and Lianne Tendler, "Understanding and Addressing Teen Sexual Assault: A Parent's Guide," Evolve, October 30, 2023, https://evolvetreatment.com/parent-guides/teen-sexual-assault/.

20. Eugenia Torazzi, Vera Merelli, Giussy Barbara, Alessandra Kustermann, Laura Marasciuolo, Federica Collini, and Cristina Cattaneo, "Similarity and Differences in Sexual Violence against Adolescents and Adult Women: The Need to Focus on Adolescent Victims." *Journal of Pediatric and Adolescent Gynecology* 34, no. 3 (June 2021): 302–10.

## CHAPTER THREE

1. "8 Ways Covid Has Impacted Teen Mental Health, and What We Can Do about It," *St. Louis Jewish Light*, September 26, 2021, https://stljewishlight.org/news/world-news/8-ways-covid-has-impacted-teen-mental-health-and-what-we-can-do-about-it.

2. "Israeli Study: 1 in 4 Kids Became More Violent during COVID Era," *Times of Israel*, September 2, 2021, https://www.timesofisrael.com/study-1-in-4-israeli-kids-became-more-violent-during-Covid-era/.

3. "8 Ways Covid Has Impacted Teen Mental Health," *St. Louis Jewish Light*.

4. Sandra Lopez-Leon, Talia Wegman-Ostrosky, Norma Cipatli Ayuzo del Valle, Carol Perelman, Rosalinda Sepulveda, Paulina A. Rebolledo, Angelica Cuapio, and Sonia Villapol, "Long-COVID in Children and Adolescents: A Systematic Review and Meta-Analyses," *Scientific Reports* 12, no. 9950 (June 13, 2022).

5. Kelly Y. L. Ku, Qiuyi Kong, Yunya Song, Lipeng Deng, Yi Kang, and Aihua Hu, "What Predicts Adolescents' Critical Thinking about Real-Life News? The Roles of Social Media News Consumption and News Media Literacy," *Thinking Skills and Creativity* 33 (September 2019).

6. "Gun Safety Policies Save Lives," 2024 Everytown Gun Law Rankings, January 4, 2024, https://everytownresearch.org/rankings/.

7. Jeffrey Gottfried and Olivia Sidoti, "Teens and Video Games Today," Pew Research Center, May 9, 2024, https://www.pewresearch.org/internet/2024/05/09/teens-and-video-games-today.

8. L. Rowell Huesman, Eric F. Dubow, Paul B. Boxer, Brad B. Bushman, Cathy S. Smith, Meagan A. Docherty, and Maureen J. O'Brien, "Longitudinal Predictions of Young Adults' Weapons Use and Criminal Behavior from Their Childhood Exposure to Violence," *Aggressive Behavior* 47, no. 6 (June 19, 2021): 621–34.

9. "A Partial List of Mass Shootings in the United States in 2022," *New York Times*, January 24, 2023, https://www.nytimes.com/article/mass-shootings-2022.html.

10. "Parenting, Media, and Everything in Between," Common Sense Media, 2024, https://www.commonsensemedia.org/articles/online-safety.

11. Dieter Luthi, Martine Le Floch, Bernhard Bereiter, Thomas Blunier, Jean-Marc Barnola, Urs Siegenthaler, Dominique Raynaud, Jean Jouzel, Hubertus Fischer, Kenji Kawamura, and Thomas F. Stocker, "High-Resolution Carbon Dioxide Concentration Record 650,000–800,000 Years before Present," *Nature* 453 (May 15, 2008): 379–82.

12. Jinho Ahn, Edward J. Brook, Logan Mitchell, Julia Rosen, Joseph R. McConnell, Kendrick Taylor, David Etheridge, and Mauro Rubino, "Atmospheric $CO_2$ over the Last 1000 Years: A High-Resolution Record from the West Antarctic Ice Sheet (WAIS) Divide Ice Core," *Global Biogeochemical Cycles* 26, no. 2 (May 26, 2012): GB2027.

13. "WMO Confirms That 2023 Smashes Global Temperature Record," World Meteorological Organization, January 12, 2024, https://wmo.int/news/media-centre/wmo-confirms-2023-smashes-global-temperature-record.

14. "38°C Record Arctic Temperature Confirmed, Others Likely to Follow: WMO," UN News, December 14, 2021, https://news.un.org/en/story/2021/12/1107872.

15. "Progress Cleaning the Air and Improving People's Health," United States Environmental Protection Agency, 2024, https://www.epa.gov/clean-air-act-overview/progress-cleaning-air-and-improving-peoples-health.

16. "Alcohol's Effects on Health: Research-Based Information on Drinking and Its Impact," National Institute on Alcohol Abuse and Alcoholism, February 2024, https://www.niaaa.nih.gov/publications/brochures-and-fact-sheets/underage-drinking.

17. "Traffic Safety Facts," National Highway Traffic and Safety Administration, June 2022, https://crashstats.nhtsa.dot.gov/Api/Public/ViewPublication/813313.

18. "Monitoring the Future," National Institute on Drug Abuse, June 2024, https://nida.nih.gov/research-topics/trends-statistics/monitoring-future.

19. CDC National Center for Health Statistics, "U.S. Overdose Deaths Decrease in 2023, First Time since 2018," May 15, 2024, https://www.cdc.gov/nchs/pressroom/nchs_press_releases/2024/20240515.htm.

20. Rachel N. Lipari and Arthur Hughes, "How People Obtain the Prescription Pain Relievers They Misuse" (Rockville, MD: The CBHSQ Report, 2017).

21. "Why You Should Talk with Your Child about Alcohol and Other Drugs," Substance Abuse and Mental Health Services Administration, August 2019, https://library.samhsa.gov/product/talk-they-hear-you-why-you-should-talk-your-child-about-alcohol-and-other-drugs-fact-sheet.

22. "Parents Talking about Their Own Drug Use to Children Could Be Detrimental," *Science Daily*, February 22, 2013, https://www.sciencedaily.com/releases/2013/02/130222083127.htm.

23. Mitch Abblett, "Open Book: A Parent's Guide to Self-Disclosure with Kids," *Psychology Today*, January 25, 2011, https://www.psychologytoday.com/us/blog/special-education/201101/open-book-parents-guide-self-disclosure-kids.

## CHAPTER FOUR

1. Deborah Christie and Russell Viner, "Adolescent Development," *BMJ* 330, no. 7486 (2005): 301–4.

2. John Gottman and Nan Silver, *The Seven Principles for Making Marriage Work: A Practical Guide from the Country's Foremost Relationship Expert* (San Jose, CA: Harmony Press, 2015).

3. John Gottman, Joan Declaire, and Daniel Goleman, *Raising an Emotionally Intelligent Child: The Heart of Parenting* (New York: Simon and Schuster, 1998).

4. Christie and Viner, "Adolescent Development," 301.

5. Alannah Shelby Rivers, "Not Just Mothers: Understanding the Unique Role of Attachment to Fathers," Society for Couple & Family Psychology, March 1, 2022, https://www.apadivisions.org/division-43/publications/blog/research/attachment-fathers.

6. Christie and Viner, "Adolescent Development," 301; Melissa Benaroya, "How to Bond with Your Child by Sharing Fondness and Admiration," The Gottman Institute, November 9, 2021, https://www.gottman.com/blog/how-to-bond-with-your-child-by-sharing-fondness-and-admiration/.

7. Fiona White, David Livesey, and Brett Hayes, *Developmental Psychology: From Infancy to Development*, 3rd ed. (Camberwell: Pearson Australia, 2012).

8. Cynthia E. Foster, Adam Horwitz, Alvin Thomas, Kiel Opperman, Polly Gipson, Amanda Burnside, Deborah M. Stone, and Cheryl A. King, "Connectedness to Family, School, Peers, and Community in Socially Vulnerable Adolescents," *Child and Youth Services Review* 81 (October 2017): 321–31.

9. Marlene M. Moretti and Maya Peled, "Adolescent-Parent Attachment: Bonds That Support Healthy Development," *Paediatrics & Child Health* 9, no. 8 (October 2004): 551–55.

10. Benaroya, "How to Bond with Your Child by Sharing Fondness and Admiration."

11. Ellen Boeder, "Emotional Safety Is Necessary for Emotional Connection," The Gottman Institute, 2017, https://www.gottman.com/blog/emotional-safety-is-necessary-for-emotional-connection/.

12. Jeffrey J. Kim, Stacey L. Parker, James R. Doty, Ross Cunnington, Paul Gilbert, and James N. Kirby, "Neurophysiological and Behavioural Markers of Compassion," *Scientific Reports* 10, no. 6789 (April 22, 2020).

13. Daniel J. Siegel and Tina Payne Bryson, *The Power of Showing Up: How Parental Presence Shapes Who Our Kids Become and How Their Brains Get Wired* (New York: Ballantine Books, 2020).

14. Daniel Siegel and Mary Hartzell, *Parenting from the Inside Out: How a Deeper Self-Understanding Can Help You Raise Children Who Thrive* (New York: TarcherPerigee, 2014).

15. Kim, Parker, Doty, Cunnington, Gilbert, and Kirby, "Neurophysiological and Behavioural Markers of Compassion."

16. *Parents under Pressure: The U.S. Surgeon General Advisory on the Mental Health and Well-Being of Parents* (Washington, DC: US Department of Health and Human Services, Office of the Surgeon General, 2024), https://www.hhs.gov/surgeongeneral/priorities/parents/index.html.

## CHAPTER FIVE

1. Nicola S. Schutte and John M. Malouff, "A Meta-Analytic Review of the Effects of Mindfulness Meditation on Telomerase Activity,"

*Psychoneuroendocrinology* 42 (April 2014): 45–48; Elizabeth H. Blackburn, "Telomere States and Cell Fates," *Nature* 408, no. 6808 (November 2, 2000): 53–56.

2. John M. Darley and Daniel C. Batson, "'From Jerusalem to Jericho': A Study of Situational and Dispositional Variables in Helping Behavior," *Journal of Personality and Social Psychology* 27, no. 1 (1973): 100–108.

3. Daniel Lim, Paul Condon, and David DeSteno, "Mindfulness and Compassion: An Examination of Mechanism and Scalability," *PLOS ONE* 10, no. 2 (2015): e0118221. doi:10.1371/journal.pone.0118221.

4. Paul Condon, Gaelle Desbordes, Willa B. Miller, and David DeSteno, "Meditation Increases Compassionate Responses to Suffering," *Psychological Science* 24, no. 10 (Aug 2013): 2125–27.

5. Lim, Condon, and DeSteno, "Mindfulness and Compassion," e0118221.

6. Kelly H. Werner, Hooria Jazaieri, Phillipe R. Goldin, Michal Ziv, Richard G. Heimberg, and James J. Gross, "Self-Compassion and Social Anxiety Disorder," *Anxiety, Stress & Coping* 25, no. 5 (September 2011): 543–58.

7. Mark R. Leary, Eleanor B. Tate, Claire E. Adams, Allen Batts, and Jessica Hancock, "Self-Compassion and Reactions to Unpleasant Self-Relevant Events: The Implications of Treating Oneself Kindly," *Journal of Personality and Social Psychology* 92, no. 5 (May 2007): 887–904.

8. Kristin Neff, "Comparing Compassion for Self and Others: Impacts on Personal and Interpersonal Well-Being," *Human Development* 52, no. 4 (June 2009): 211–14.

9. Parissa Ballard, Lindsay T. Hoyt, and Mark C. Pachucki, "Impacts of Adolescent and Young Adult Civic Engagement on Health and Socioeconomic Status in Adulthood," *Child Development* 90, no. 4 (January 23, 2018): 1138–54.

10. Kayla J. Fike, Jacqueline S. Mattis, Kyle Nickodem, and Casta Guillaume, "Black Adolescent Altruism: Exploring the Role of Racial Discrimination and Empathy," *Children and Youth Services Review* 150 (2023): 106990.

11. Brennan McDonald and Phillipp Kanske, "Gender Differences in Empathy, Compassion, and Prosocial Donations, but Not Theory of Mind in a Naturalistic Social Task," *Scientific Reports* 13, no. 20748 (2023).

12. J. G. Breines and S. Chen, "Self-Compassion Increases Self-Improvement Motivation," *Personality and Social Psychology Bulletin* 38, no. 9 (2012): 1–11.

13. Belén Mesurado, María E. Oñate, Lucas M. Rodriguez, Natalia Putrino, Paulina Guerra, and Claudia E. Vanney, "Study of the Efficacy of the

Hero Program: Cross-National Evidence," *PLOS ONE* 16, no. 4 (April 2021): e0250287. doi:10.1371/journal.pone.0238442.

14. Everett Worthington, *Five Steps to Forgiveness: The Art and Science of Forgiving* (New York: Crown, 2001).

15. Jakob H. Eklund and Martina S. Meranius, "Toward a Consensus on the Nature of Empathy: A Review of Reviews," *Patient Education and Counseling* 104, no. 2 (February 2021): 300–307.

16. Xingchao Wang, Li Lei, Jiping Yang, Ling Gao, and Fengqing Zhao, "Moral Disengagement as Mediator and Moderator of the Relation between Empathy and Aggression among Chinese Male Juvenile Delinquents," *Child Psychiatry and Human Development* 48, no. 2 (April 2017): 316–26.

17. Mary Hylton, "The Role of Civic Literacy and Social Empathy on Rates of Civic Engagement among University Students," *Journal of Higher Education Outreach and Engagement* 22, no.1 (March 2018): 87–106.

## CHAPTER SIX

1. Jon Kabat-Zinn, *Mindfulness for Beginners: Reclaiming the Present Moment—and Your Life*, (Louisville, CO: Sounds True Adult, 2016).

2. Laura G. Kiken, Eric L. Garland, Karen Bluth, Olafur S. Palsson, and Susan A. Gaylord, "From a State to a Trait: Trajectories of State Mindfulness in Meditation during Intervention Predict Changes in Trait Mindfulness," *Personality and Individual Differences* 1, no. 81 (2015): 41–46; Jonathan Gibson, "Mindfulness, Interoception, and the Body: A Contemporary Perspective," *Frontiers in Psychology* 10 (2019). doi:10.3389/fpsyg.2019.02012.

3. Jon Kabat-Zinn, "Some Reflections on the Origins of MBSR, Skillful Means, and the Trouble with Maps," *Contemporary Buddhism* 12, no. 1 (2013): 281–306.

4. Howard E. LeWine, "Understanding the Stress Response," Harvard Health Publishing, April 3, 2024, https://www.health.harvard.edu/staying-healthy/understanding-the-stress-response.

5. "Long Telomeres, the Endcaps on DNA, Not the Fountain of Youth Once Thought—Scientists May Now Know Why," Johns Hopkins Medicine Newsroom, May 4, 2024, https://www.hopkinsmedicine.org/news/newsroom/news-releases/2023/05/long-telomeres-the-endcaps-on-dna-not-the-fountain-of-youth-once-thought--scientists-may-now-know-why.

6. Ann MacDonald, "Using the Relaxation Response to Reduce Stress," Harvard Health Publishing, November 20, 2010, https://www.health.harvard.edu/blog/using-the-relaxation-response-to-reduce-stress-20101110780.

7. Valentin Magnon, Frédéric Dutheil, and Guillaume T. Vallet, "Benefits from One Session of Deep and Slow Breathing on Vagal Tone and Anxiety in Young and Older Adults," *Scientific Reports* 11, no. 19267 (September 2021). doi:10.1038/s41598-021-98736-9.

8. Paul Ekman and Wallace V. Friesen, *Unmasking the Face: A Guide to Recognizing Emotions from Facial Expressions* (Saddle River, NJ: Prentice Hall, 1975).

9. Eduardo L. Bunge, Javier Mandil, Andrés J. Consoli, and Martín Gomar, *CBT Strategies for Anxious and Depressed Children and Adolescents: A Clinician's Toolkit* (New York: Guilford Press, 2017).

10. Dennis Greenberger and Christine A. Padesky, *Mind over Mood*, 2nd ed. (New York: Guilford Press, 2015).

11. David D. Burns, *The Feeling Good Handbook: Using the New Mood Therapy in Everyday Life* (New York: Plume Publishing, 1999).

12. Marshall Hagins and Andrew Rundle, "Yoga Improves Academic Performance in Urban High School Students Compared to Physical Education: A Randomized Controlled Trial," *Mind, Brain, and Education* 10, no. 2 (2016): 105–16.

13. Christina F. Chick, Anisha Singh, Lauren A. Anker, Casey Buck, Makoto Kawai, Christine Gould, Isabelle Cotto, Logan Schneider, Omer Linkovski, Rosy Karna, Sophia Pirog, Kai Parker-Fong, Christian R. Nolan, Deanna N. Shinsky, Priyanka N. Hiteshi, Oscar Leyva, Brenda Flores, Ryan Matlow, Travis Bradley, Josh Jordan, Victor Carrion, and Ruth O'Hara, "A School-Based Health and Mindfulness Curriculum Improves Children's Objectively Measured Sleep: A Prospective Observational Cohort Study," *Journal of Clinical Sleep Medicine* 18, no. 9 (2022): 2261–71.

14. Tara Brach, "RAIN: A Practice of Radical Compassion," *Tara Brach*, August 2024, https://www.tarabrach.com/rain/.

15. Kristin Neff, "Self-Compassion Exercise 1: How Would You Treat a Friend?" *Self-Compassion*, 2024, https://self-compassion.org/exercise-1-treat-friend/.

16. Kristin Neff, "The Criticizer, the Criticized, and the Compassionate Observer," *Self-Compassion*, February 23, 2023, https://self-compassion.org/exercise-4-supportive-touch/.

## CHAPTER SEVEN

1. Sam Goldstein and Jack A. Naglieri, *Encyclopedia of Child Behavior and Development* (Boston: Springer, 2011).

2. *Tibetan Buddhist Dictionary*, s.v. "Ksanti," December 21, 2023, https://www.tibetanbuddhistencyclopedia.com/en/index.php?title=Ksanti.

3. Alex M. Wood, Jeffrey J. Froh, and Adam W. A. Geraghty, "Gratitude and Well-Being: A Review and Theoretical Integration," *Clinical Psychology Review* 30, no. 7 (November 2010): 890–905. doi:10.1016/j.cpr.2010.03.005.

4. J. Bryan Sexton and Kathryn C. Adair, "Forty-Five Good Things: A Prospective Pilot Study of the Three Good Things Well-Being Intervention in the USA for Healthcare Worker Emotional Exhaustion, Depression, Work-Life Balance and Happiness," *BMJ Open* 9, no. 3 (2019): e022695. doi:10.1136/bmjopen-2018-022695.

5. Kathryn C. Adair, Lindsay A. Kennedy, and Bryan Sexton, "Three Good Tools: Positively Reflecting Backwards and Forwards Is Associated with Robust Improvements in Well-Being across Three Distinct Interventions," *Journal of Positive Psychology* 15, no. 5 (July 9, 2020): 613–22.

6. Charlotte vanOyen Witvliet, Fallon J. Richie, Lindsey M. Root Luna, and Daryl R. Van Tongeren, "Gratitude Predicts Hope and Happiness: A Two-Study Assessment of Traits and States," *Journal of Positive Psychology* 14, no. 3 (2018): 271–82. doi:10.1080/17439760.2018.1424924.

7. Nicola S. Schutte, Suresh K. A. Palanisamy, and James R. McFarlane, "The Relationship between Positive Psychological Characteristics and Longer Telomeres," *Psychology and Health* 31, no. 12 (2016): 1466–80.

8. Laura S. Redwine, Brook L. Henry, Meredith A. Pung, Kathleen Wilson, Kelly Chinh, Brian Knight, Shamini Jain, Thomas Rutledge, Barry Greenberg, Alan Maisel, and Paul J. Mills, "Pilot Randomized Study of a Gratitude Journaling Intervention on Heart Rate Variability and Inflammatory Biomarkers in Patients with Stage B Heart Failure," *Psychosomatic Medicine* 78, no. 6 (July–August 2016): 667–76.

9. Barbara L. Fredrickson, "The Broaden-and-Build Theory of Positive Emotions," *Philosophical Transactions of the Royal Society, Series B, Biological Sciences* 359, no. 1449 (September 29, 2004): 1367–78.

10. Glenn R. Fox, Jonas Kaplan, Hanna Damasio, and Antonio Damasio, "Neural Correlates of Gratitude," *Frontiers in Psychology* 6 (September 29, 2015): 1491.

## CHAPTER EIGHT

1. Attributed to Reinhold Niebuhr (1892–1971), 1943.

2. "The Law of Least Effort," Chopra, May 23, 2015, https://chopra.com/blogs/meditation/the-law-of-least-effort.

3. Rachel I. Rosner, "Aaron T. Beck's Drawings and the Psychoanalytic Story of Cognitive Therapy," *History of Psychology* 15, no. 1 (February 2012): 1–18.

4. Jinping Ma, Lili Ji, and Guohua Lu, "Adolescents' Experiences of Acceptance and Commitment Therapy for Depression: An Interpretative Phenomenological Analysis of Good-Outcome Cases," *Frontiers in Psychology* 14, no. 1 (March 22, 2023): 1050227.

## CHAPTER NINE

1. Jon Kabat-Zinn, "Defining Mindfulness," Mindful, January 17, 2017, https://www.mindful.org/jon-kabat-zinn-defining-mindfulness/.

2. David Emerald, *The Power of TED: The Empowerment Dynamic* (Edinburgh, Scotland: Polaris Publishing, 2015).

3. Michelle R. Nelson, Xuan Zhu, Yingying Li, Barbara Fiese, and Brenda Koester, "Get Real: How Current Behavior Influences Perceptions of Realism and Behavioral Intent for Public Service Announcements," *Health Communication* 30, no. 7 (August 4, 2014): 669–79.

4. Eileen S. Anderson, Richard A. Winett, and Janet R. Wojcik, "Self-Regulation, Self-Efficacy, Outcome Expectations, and Social Support: Social Cognitive Theory and Nutrition Behavior," *Annals of Behavioral Medicine* 34, no. 3 (October 1, 2007): 304–12.

5. Kevin G. Volpp, George Loewenstein, Andrea B. Troxel, Jalpa Doshi, Maureen Price, Mitchell Laskin, and Stephen E. Kimmel, "A Test of Financial Incentives to Improve Warfarin Adherence," *BMC Health Services Research* 8, no. 272 (December 23, 2008); Kevin G. Volpp, Andrea B. Troxel, Mark V. Pauly, Henry A. Glick, Andrea Puig, David A. Asch, Robert Galvin, Jingsan Zhu, Fei Wan, Jill DeGuzman, Elizabeth Corbett, Janet Weiner, and Janet Audrain-McGovern, "A Randomized, Controlled Trial of Financial Incentives for Smoking Cessation," *New England Journal of Medicine* 360, no. 7 (February 12, 2009): 699–709.

6. E. L. Deci, R. Koestner, and R. M. Ryan, "A Meta-Analytic Review of Experiments Examining the Effects of Extrinsic Rewards on Intrinsic Motivation," *Psychological Bulletin* 125, no. 6 (November 1999): 627–88.

7. Lucy J. Cooke, Lucy C. Chambers, Elizabeth V. Añez, and Jane Wardle, "Facilitating or Undermining? The Effect of Reward on Food Acceptance. A Narrative Review," *Appetite* 57, no. 2 (October 2011): 493–97.

8. Nienke M. J. Hensen and Olle ten Cate, "How to Deal with the Unmotivated Medical Student in Small Group Sessions?" *MedEdPublish* 6 (May 19, 2017): 86.

## CHAPTER TEN

1. *American Heritage Dictionary of the English Language*, 5th ed. (Boston: Houghton Mifflin Harcourt, 2016).

2. Jon Kabat-Zinn, *Full Catastrophe Living: Using the Wisdom of Your Body and Mind to Face Stress, Pain, and Illness* (New York: Bantam Books, 2013).

3. Kabat-Zinn, *Full Catastrophe Living*.

4. G. Downey and S. I. Feldman, "Implications of Rejection Sensitivity for Intimate Relationships," *Journal of Personality and Social Psychology* 70, no. 6 (June 1996): 1327–43.

5. Jessica R. Peters, Tory A. Eisenlohr-Moul, and Laura M. Smart, "Dispositional Mindfulness and Rejection Sensitivity: The Critical Role of Nonjudgment," *Personality and Individual Differences* 93 (April 1, 2016): 125–29.

6. Downey and Feldman, "Implications of Rejection Sensitivity for Intimate Relationships," 1327.

7. Malek Mneimne, Samantha Dashineau, and K. Lira Yoon, "Mindfulness and Negative Affectivity in Real Time: A Within-Person Process Model," *Cognition and Emotion* 33, no. 8 (March 25, 2019): 1687–1701.

8. Jeffrey A. Ciesla, Laura C. Reilly, Kelsey S. Dickson, Amber S. Emanuel, and John A. Updegraff, "Dispositional Mindfulness Moderates the Effects of Stress among Adolescents: Rumination as a Mediator," *Journal of Clinical Child and Adolescent Psychology* 41, no. 6 (July 9, 2012): 760–70; Miachael J. Tumminia, Blake A. Colaianne, Robert W. Roeser, and Brian M. Galla, "How Is Mindfulness Linked to Negative and Positive Affect? Rumination as an Explanatory Process in a Prospective Longitudinal Study of Adolescents," *Journal of Youth and Adolescence* 49, no. 10 (May 7, 2020): 2136–48.

9. Emily C. Helminen, Tory L. Ash, Emily L. Cary, Samantha E. Sinegar, Pam Janack, Robert DiFlorio, and Joshua C. Felver, "Gender Differences in the Stress-Buffering Effects of Mindfulness Facets on Substance Use among Low-Income Adolescents," *Addiction Behaviors* 136 (January 2023): 107491.

10. Kristen M. Kraemer, Emily M. O'Bryan, Adrienne L. Johnson, and Alison C. McLeish, "The Role of Mindfulness Skills in Terms of Anxiety-Related Cognitive Risk Factors among College Students with Problematic Alcohol Use," *Substance Abuse* 38, no. 3 (July–September 2017): 337–43.

11. Tiffany M. Stewart, "Light on Body Image Treatment: Acceptance through Mindfulness," *Behavior Modification* 28, no. 6 (November 2004): 783–811.

12. Joachim Stoeber, Natalia Schneider, Rimi Hussain, and Kelly Matthews, "Perfectionism and Negative Affect after Repeated Failure: Anxiety, Depression, and Anger," *Journal of Individual Differences* 35, no. 2 (January 1, 2014): 87–94.

13. Hannah R. Koerten, Tanya S. Watford, Eric F. Dubow, and William H. O'Brien, "Cardiovascular Effects of Brief Mindfulness Meditation among Perfectionists Experiencing Failure," *Psychophysiology* 57, no. 4 (April 5, 2020): e13517.

14. Ana Telma Pereira, Carolina Cabaços, Ana Araújo, Ana Paula Amaral, Frederica Carvalho, and António Macedo, "COVID Psychological Impact: The Role of Perfectionism," *Personality and Individual Differences* 184 (January 2022): 111160.

15. Tumminia, Colaianne, Roeser, and Galla, "How Is Mindfulness Linked to Negative and Positive Affect?" 2136.

## CHAPTER ELEVEN

1. Jon Kabat-Zinn, *Full Catastrophe Living: Using the Wisdom of Your Body and Mind to Face Stress, Pain, and Illness* (New York: Delta, 2005).

2. Britta K. Hölzel, James Carmody, Mark Vangel, Christina Congleton, Sita M. Yerramsetti, Tim Gard, and Sara W. Lazar, "Mindfulness Practice Leads to Increases in Regional Brain Matter Density," *Psychiatric Research* 191 (January 30, 2011): 36–43.

3. Norman A. S. Farb, Zindel V. Segal, Helen Mayberg, Jim Bean, Deborah McKeon, Zainab Fatima, and Adam K. Anderson, "Attending to the Present: Mindfulness Meditation Reveals Distinct Neural Modes of Self-Reference," *SCAN* 2, no. 4 (August 13, 2007): 313–17.

4. Jack Kornfield, *The Art of Forgiveness, Loving-Kindness, and Peace* (London: Bantam Press, 2008).

5. Melissa A. Rosenkranz, Richard J. Davidson, Donal G. Maccoon, John F. Sheridan, Ned H. Kalin, and Antoine Lutz, "A Comparison of Mindfulness-Based Stress Reduction and an Active Control in Modulation of Neurogenic Inflammation," *Brain, Behavior, and Immunity* 27, no. 1 (January 2013): 313–22.

6. J. Kabat-Zinn, E. Wheeler, T. Light, A. Skillings, M. J. Scharf, T. G. Cropley, D. Hosmer, and J. D. Bernhard, "Influence of a Mindfulness-Based Stress Reduction Intervention on Rates of Skin Clearing in Patients with Moderate-to-Severe Psoriasis Undergoing Phototherapy (UVB) and Photo-chemotherapy (PUVA)," *Psychosomatic Medicine* 60, no. 5 (September–October 1998): 625–32.

7. Richard J. Davidson, Jon Kabat-Zinn, Jessica Schumacher, Melissa Rosenkranz, Daniel Muller, Saki F. Santorelli, Ferris Urbanowski, Anne Harrington, Katherine Bonus, and John F. Sheridan, "Alterations in Brain and Immune Function Produced by Mindfulness Meditation," *Psychosomatic Medicine* 65, no. 4 (July–August 2003): 564–70.

8. J. David Creswell, Michael R. Irwin, Lisa J. Burklund, Matthew D. Lieberman, Jesusa M. G. Arevalo, Jeffrey Ma, Elizabeth Crabb Breen, and Steven W. Cole, "Mindfulness-Based Stress Reduction Training Reduces Loneliness and Proinflammatory Gene Expression in Older Adults: A Small Randomized Controlled Trial," *Brain, Behavior, and Immunity* 26, no. 7 (July 20, 2012): 1095–1101.

9. Ravinder Jerath, John W. Edry, Vernon A. Barnes, and Vandna Jerath, "Physiology of Long Pranayama Breathing: Neural Respiratory Elements May Provide a Mechanism That Explains How Slow Deep Breathing Shifts the Autonomic Nervous System," *Medican Hypotheses* 67, no. 3 (April 18, 2006): 566–71; Rajeev Mohan Kaushik, Reshma Kaushik, Sukhdev Krishan Mahajan, and Vemreddi Rajesh, "Effects of Mental Relaxation and Slow Breathing in Essential Hypertension," *Complementary Therapies in Medicine* 14, no. 2 (June 2006): 120–26; D. R. Seals, N. O. Suwarno, M. J. Joyner, C. Iber, J. G. Copeland, and J. A. Dempsey, "Respiratory Modulation of Muscle Sympathetic Nerve Activity in Intact and Lung Denervated Humans," *Circulation Research* 72, no. 2 (February 1, 1993): 440–54.

10. Paul Knytl and Bertram Opitz, "Meditation Experience Predicts Negative Reinforcement Learning and Is Associated with Attenuated FRN Amplitude," *Cognative, Affective, and Behavioral Neuroscience* 19, no. 2 (April 2019): 268–82. doi:10.3758/s13415-018-00665-0.

11. Britta K. Hölzel, Ulrich Ott, Hannes Hempel, Andrea Hackl, Katharina Wolf, Rudolf Stark, and Dieter Vaitl, "Differential Engagement of Anterior Cingulate and Adjacent Medial Frontal Cortex in Adept Meditators and Non-Meditators," *Neuroscience Letters* 421, no. 1 (May 25, 2007): 16–21.

12. Sara W. Lazar, Catherine E. Kerr, Rachel H. Wasserman, Jeremy R. Gray, and Douglas N. Greve, "Meditation Experience Is Associated with Increased Cortical Thickness," *NeuroReport* 16, no. 17 (November 28, 2005): 1893–97.

13. Eileen Luders, Arthur W. Toga, Natasha Lepore, and Christian Gaser, "The Underlying Anatomical Correlates of Long-Term Meditation: Larger Hippocampal and Frontal Volumes of Gray Matter," *NeuroImage* 45, no. 3 (April 15, 2009): 672–78.

14. Julie A. Alvarez and Eugene Emory, "Executive Function and the Frontal Lobes: A Meta-Analytic Review," *Neuropsychology Review* 16, no. 1 (March 2006): 17–42.

15. E. Mohandas, "Neurobiology of Spirituality," *Mens Sana Monographs* 6, no. 1 (January–December 2008): 63–80.

16. Grant S. Shields, Wesley G. Moons, and George M. Slavich, "Inflammation, Self-Regulation, and Health: An Immunologic Model of Self-Regulatory Failure," *Perspectives on Psychological Science* (July 5, 2017): 588–612.

17. Grant S. Shields, Alea C. Skwara, Brandon G. King, Anthony P. Zanesco, Firdaus S. Dhabhar, and Clifford D. Saron, "Deconstructing the Effects of Concentration Meditation Practice on Interference Control: The Roles of Controlled Attention and Inflammatory Activity," *Brain, Behavior, and Immunity* 89 (October 2020): 256–67.

18. María José Fernández-Serrano, Miguel Pérez-García, Jacqueline Schmidt Río-Valle, and Antonio Verdejo-García, "Neuropsychological Consequences of Alcohol and Drug Abuse on Different Components of Executive Functions," *Journal of Psychopharmacology* 24, no. 9 (September 2010): 1317–32.

19. Hannah Bigelow, Marcus D. Gottlieb, Michelle Ogrodnik, Jeffrey D. Graham, and Barbara Fenesi, "The Differential Impact of Acute Exercise and Mindfulness Meditation on Executive Functioning and Psycho-Emotional Well-Being in Children and Youth with ADHD," *Frontiers in Psychology* 12 (June 14, 2021): 660845.

20. Katherine A. Cohen, Sakura Ito, Isaac L. Ahuvia, Yuanyuan Yang, and Yanchen Zhang, "Brief School-Based Interventions Targeting Student Mental Health or Well-Being: A Systematic Review and Meta-Analysis," *Clinical Child and Family Psychology Review* 27, no. 2 (June 17, 2024).

21. Drew E. Winters and Emily Beerbower, "Mindfulness and Meditation as an Adjunctive Treatment for Adolescents Involved in the Juvenile Justice System: Is Repairing the Brain and Nervous System Possible?" *Social Work in Health Care* 56, no. 4 (May 2017): 615–35.

## CHAPTER TWELVE

1. "The State of Girls and Women in STEM," NGCP, February 26, 2024, https://ngcproject.org/resources/state-girls-and-women-stem.

2. Mary Ellen Flannery, "Esports See Explosive Growth in U.S. High Schools," *NEA News*, September 16, 2021, https://www.nea.org/nea-today/all-news-articles/esports-see-explosive-growth-us-high-schools.

3. "High School Sports Participation Continues Rebound toward Pre-Pandemic Levels," *NFHS News*, September 21, 2023, https://www.nfhs.org/articles/high-school-sports-participation-continues-rebound-toward-pre-pandemic-levels/.

4. Brian J. Foster and Graig Chow, "The Effects of Psychological Skills and Mindfulness on Well-Being of Student-Athletes: A Path Analysis," *Performance Enhancement & Health* 8, nos. 2–3 (August 2020): 100180; Lucia Bühlmayer, Daniel Birrer, Philipp Röthlin, Oliver Faude, and Lars Doath, "Effects of Mindfulness Practice on Performance-Relevant Parameters and

Performance Outcomes in Sports: A Metanalytical Review," *Sports Medicine* 47 (2017): 2309–21.

5. Annemarie S. Dimech and Roland Seiler, "The Association between Extra-Curricular Sport Participation and Social Anxiety Symptoms in Children," *Journal of Clinical Sport Psychology* 4 (2010): 191–203.

6. "High School Sports Participation Continues Rebound toward Pre-Pandemic Levels."

7. "High School Sports Participation Continues Rebound toward Pre-Pandemic Levels."

8. Chunxiao Li, Yuxin Zhu, Mengge Zhang, Henrik Gustafsson, and Tao Chen, "Mindfulness and Athlete Burnout: A Systematic Review and Meta-Analysis," *International Journal of Environmental Research and Public Health* 16 (2019): 449.

9. Ryan Sappington and Kathryn Longshore, "Systematically Reviewing the Efficacy of Mindfulness-Based Interventions for Enhanced Athletic Performance," *Journal of Clinical Sport Psychology* 9, no. 3 (September 2015): 232–62.

10. "5 Awesome Mindset Hacks for Athletes," The Underground Savages, September 6, 2024, https://tusmindset.wordpress.com/2024/09/06/5-awesome-mindset-hacks-for-athletes/.

11. Ben Pickman, "With Eyes on a Final Four Return, Stanford Is Leaning Heavily on Its 'Happiness Professor,'" *SI*, November 18, 2022, https://www.si.com/college/2022/11/18/stanford-womens-basketball-haley-jones-happiness-professor.

## CONCLUSION

1. Laurence Steinberg, "Cognitive and Affective Development in Adolescence," *Trends in Cognitive Sciences* 9, no. 2 (February 2005): 69–74.

2. Deborah Christie and Russell Viner, "Adolescent Development," *BMJ* 330, no. 7486 (February 2005): 301–4.

3. Christie and Viner, "Adolescent Development," 301.

4. Daniel J. Siegel, *Brainstorm: The Power and Purpose of the Teenage Brain* (New York: TarcherPerigree), 2014.

5. Rachel K. Narr, Joseph P. Allen, Joseph S. Tan, and Emily L. Loeb, "Close Friendship Strength and Broader Peer Group Desirability as Differential Predictors of Adult Mental Health," *Child Development* 90, no. 1 (January 2019): 298–313.

6. "Leading Causes of Death," National Center for Health Statistics, May 2, 2024, https://www.cdc.gov/nchs/fastats/leading-causes-of-death.htm.

7. "AAP-AACAP-CHA Declaration of a National Emergency in Child and Adolescent Mental Health," American Academy of Pediatrics, October 19, 2021, https://www.aap.org/en/advocacy/child-and-adolescent-healthy-mental-development/aap-aacap-cha-declaration-of-a-national-emergency-in-child-and-adolescent-mental-health.

8. Gene Bernstein, "Stress in Teenagers," Mass General Brigham, August 12, 2024, https://www.massgeneralbrigham.org/en/about/newsroom/articles/stress-in-teenagers.

9. *Protecting Youth Mental Health: The U.S. Surgeon General's Advisory* (Washington, DC: Office of the Surgeon General, 2021), https://www.hhs.gov/sites/default/files/surgeon-general-youth-mental-health-advisory.pdf.

10. Daniel G. Whitney and Mark D. Peterson, "US National and State-Level Prevalence of Mental Health Disorders and Disparities of Mental Health Care Use in Children," *JAMA Pediatrics* 173, no. 4 (April 1, 2019): 389–91.

11. Lars Lange, Ludger Klimek, Kirsten Beyer, Katharina Blümchen, Natalija Novak, Eckard Hamelmann, Andrea Bauer, Hans Merk, Uta Rabe, Kirsten Jung, Wolfgang Schlenter, Johannes Ring, Adam Chaker, Wolfgang Wehrmann, Sven Becker, Norbert Mülleneisen, Katja Nemat, Wolfgang Czech, Holger Wrede, Randolf Brehler, Thomas Fuchs, Thilo Jakob, Tobias Ankermann, Sebastian M. Schmidt, Michael Gerstlauer, Torsten Zuberbier, Thomas Spindler, and Christian Vogelberg, "White Paper on Peanut Allergy—Part 1: Epidemiology, Burden of Disease, Health Economic Aspects," *Allergo Journal International* 30, no. 8 (2021): 261–69. doi:10.1007/s40629-021-00189-z.

12. Michelle L. Sever, Agustin Calatroni, Graham Roberts, George du Toit, Henry T. Bahnson, Suzana Radulovic, David Larson, Margie Byron, Alexandra F. Santos, Michelle F. Huffaker, Lisa M. Wheatley, and Gideon Lack, "Developing a Prediction Model for Determination of Peanut Allergy Status in the Learning Early about Peanut Allergy (LEAP) Studies," *Journal of Allergy and Clinical Immunology in Practice* 11, no. 7 (2023): 2217–27.e9.

13. The Learning Network, "Teenagers on the Best Thing about Being Their Age," *New York Times*, April 27, 2023, https://www.nytimes.com/2023/04/27/learning/teenagers-on-the-best-thing-about-being-their-age.html.

# BIBLIOGRAPHY

## BOOKS

Bunge, Eduardo L., Javier Mandil, Andrés J. Consoli, and Martín Gomar. *CBT Strategies for Anxious and Depressed Children and Adolescents: A Clinician's Toolkit.* New York: Guilford Press, 2017.

Burns, David D. *The Feeling Good Handbook: Using the New Mood Therapy in Everyday Life.* New York: Plume Publishing, 1999.

Eckman, Paul, and Wallace V. Friesen. *Unmasking the Face: A Guide to Recognizing Emotions from Facial Expressions.* Saddle River, NJ: Prentice Hall, 1975.

Emerald, David. *The Power of TED: The Empowerment Dynamic.* Edinburgh, Scotland: Polaris Publishing, 2015.

Gottman, John, Joan Declaire, and Daniel Golman. *Raising an Emotionally Intelligent Child: The Heart of Parenting.* New York: Simon and Schuster, 1998.

Gottman, John, and Nan Silver. *The Seven Principles for Making Marriage Work: A Practical Guide from the Country's Foremost Relationship Expert.* San Jose, CA: Harmony Press, 2015.

Greenberger, Dennis, and Christine A. Padesky. *Mind over Mood.* 2nd ed. New York: Guilford Press, 2015.

Haidt, Jonathan. *The Anxious Generation: How the Great Rewiring of Childhood Is Causing and Epidemic of Mental Illness.* New York: Penguin, 2024.

Hefferman, Lisa, and Mary Dell Harrigton. *Grown & Flown: How to Support Your Teen, Stay Close as a Family, and Raise Independent Adults.* New York: Flatiron Books, 2019.

Kabat-Zinn, Jon. *Full Catastrophe Living: Using the Wisdom of Your Body and Mind to Face Stress, Pain, and Illness.* Rev. ed. New York: Bantam Books, 2013.

Kabat-Zinn, Jon. *Full Catastrophe Living: Using the Wisdom of Your Body and Mind to Face Stress, Pain, and Illness.* New York: Delta Trade Paperbacks, 2005.

Kabat-Zinn, Jon. *Mindfulness for Beginners: Reclaiming the Present Moment—and Your Life.* Louisville, CO: Sounds True Adult, 2016.

Kornfield, Jack. *The Art of Forgiveness, Loving-Kindness, and Peace.* London: Bantam Press, 2008.

Leahy, Michael. *Porn University: What College Students Are Saying about Sex on Campus*. Northfield, VT: Northfield Publishing, 2009.

Lythcott-Haims, Julie. *How to Raise an Adult: Break Free of the Overparenting Trap and Prepare Your Kid for Success*. New York: St. Martin's Press, 2016.

Selby, John. *Seven Masters, One Path*. San Francisco: HarperCollins, 2003.

Siegel, Daniel J. *Brainstorm: The Power and Purpose of the Teenage Brain*. New York: TarcherPerigree, 2014.

Siegel, Daniel J., and Tina Payne Bryson. *The Power of Showing Up: How Parental Presence Shapes Who Our Kids Become and How Their Brains Get Wired*. New York: Ballantine Books, 2020.

Siegel, Daniel, and Mary Hartzell. *Parenting from the Inside Out: How a Deeper Self-Understanding Can Help You Raise Children Who Thrive*. New York: TarcherPerigee, 2014.

Tsabary, Shefali. *The Conscious Parent: Transforming Ourselves, Empowering Our Children*. Vancouver: Namaste Publishing, 2012.

Weinstein, Emily, and Carrie James. *Behind Their Screens: What Teens Are Facing (And Adults Are Missing)*. Cambridge, MA: MIT Press, 2022.

White, Fiona, David Livesey, and Brett Hayes. *Developmental Psychology: From Infancy to Development*. 3rd ed. Camberwell: Pearson Australia, 2012.

Wojcicki, Esther. *How to Raise Successful People: Simple Lessons for Radical Results*. New York: Houghton Mifflin Harcourt, 2019.

Worthington, Everett. *Five Steps to Forgiveness: The Art and Science of Forgiving*. New York: Crown, 2001.

Zaloom, Shafia. *Sex, Teens, & Everything in Between: The New and Necessary Conversations Today's Teenagers Need to Have about Consent, Sexual Harassment, Healthy Relationships, Love, and More*. Naperville, IL: Sourcebooks, 2019.

## JOURNAL ARTICLES AND MAGAZINES

Abi-Jaoude, Elia, Karline Treurnicht Naylor, and Antonio Pignatiello. "Smartphones, Social Media Use and Youth Mental Health." *Canadian Medical Association Journal* 192, no. 6 (February 10, 2020): E136–41.

Adair, Kathryn C., Lindsay A. Kennedy, and Bryan Sexton. "Three Good Tools: Positively Reflecting Backwards and Forwards Is Associated with Robust Improvements in Well-Being across Three Distinct Interventions." *Journal of Positive Psychology* 15, no. 5 (July 9, 2020): 613–22.

Ahn, Jinho, Edward J. Brook, Logan Mitchell, Julia Rosen, Joseph R. McConnell, Kendrick Taylor, David Etheridge, and Mauro Rubino. "Atmospheric

$CO_2$ over the Last 1000 Years: A High-Resolution Record from the West Antarctic Ice Sheet (WAIS) Divide Ice Core." *Global Biogeochemical Cycles* 26, no. 2 (May 26, 2012): GB2027.

Alvarez, Julie A., and Eugene Emory. "Executive Function and the Frontal Lobes: A Meta-Analytic Review." *Neuropsychology Review* 16, no. 1 (March 2006): 17–42.

Anderson, Eileen S., Richard A. Winett, and Janet R. Wojcik. "Self-Regulation, Self-Efficacy, Outcome Expectations, and Social Support: Social Cognitive Theory and Nutrition Behavior." *Annals of Behavioral Medicine* 34, no. 3 (October 1, 2007): 304–12.

Ballard, Parissa, Lindsay T. Hoyt, and Mark C. Pachucki. "Impacts of Adolescent and Young Adult Civic Engagement on Health and Socioeconomic Status in Adulthood." *Child Development* 90, no. 4 (January 23, 2018): 1138–54.

Beal, Judy A. "Impact of Social Media on Adolescents." *MCN, The American Journal of Maternal/Child Nursing* 47, no. 2 (March/April 2022): 108. doi:10.1097/NMC.0000000000000799.

Bigelow, Hannah, Marcus D. Gottlieb, Michelle Ogrodnik, Jeffrey D. Graham, and Barbara Fenesi. "The Differential Impact of Acute Exercise and Mindfulness Meditation on Executive Functioning and Psycho-Emotional Well-Being in Children and Youth with ADHD." *Frontiers in Psychology* 12 (June 14, 2021): 660845.

Bridges Ana J., and Robert Wosnitzer, Erica Scharrer, Chyng Sun, and Rachael Lieberman. "Aggression and Sexual Behavior in Best-Selling Pornography Videos: A Content Analysis Update." *Violence against Women* 16, no. 10 (October 2010): 1065–85.

Bühlmayer, Lucia, Daniel Birrer, Philipp Röthlin, Oliver Faude, and Lars Doath. "Effects of Mindfulness Practice on Performance-Relevant Parameters and Performance Outcomes in Sports: A Metanalytical Review." *Sports Medicine* 47 (2017): 2309–21.

Christie, Deborah, and Russell Viner. "Adolescent Development." *BMJ* 330, no. 7486 (February 2005): 301–4.

Ciesla, Jeffrey A., Laura C. Reilly, Kelsey S. Dickson, Amber S. Emanuel, and John A. Updegraff. "Dispositional Mindfulness Moderates the Effects of Stress among Adolescents: Rumination as a Mediator." *Journal of Clinical and Child Adolescent Psychology* 41, no. 6 (July 9, 2012): 760–70.

Cohen, Katherine A., Sakura Ito, Isaac L. Ahuvia, Yuanyuan Yang, and Yanchen Zhang. "Brief School-Based Interventions Targeting Student Mental Health or Well-Being: A Systematic Review and Meta-Analysis." *Clinical Child and Family Psychology Review* 27, no. 2 (June 17, 2024).

Condon, Paul, Gaelle Desbordes, Willa B. Miller, and David DeSteno. "Meditation Increases Compassionate Responses to Suffering." *Psychological Science* 24, no. 10 (August 2013): 2125–27.

Cooke, Lucy J., Lucy C. Chambers, Elizabeth V. Añez, and Jane Wardle. "Facilitating or Undermining? The Effect of Reward on Food Acceptance. A Narrative Review." *Appetite* 57, no. 2 (July 2, 2011): 493–97.

Corcoran, J. L., P. Li, S. L. Davies, C. C. Knight, R. G. Lanzi, and S. L. Ladores. "Adolescent Chlamydia Rates by Region, Race, and Sex: Trends from 2013 to 2017." *Journal of Pediatric Health Care* 35, no. 2 (2021): 172–79. doi:10.1016/j.pedhc.2020.09.004.

Creswell, J. David, Michael R. Irwin, Lisa J. Burklund, Matthew D. Lieberman, Jesusa M. G. Arevalo, Jeffrey Ma, Elizabeth Crabb Breen, and Steven W. Cole. "Mindfulness-Based Stress Reduction Training Reduces Loneliness and Proinflammatory Gene Expression in Older Adults: A Small Randomized Controlled Trial." *Brain, Behavior, and Immunity* 26, no. 7 (July 20, 2012): 1095–1101.

Darley, John M., and Daniel C. Batson. "'From Jerusalem to Jericho': A Study of Situational and Dispositional Variables in Helping Behavior." *Journal of Personality and Social Psychology* 27, no. 1 (1973): 100–108.

Davidson, Richard J., and Jon Kabat-Zinn, Jessica Schumacher, Melissa Rosenkranz, Daniel Muller, Saki F. Santorelli, Ferris Urbanowski, Anne Harrington, Katherine Bonus, and John F. Sheridan. "Alterations in Brain and Immune Function Produced by Mindfulness Meditation." *Psychosomatic Medicine* 65, no. 4 (July–August 2003): 564–70.

Deci, Edward L., Richard Koestner, and Richard M. Ryan. "A Meta-Analytic Review of Experiments Examining the Effects of Extrinsic Rewards on Intrinsic Motivation." *Psychological Bulletin* 125, no. 6 (November 1999): 627–88.

Dennis, P. M. "Chills and Thrills: Does Radio Harm Our Children? The Controversy over Program Violence during the Age of Radio." *Journal of the History of the Behavioral Sciences* 34, no. 1 (winter 1998): 33–50.

Dimech, Annemarie S., and Roland Seiler. "The Association between Extra-Curricular Sport Participation and Social Anxiety Symptoms in Children." *Journal of Clinical Sport Psychology* 4 (2010): 191–203.

Downey, G., and S. I. Feldman. "Implications of Rejection Sensitivity for Intimate Relationships." *Journal of Personality and Social Psychology* 70, no. 6 (June 1996): 1327–43.

Eklund, Jakob H., and Martina S. Meranius. "Toward a Consensus on the Nature of Empathy: A Review of Reviews." *Patient Education and Counseling* 104, no. 2 (February 2021): 300–307.

Farb, Norman A. S., Zindel V. Segal, Helen Mayberg, Jim Bean, Deborah McKeon, Zainab Fatima, and Adam K. Anderson. "Attending to the Present: Mindfulness Meditation Reveals Distinct Neural Modes of Self-Reference." *SCAN* 2, no. 4 (August 13, 2007): 313–17.

Fernández-Serrano, María José, Miguel Pérez-García, Jacqueline Schmidt Río-Valle, Antonio Verdejo-García. "Neuropsychological Consequences of Alcohol and Drug Abuse on Different Components of Executive Functions." *Journal of Psychopharmacology* 24, no. 9 (September 2010): 1317–32.

Fike, Kayla J., Jacqueline S. Mattis, Kyle Nickodem, and Casta Guillaume. "Black Adolescent Altruism: Exploring the Role of Racial Discrimination and Empathy." *Children and Youth Services Review*, 150 (2023): 106990.

Finer, Lawrence B., and Jesse M. Philbin. "Sexual Initiation, Contraceptive Use, and Pregnancy among Young Adolescents." *Pediatrics* 131, no. 5 (2013): 886–91, https://publications.aap.org/pediatrics/article-abstract/131/5/886/31308/Sexual-Initiation-Contraceptive-Use-and-Pregnancy.

Foster, Brian J., and Graig Chow. "The Effects of Psychological Skills and Mindfulness on Well-Being of Student-Athletes: A Path Analysis." *Performance Enhancement & Health* 8, nos. 2–3 (August 2020): 100180.

Foster, Cynthia E., Adam Horwitz, Alvin Thomas, Kiel Opperman, Polly Gipson, Amanda Burnside, Deborah M. Stone, and Cheryl A. King. "Connectedness to Family, School, Peers, and Community in Socially Vulnerable Adolescents." *Child and Youth Services Review* 81 (October 2017): 321–31.

Fox, Glenn R., Jonas Kaplan, Hanna Damasio, and Antonio Damasio. "Neural Correlates of Gratitude." *Frontiers in Psychology* 6 (September 29, 2015): 1491.

Fredrickson, Barbara L. "The Broaden-and-Build Theory of Positive Emotions." *Philosophical Transactions of the Royal Society of London, Series B, Biological Sciences* 359, no. 1449 (September 29, 2004): 1367–78.

Furedi, Frank. "The Media's First Moral Panic." *History Today* 65, no. 11 (October 2015).

Garrett, S. L., K. Burnell, E. L. Armstrong-Carter, M. J. Prinstein, and E. H. Telzer. "Linking Video Chatting, Phone Calling, Text Messaging, and Social Media with Peers to Adolescent Connectedness." *Journal of Research on Adolescence* 33, no. 4 (December 2023): 1222–34.

Gasso, Aina M., Katrin Mueller-Johnson, and Irene Montiel. "Sexting, Online Sexual Victimization, and Psychopathology Correlates by Sex: Depression, Anxiety, and Global Psychopathology." *International Journal of Environmental Research and Public Health* 17, no. 3 (February 6, 2020): 1018.

Gibson, Jonathan, "Mindfulness, Interoception, and the Body: A Contemporary Perspective." *Frontiers in Psychology* 10 (September 12, 2019). doi:10.3389/fpsyg.2019.02012.

Haidt, Jonathan. "End the Phone-Based Childhood Now." *The Atlantic*, March 13, 2024.

Helminen, Emily C., Tory L. Ash, Emily L. Cary, Samantha E. Sinegar, Pam Janack, Robert DiFlorio, and Joshua C. Felver. "Gender Differences in the Stress-Buffering Effects of Mindfulness Facets on Substance Use among Low-Income Adolescents." *Addictive Behaviors* 136 (January 2023): 107491.

Hensen, Nienke M. J., and Olle ten Cate. "How to Deal with the Unmotivated Medical Student in Small Group Sessions?" *MedEdPublish* 6 (May 19, 2017): 86.

Hölzel, Britta K., James Carmody, Mark Vangel, Christina Congleton, Sita M. Yerramsetti, Tim Gard, and Sara W. Lazar, "Mindfulness Practice Leads to Increases in Regional Brain Matter Density." *Psychology Research* 191 (January 30, 2011): 36–43.

Hölzel, Britta K., and Ulrich Ott, Hannes Hempel, Andrea Hackl, Katharina Wolf, Rudolf Stark, and Dieter Vaitl. "Differential Engagement of Anterior Cingulate and Adjacent Medial Frontal Cortex in Adept Meditators and Non-Meditators." *Neuroscience Letters* 421, no. 1 (May 25, 2007): 16–21.

Huesman, L. Rowell, Eric F. Dubow, Paul B. Boxer, Brad B. Bushman, Cathy S. Smith, Meagan A. Docherty, and Maureen J. O'Brien. "Longitudinal Predictions of Young Adults' Weapons Use and Criminal Behavior from Their Childhood Exposure to Violence." *Aggressive Behavior* 47, no. 6 (June 19, 2021): 621–34.

Hylton, Mary. "The Role of Civic Literacy and Social Empathy on Rates of Civic Engagement among University Students." *Journal of Higher Education Outreach and Engagement* 22, no. 1 (March 2018): 87–106.

Janusek, Linda Witek, Dina Tel, and Herbert L. Mathews. "Mindfulness Predicts Psycho-Behavioral Improvement after Breast Cancer Diagnosis: Influence of Childhood Adversity." *Western Journal of Nursing Research* 43, no. 3 (June 7, 2020).

Jerath, Ravinder, John W. Edry, Vernon A. Barnes, and Vandna Jerath. "Physiology of Long Pranayama Breathing: Neural Respiratory Elements May Provide a Mechanism That Explains How Slow Deep Breathing Shifts the Autonomic Nervous System." *Medical Hypotheses* 67, no. 3 (April 18, 2006): 566–71.

Kabat-Zinn, J., E. Wheeler, T. Light, A. Skillings, M. J. Scharf, T. G. Cropley, D. Hosmer, and J. D. Bernhard. "Influence of a Mindfulness-Based Stress Reduction Intervention on Rates of Skin Clearing in Patients with

Moderate-to-Severe Psoriasis Undergoing Phototherapy (UVB) and Photochemotherapy (PUVA)." *Psychosomatic Medicine* 60, no. 5 (September–October 1998): 625–32.

Kabat-Zinn, Jon. "Some Reflections on the Origins of MBSR, Skillful Means, and the Trouble with Maps." *Contemporary Buddhism* 12, no. 1 (2013): 281–306.

Kann L., T. McManus, W. A. Harris, S. L. Shanklin, K. H. Flint, B. Queen, R. Lowry, D. Chyen, L. Whittle, J. Thornton, C. Lim, D. Bradford, Y. Yamakawa, M. Leon, N. Brener, and K. A. Ethier. "Youth Risk Behavior Surveillance—United States, 2017." *Morbidity and Mortality Weekly Report Surveillance Summaries* 67, no. 8 (2018): 1–114.

Kaushik, Rajeev Mohan, Reshma Kaushik, Sukhdev Krishan Mahajan, and Vemreddi Rajesh. "Effects of Mental Relaxation and Slow Breathing in Essential Hypertension." *Complementary Therapeutic Medicine* 14, no. 2 (June 2006): 120–26.

Kiken, Laura G., Eric L. Garland, Karen Bluth, Olafur S. Palsson, and Susan A. Gaylord. "From a State to a Trait: Trajectories of State Mindfulness in Meditation during Intervention Predict Changes in Trait Mindfulness." *Personality and Individual Differences* 1, no. 81 (2015): 41–46.

Kim, Jeffrey J., Stacey L. Parker, James R. Doty, Ross Cunnington, Paul Gilbert, and James N. Kirby. "Neurophysiological and Behavioral Markers of Compassion." *Scientific Reports* 10, no. 6789 (April 22, 2020).

Knytl, Paul, and Bertram Opitz. "Meditation Experience Predicts Negative Reinforcement Learning and Is Associated with Attenuated FRN Amplitude." *Cognitive, Affective, and Behavioral Neuroscience* 19, no. 2 (April 2019): 268–82. doi:10.3758/s13415-018-00665-0.

Koerten, Hannah R., Tanya S. Watford, Eric F. Dubow, and William H. O'Brien. "Cardiovascular Effects of Brief Mindfulness Meditation among Perfectionists Experiencing Failure." *Psychophysiology* 57, no. 4 (April 5, 2020): e13517.

Kraemer, Kristen M., Emily M. O'Bryan, Adrienne L. Johnson, and Alison C. McLeish. "The Role of Mindfulness Skills in Terms of Anxiety-Related Cognitive Risk Factors among College Students with Problematic Alcohol Use." *Substance Abuse* 38, no. 3 (July–September 2017): 337–43.

Ku, Kelly Y. L., Qiuyi Kong, Yunya Song, Lipeng Deng, Yi Kang, and Aihua Hu. "What Predicts Adolescents' Critical Thinking about Real-Life News? The Roles of Social Media News Consumption and News Media Literacy." *Thinking Skills and Creativity* 33 (September 2019).

Lange, Lars, Ludger Klimek, Kirsten Beyer, Katharina Blümchen, Natalija Novak, Eckard Hamelmann, Andrea Bauer, Hans Merk, Uta Rabe, Kirsten

Jung, Wolfgang Schlenter, Johannes Ring, Adam Chaker, Wolfgang Wehrmann, Sven Becker, Norbert Mülleneisen, Katja Nemat, Wolfgang Czech, Holger Wrede, Randolf Brehler, Thomas Fuchs, Thilo Jakob, Tobias Ankermann, Sebastian M. Schmidt, Michael Gerstlauer, Torsten Zuberbier, Thomas Spindler, and Christian Vogelberg. "White Paper on Peanut Allergy—Part 1: Epidemiology, Burden of Disease, Health Economic Aspects." *Allergo Journal International* 30, no. 8 (2021): 261–69. doi:10.1007/s40629-021-00189-z.

Lazar, Sara W., Catherine E. Kerr, Rachel H. Wasserman, Jeremy R. Gray, and Douglas N. Greve. "Meditation Experience Is Associated with Increased Cortical Thickness." *Neuroscience Report* 16, no. 17 (November 28, 2005): 1893–97.

Leary, Mark R., Eleanor B. Tate, Claire E. Adams, Allen Batts, and Jessica Hancock. "Self-Compassion and Reactions to Unpleasant Self-Relevant Events: The Implications of Treating Oneself Kindly." *Journal of Personality and Social Psychology* 92, no. 5 (May 2007): 887–904.

Li, Chunxiao, Yuxin Zhu, Mengge Zhang, Henrik Gustafsson, and Tao Chen. "Mindfulness and Athlete Burnout: A Systematic Review and Meta-Analysis." *International Journal of Environmental Research and Public Health* 16 (2019): 449.

Lim, Daniel, Paul Condon, and David DeSteno. "Mindfulness and Compassion: An Examination of Mechanism and Scalability." *PLOS ONE* 10, no. 2 (2015): e0118221. doi:10.1371/journal.pone.0118221.

Lipari, Rachel N., and Arthur Hughes. *How People Obtain the Prescription Pain Relievers They Misuse.* Rockville, MD: Center for Behavioral Health Statistics and Quality, Substance Abuse and Mental Health Services Administration, 2017.

Little, Craig B., and Andrea Rankin. "Why Do They Start It? Explaining Reported Early-Teen Sexual Activity." *Sociological Forum* 16 (2001): 703–29.

Lopez-Leon, Sandra, Talia Wegman-Ostrosky, Norma Cipatli Ayuzo del Valle, Carol Perelman, Rosalinda Sepulveda, Paulina A. Rebolledo, Angelica Cuapio, and Sonia Villapol. "Long-COVID in Children and Adolescents: A Systematic Review and Meta-Analysis." *Scientific Reports* 12, no. 9950 (June 13, 2022).

Luders, Eileen, Arther W. Toga, Natasha Lepore, and Christian Gaser. "The Underlying Anatomical Correlates of Long-Term Meditation: Larger Hippocampal and Frontal Volumes of Gray Matter." *NeuroImage* 45, no. 3 (April 15, 2009): 672–78.

Luthi, Dieter, Martine Le Floch, Bernhard Bereiter, Thomas Blunier, Jean-Marc Barnola, Urs Siegenthaler, Dominique Raynaud, Jean Jouzel,

Hubertus Fischer, Kenji Kawamura, and Thomas F. Stocker. "High-Resolution Carbon Dioxide Concentration Record 650,000–800,000 Years before Present." *Nature* 453 (May 15, 2008): 379–82.

Ma, Jinping, Lili Ji, and Guohua Lu. "Adolescents' Experiences of Acceptance and Commitment Therapy for Depression: An Interpretative Phenomenological Analysis of Good-Outcome Cases." *Frontiers in Psychology* 14, no. 1 (March 22, 2023): 1050227.

Madigan, Sheri, Ahn Ly, Christiana L. Rash, Joris Van Ouytsel, and Jeff R. Temple. "Prevalence of Multiple Forms of Sexting Behavior among Youth." *JAMA Pediatrics* 172, no. 4 (April 2018): 327–35.

Magnon, Valentin, Frédéric Dutheil, and Guillaume T. Vallet. "Benefits from One Session of Deep and Slow Breathing on Vagal Tone and Anxiety in Young and Older Adults." *Scientific Reports* 11, no. 19267 (September 2021). doi:10.1038/s41598-021-98736-9.

Maza, Maria T., Kara A. Fox, Seh-Joo Kwon, Jessica E. Flannery, Kristen A. Lindquist, Mitchell J. Prinstein, and Eva H. Telzer. "Association of Habitual Checking Behaviors on Social Media with Longitudinal Functional Brain Development." *JAMA Pediatrics* 177, no. 2 (2023): 160–67. doi:10.1001/jamapediatrics.2022.4924.

Mesurado, Belén, Maria E. Oñate, Lucas M. Rodriguez, Natalia Putrino, Paulina Guerra, and Claudia E. Vanney. "Study of the Efficacy of the Hero Program: Cross-National Evidence." *PLOS ONE* 16, no. 4 (April 2021): e0250287. doi:10.1371/journal.pone.0238442.

Mneimne, Malek, and Samantha Dashineau, and K. Lira Yoon. "Mindfulness and Negative Affectivity in Real Time: A Within-Person Process Model." *Cognition and Emotion* 33, no. 8 (March 25, 2019): 1687–1701.

Mohandas, E. "Neurobiology of Spirituality." *Mens.Sana Monographs* 6, no.1 (January–December 2008): 63–80.

Moretti, Marlene M., and Maya Peled. "Adolescent-Parent Attachment: Bonds That Support Healthy Development." *Paediatrics & Child Health* 9, no. 8 (October 2004): 551–55.

Narr, Rachel K., Joseph P. Allen, Joseph S. Tan, and Emily L. Loeb. "Close Friendship Strength and Broader Peer Group Desirability as Differential Predictors of Adult Mental Health." *Child Development* 90, no. 1 (January 2019): 298–313.

Neff, Kristin. "Comparing Compassion for Self and Others: Impacts on Personal and Interpersonal Well-Being." *Human Development* 52, no. 4 (June 2009): 211–14.

Nelson, Michelle R., Xuan Zhu, Yingying Li, Barbara Fiese, and Brenda Koester. "Get Real: How Current Behavior Influences Perceptions of

Realism and Behavioral Intent for Public Service Announcements." *Health Communication* 30, no. 7 (August 4, 2014): 669–79.

Nixon, Charisse L. "Current Perspectives: The Impact of Cyberbullying on Adolescent Health." *Adolescent Health, Medicine, and Therapeutics* 5 (2014): 143–58. doi:10.2147/AHMT.S36456.

Orben, Amy. "The Sisyphean Cycle of Technology Panics." *Perspectives on Psychological Science* 15, no. 5 (September 2020): 1143–57.

Pereira, Ana Telma, Carolina Cabaços, Ana Araújo, Ana Paula Amaral, Frederica Carvalho, and António Macedo. "COVID Psychological Impact: The Role of Perfectionism." *Personality and Individual Differences* 184 (January 2022): 111160.

Peters, Jessica R., Tory A. Eisenlohr-Moul, and Laura M. Smart. "Dispositional Mindfulness and Rejection Sensitivity: The Critical Role of Nonjudgment." *Personality and Individual Differences* 93 (April 1, 2016): 125–29.

Preston, Mary I. "Children's Reactions to Movie Horrors and Radio Crime." *Journal of Pediatrics* 19 (1941): 147–68.

Redwine, Laura S., Brook L. Henry, Meredith A. Pung, Kathleen Wilson, Kelly Chinh, Brian Knight, Shamini Jain, Thomas Rutledge, Barry Greenberg, Alan Maisel, and Paul J. Mills. "Pilot Randomized Study of a Gratitude Journaling Intervention on Heart Rate Variability and Inflammatory Biomarkers in Patients with Stage B Heart Failure." *Psychological Medicine* 78, no. 6 (July–August 2016): 667–76.

Rosenkranz, Melissa A., and Richard J. Davidson, Donal G. MacCoon, John F. Sheridan, Ned H. Kalin, and Antoine Lutz. "A Comparison of Mindfulness-Based Stress Reduction and an Active Control in Modulation of Neurogenic Inflammation." *Brain Behavior and Immunity* 27, no. 1 (January 2013): 313–22.

Rosner, Rachel I. "Aaron T. Beck's Drawings and the Psychoanalytic Story of Cognitive Therapy." *History of Psychology* 15, no. 1 (February 2012): 1–18.

Santos, Renata Maria Silva, Camila Guimaraes Mendes, Guilherme Yang Sen Bressani, G. Samara de Alcantara Ventura, Yago Jean de Almeida Nogueira, Débora Marques de Miranda, and Marco Aurélio Romano-Silva. "The Associations between Screen Time and Mental Health in Adolescents: A Systematic Review." *BMC Psychology* 11, no. 127 (April 20, 2023). doi:10.1186/s40359-023-01166-7.

Sappington, Ryan, and Kathryn Longshore. "Systematically Reviewing the Efficacy of Mindfulness-Based Interventions for Enhanced Athletic Performance." *Journal of Clinical Sport Psychology* 9, no. 3 (September 2015): 232–62.

Schutte, Nicola S., Suresh K. A. Palanisamy, and James R. McFarlane. "The Relationship between Positive Psychological Characteristics and Longer Telomeres." *Psychology and Health* 31, no. 12 (2016): 1466–80.

Seals, D. R., N. O. Suwarno, M. J. Joyner, C. Iber, J. G. Copeland, and J. A. Dempsey. "Respiratory Modulation of Muscle Sympathetic Nerve Activity in Intact and Lung Denervated Humans." *Circulation Research* 72, no. 2 (February 1, 1993): 440–54.

Sever, Michelle L., Agustin Calatroni, Graham Roberts, George du Toit, Henry T. Bahnson, Suzana Radulovic, David Larson, Margie Byron, Alexandra F. Santos, Michelle F. Huffaker, Lisa M. Wheatley, and Gideon Lack. "Developing a Prediction Model for Determination of Peanut Allergy Status in the Learning Early about Peanut Allergy (LEAP) Studies." *Journal of Allergy and Clinical Immunology in Practice* 11, no. 7 (2023): 2217–2227.e9.

Sexton, J. Bryan, and Kathryn C. Adair. "Forty-Five Good Things: A Prospective Pilot Study of the Three Good Things Well-Being Intervention in the USA for Healthcare Worker Emotional Exhaustion, Depression, Work-Life Balance and Happiness." *BMJ Open* 9, no. 3 (2019): e022695. doi:10.1136/bmjopen-2018-022695.

Shields, Grant S., Wesley G. Moons, and George M. Slavich. "Inflammation, Self-Regulation, and Health: An Immunologic Model of Self-Regulatory Failure." *Perspectives on Psychological Science* (July 5, 2017): 588–612.

Shields, Grant S., Alea C. Skwara, Brandon G. King, Anthony P. Zanesco, Firdaus S. Dhabhar, and Clifford D. Saron. "Deconstructing the Effects of Concentration Meditation Practice on Interference Control: The Roles of Controlled Attention and Inflammatory Activity." *Brain, Behavior, and Immunity* 89 (October 2020): 256–67.

Spicknall, I. H., E. E. Flagg, and E. A. Torrone. "Estimates of the Prevalence and Incidence of Genital Herpes, United States, 2018." *Sexually Transmitted Diseases* 48, no. 4 (April 1, 2021): 260–65.

Steinberg, Laurence. "Cognitive and Affective Development in Adolescence." *Trends in Cognitive Sciences* 9, no. 2 (February 2005): 69–74.

Stewart, Tiffany M. "Light on Body Image Treatment: Acceptance through Mindfulness." *Behavior Modification* 28, no. 6 (November 2004): 783–811.

Stoeber, Joachim, Natalia Schneider, Rimi Hussain, and Kelly Matthews. "Perfectionism and Negative Affect after Repeated Failure: Anxiety, Depression, and Anger." *Journal of Independent Differences* 35, no. 2 (January 1, 2014): 87–94.

Strassberg, Donald S., Deanna Cann, and Valeri Velarde. "Sexting by High School Students." *Archives of Sexual Behavior* 46, no. 6 (August 2017): 1667–72.

Torazzi, Eugenia, Vera Merelli, Giussy Barbara, Alessandra Kustermann, Laura Marasciuolo, Federica Collini, and Cristina Cattaneo. "Similarity and Differences in Sexual Violence against Adolescents and Adult Women: The Need to Focus on Adolescent Victims." *Journal of Pediatric and Adolescent Gynecology* 34, no. 3 (June 2021): 302–10.

Tumminia, Miachael J., Blake A. Colaianne, Robert W. Roeser, and Brian M. Galla. "How Is Mindfulness Linked to Negative and Positive Affect? Rumination as an Explanatory Process in a Prospective Longitudinal Study of Adolescents." *Journal of Youth and Adolescents* 49, no. 10 (May 7, 2020): 2136–48.

VanOyen Witvliet, Charlotte, Fallon J. Richie, Lindsey M. Root Luna, and Daryl R. Van Tongeren. "Gratitude Predicts Hope and Happiness: A Two-Study Assessment of Traits and States." *Journal of Positive Psychology* 14, no. 3 (January 15, 2018): 271–82. doi:10.1080/17439760.2018.1424924.

Volpp, Kevin G., George Loewenstein, Andrea B. Troxel, Jalpa Doshi, Maureen Price, Mitchell Laskin, and Stephen E. Kimmel. "A Test of Financial Incentives to Improve Warfarin Adherence." *BMC Health Services Research* 8, no. 272 (December 23, 2008): 272.

Volpp, Kevin G., Andrea B. Troxel, Mark V. Pauly, Henry A. Glick, Andrea Puig, David A. Asch, Robert Galvin, Jingsan Zhu, Fei Wan, Jill DeGuzman, Elizabeth Corbett, Janet Weiner, and Janet Audrain-McGovern. "A Randomized, Controlled Trial of Financial Incentives for Smoking Cessation." *New England Journal of Medicine* 360, no. 7 (February 12, 2009): 699–709.

Walsh, Wendy A., and Dafna Tener. "'If You Don't Send Me Five Other Pictures, I Am Going to Post the Photo Online': A Qualitative Analysis of Experiences of Survivors of Sextortion." *Journal of Child Sexual Abuse* 31, no. 4 (April 21, 2022): 447–65.

Wang, Xingchao, Li Lei, Jiping Yang, Ling Gao, and Fengqing Zhao. "Moral Disengagement as Mediator and Moderator of the Relation between Empathy and Aggression among Chinese Male Juvenile Delinquents." *Child Psychiatry and Human Development* 48, no. 2 (April 2017): 316–26.

Werner, Kelly H., Horria Jazaieri, Phillipe R. Goldin, Michal Ziv, Richard G. Heimberg, and James J. Gross. "Self-Compassion and Social Anxiety Disorder." *Anxiety, Stress & Coping* 25, no. 5 (September 2011): 543–58.

Whitney, Daniel G., and Mark D. Peterson. "US National and State-Level Prevalence of Mental Health Disorders and Disparities of Mental Health Care Use in Children." *JAMA Pediatrics* 173, no. 4 (April 1, 2019): 389–91.

Winters, Drew E., and Emily Beerbower. "Mindfulness and Meditation as an Adjunctive Treatment for Adolescents Involved in the Juvenile Justice System: Is Repairing the Brain and Nervous System Possible?" *Social Work Health Care* 56, no. 4 (May 2017): 615–35.

Wood, Alex M., Jeffrey J. Froh, and Adam W. A. Geraghty, "Gratitude and Well-Being: A Review and Theoretical Integration," *Clinical Psychology Review* 30, no. 7 (November 2010): 890–905. doi:10.1016/j.cpr.2010.03.005.

## INTERNET REFERENCES

"5 Awesome Mindset Hacks for Athletes." *The Underground Savages*, September 6, 2024, https://tusmindset.wordpress.com/2024/09/06/5-awesome-mindset-hacks-for-athletes/.

"8 Ways Covid Has Impacted Teen Mental Health, and What We Can Do about It." *St. Louis Jewish Light*, September 26, 2021, https://stljewishlight.org/news/world-news/8-ways-Covid-has-impacted-teen-mental-health-and-what-we-can-do-about-it.

"38°C Record Arctic Temperature Confirmed, Others Likely to Follow: WMO." UN News, December 14, 2021, https://news.un.org/en/story/2021/12/1107872.

"2023 State of Deepfakes: Realities, Threats, and Impact." Security Hero, January 9, 2025, https://www.securityhero.io/state-of-deepfakes.

"AAP-AACAP-CHA Declaration of a National Emergency in Child and Adolescent Mental Health." American Academy of Pediatrics, October 19, 2021, https://www.aap.org/en/advocacy/child-and-adolescent-healthy-mental-development/aap-aacap-cha-declaration-of-a-national-emergency-in-child-and-adolescent-mental-health.

"Alcohol's Effects on Health: Research-Based Information on Drinking and Its Impact." National Institute on Alcohol Abuse and Alcoholism, February 2024, https://www.niaaa.nih.gov/publications/brochures-and-fact-sheets/underage-drinking.

*The Annual Bullying Survey 2017*. Ditch the Label, 2017, https://dtl-beta-website-assets.s3.amazonaws.com/ABS_2017_1_ae04a7734b.pdf.

"Average Screen Time for Teenagers in 2024," Cosmo, February 14, 2024, https://cosmotogether.com/blogs/news/average-screen-time-for-teenagers-in-2024.

Babida, Blair. "Hollow Flashlight." EEWeb, July 13, 2018, https://www.eeweb.com/hollow-flashlight/.

Benaroya, Melissa. "How to Bond with Your Child by Sharing Fondness and Admiration." The Gottman Institute, November 9, 2021, https://www.gottman.com/blog/how-to-bond-with-your-child-by-sharing-fondness-and-admiration/.

Bernstein, Gene, "Stress in Teenagers." Mass General Brigham, August 12, 2024, https://www.massgeneralbrigham.org/en/about/newsroom/articles/stress-in-teenagers.

Boeder, Ellen, "Emotional Safety Is Necessary for Emotional Connection." The Gottman Institute, 2017, https://www.gottman.com/blog/emotional-safety-is-necessary-for-emotional-connection/.

Brach, Tara. "RAIN: A Practice of Radical Compassion." *Tara Brach*, August 2024, https://www.tarabrach.com/rain/.

CDC National Center for Health Statistics. "U.S. Overdose Deaths Decrease in 2023, First Time since 2018," May 15, 2024, https://www.cdc.gov/nchs/pressroom/nchs_press_releases/2024/20240515.htm.

"Distracted Driving." US Centers for Disease Control and Prevention, May 16, 2024, https://www.cdc.gov/distracted-driving/about/index.html.

Flannery, Mary Ellen. "Esports See Explosive Growth in U.S. High Schools." *NEA News*, September 16, 2021, https://www.nea.org/nea-today/all-news-articles/esports-see-explosive-growth-us-high-schools.

Gecker, Jocelyn. "Kids Are Using Phones in Class, Even When It's against the Rules. Should Schools Ban Them All Day?" AP News, February 27, 2024, https://www.barchart.com/story/news/24364395/kids-are-using-phones-in-class-even-when-its-against-the-rules-should-schools-ban-them-all-day.

Goldstein, Sam, and Jack A. Naglieri. *Encyclopedia of Child Behavior and Development*. (Boston: Springer, 2011).

Gottfried, Jeffrey, and Olivia Sidoti. "Teens and Video Games Today." Pew Research Center, May 9, 2024, https://www.pewresearch.org/internet/2024/05/09/teens-and-video-games-today.

"Gun Safety Policies Save Lives." 2024 Everytown Gun Law Rankings, January 4, 2024, https://everytownresearch.org/rankings/.

"High School Sports Participation Continues Rebound toward Pre-Pandemic Levels." *NFHS News*, September 21, 2023, https://www.nfhs.org/articles/high-school-sports-participation-continues-rebound-toward-pre-pandemic-levels/.

"How Many People Are on Porn Sites Right Now? (Hint: It's a Lot)." *Fight the New Drug*, 2023, https://fightthenewdrug.org/by-the-numbers-see-how-many-people-are-watching-porn-today/.

"Israeli Study: 1 in 4 Kids Became More Violent during COVID Era." *Times of Israel*, September 2, 2021, https://www.timesofisrael.com/study-1-in-4-israeli-kids-became-more-violent-during-Covid-era/.

Jargon, Julie. "This School Took Away Smartphones. The Kids Don't Mind." *Wall Street Journal*, November 5, 2022, https://www.wsj.com/articles/this-school-took-away-smartphones-the-kids-dont-mind-11667614444.

Kirley, B. B., K. L. Robison, A. H. Goodwin, K. J. Harmon, N. P. O'Brien, A. West, S. S. Harrell, L. Thomas, and K. Brookshire. "Young Drivers." In *Countermeasures That Work: A Highway Safety Countermeasure Guide for*

*State Highway Safety Offices* Washington, DC: National Highway Traffic Safety Administration, 2023, https://www.nhtsa.gov/book/countermeasures-that-work/young-drivers.

"The Law of Least Effort," Chopra, May 23, 2015, https://chopra.com/blogs/meditation/the-law-of-least-effort.

"Leading Causes of Death." National Center for Health Statistics, May 2, 2024, https://www.cdc.gov/nchs/fastats/leading-causes-of-death.html.

The Learning Network, "Teenagers on the Best Thing about Being Their Age." *New York Times*, April 27, 2023, https://www.nytimes.com/2023/04/27/learning/teenagers-on-the-best-thing-about-being-their-age.html.

Leonhardt, David. "Smartphones in Schools." *New York Times*, September 6, 2024, https://www.nytimes.com/2024/09/06/briefing/smartphones-in-schools.html.

LeWine, Howard E. "Understanding the Stress Response." Harvard Health Publishing, April 3, 2024, https://www.health.harvard.edu/staying-healthy/understanding-the-stress-response.

"Long Telomeres, the Endcaps on DNA, Not the Fountain of Youth Once Thought—Scientists May Now Know Why," Johns Hopkins Medicine Newsroom, May 4, 2024, https://www.hopkinsmedicine.org/news/newsroom/news-releases/2023/05/long-telomeres-the-endcaps-on-dna-not-the-fountain-of-youth-once-thought--scientists-may-now-know-why.

MacDonald, Ann. "Using the Relaxation Response to Reduce Stress." Harvard Health Publishing, November 20, 2010, https://www.health.harvard.edu/blog/using-the-relaxation-response-to-reduce-stress-20101110780.

"Monitoring the Future." National Institute on Drug Abuse, June 2024, https://nida.nih.gov/research-topics/trends-statistics/monitoring-future.

Neff, Kristin. "The Criticizer, the Criticized, and the Compassionate Observer." *Self-Compassion*, February 23, 2023, https://self-compassion.org/exercise-4-supportive-touch/.

Neff, Kristin. "Self-Compassion Exercise 1: How Would You Treat a Friend?" *Self-Compassion*, 2024, https://self-compassion.org/exercise-1-treat-friend/.

"New Report Reveals Truths about How Teens Engage with Pornography." Common Sense Media, January 10, 2023, https://www.commonsensemedia.org/press-releases/new-report-reveals-truths-about-how-teens-engage-with-pornography.

Orcena, Alyson, Melissa Vallas, Shikha Verma, Ellen Bloch, and Lianne Tendler. "Understanding and Addressing Teen Sexual Assault: A Parent's Guide," Evolve, October 30, 2023, https://evolvetreatment.com/parent-guides/teen-sexual-assault/.

Osterman, M. J. K., B. E. Hamilton, J. A. Martin, A. K. Driscoll, and C. P. Valenzuela. "Births: Final Data for 2020." *National Vital Statistics Reports* 70, no. 17 (2022).

"Parenting, Media, and Everything in Between." Common Sense Media, 2024, https://www.commonsensemedia.org/articles/online-safety.

"Parents Talking about Their Own Drug Use to Children Could Be Detrimental." *Science Daily*, February 22, 2013, https://www.sciencedaily.com/releases/2013/02/130222083127.htm.

*Parents under Pressure: The U.S. Surgeon General Advisory on the Mental Health and Well-Being of Parents*. Washington, DC: US Department of Health and Human Services, Office of the Surgeon General, 2024, https://www.hhs.gov/surgeongeneral/priorities/parents/index.html.

"A Partial List of Mass Shootings in the United States in 2022." *New York Times*, January 24, 2023, https://www.nytimes.com/article/mass-shootings-2022.html.

Patchin, J. W., and Hinduja, S. "Cyberbullying Facts." Cyberbullying Research Center, 2024, https://cyberbullying.org/facts.

Pickman, Ben. "With Eyes on a Final Four Return, Stanford Is Leaning Heavily on Its 'Happiness Professor.'" *SI*, November 18, 2022, https://www.si.com/college/2022/11/18/stanford-womens-basketball-haley-jones-happiness-professor.

"Progress Cleaning the Air and Improving People's Health." United States Environmental Protection Agency, 2024, https://www.epa.gov/clean-air-act-overview/progress-cleaning-air-and-improving-peoples-health.

*Protecting Youth Mental Health: The U.S. Surgeon General's Advisory*. Washington, DC: Office of the Surgeon General, 2021, https://www.hhs.gov/sites/default/files/surgeon-general-youth-mental-health-advisory.pdf.

Randazzo, Sara, and Alyssa Lukpat. "Los Angeles School District Votes in Favor of Cellphone Ban." *Wall Street Journal*, June 18, 2024, https://www.wsj.com/us-news/education/los-angeles-school-district-votes-in-favor-of-cellphone-ban-667c1ff3.

"Ratings and Reviews Parents Trust." Common Sense Media, August 2024, https://www.commonsensemedia.org/.

Rothwell, Jonathan. "Parenting Is the Key to Adolescent Mental Health." Gallup.com, November 30, 2023, https://www.gallup.com/analytics/610151/ifs-usa-parenting-research.aspx.

Rothwell, Jonathan. "Parenting Mitigates Social Media–Linked Mental Health Issues." Gallup.com, October 27, 2023, https://news.gallup.com/poll/513248/parenting-mitigates-social-media-linked-mental-health-issues.aspx.

"Sexually Transmitted Infections Workgroup." *Healthy People 2030*, January 9, 2025, https://odphp.health.gov/healthypeople/about/workgroups/sexually-transmitted-infections-workgroup.

Shelby Rivers, Alannah. "Not Just Mothers: Understanding the Unique Role of Attachment to Fathers." Society for Couple & Family Psychology, March 1, 2022, https://www.apadivisions.org/division-43/publications/blog/research/attachment-fathers.

Soave, Robby. "People Have Been Panicking about New Media since before the Printing Press." *Reason: Free Minds and Free Markets*, November 2021, https://reason.com/2021/09/29/people-have-been-panicking-about-new-media-since-before-the-printing-press/.

"The State of Girls and Women in STEM." NGCP, February 26, 2024, https://ngcproject.org/resources/state-girls-and-women-stem.

Taylor, Petroc. "Percentage of Teenagers in the United States Who Have Access to a Smartphone at Home as of October 2023, by Gender." Statista, February 28, 2024, https://www.statista.com/statistics/256501/teen-cell-phone-and-smartphone-ownership-in-the-us-by-gender/.

*Television and Growing Up: The Impact of Television Violence.* Rockville, MD: National Institute of Mental Health, 1971, https://www.ojp.gov/ncjrs/virtual-library/abstracts/television-and-growing-impact-televised-violence.

"Traffic Safety Facts." National Highway Traffic and Safety Administration, June 2022, https://crashstats.nhtsa.dot.gov/Api/Public/ViewPublication/813313.

US Department of Health and Human Services. "Surgeon General Issues New Advisory about Effects Social Media Use Has on Youth Mental Health." May 23, 2023, https://www.hhs.gov/about/news/2023/05/23/surgeon-general-issues-new-advisory-about-effects-social-media-use-has-youth-mental-health.html.

"Why You Should Talk with Your Child about Alcohol and Other Drugs." Substance Abuse and Mental Health Services Administration, August 2019, https://library.samhsa.gov/product/talk-they-hear-you-why-you-should-talk-your-child-about-alcohol-and-other-drugs-fact-sheet.

"WMO Confirms That 2023 Smashes Global Temperature Record." World Meteorological Organization, January 12, 2024, https://wmo.int/news/media-centre/wmo-confirms-2023-smashes-global-temperature-record.

# INDEX

Alzheimer's disease, 17, 141
acceptance, 115–123
acceptance and commitment therapy (ACT), 5, 30, 32, 39, 103, 109, 117–121, 123, 146
Adderall, 55
ADHD, 41, 55, 143
adolescence, joys of, 163
adolescent egocentrism, 108
adolescents, 27, 36, 40, 43, 45, 47, 57, 108, 131–132, 143, 155–159
aggressive behavior, 45
alcohol, 25, 37, 52–53, 56–57, 132, 157, 162
American Academy of Pediatrics (AAP), 158
anemia, 26
anxiety, 9–11, 13, 25, 33, 36, 39–42, 152–163; new anxieties, 39
Apple iPhone, 4
Arbor Day Foundation, 51
attention deficit hyperactivity disorder (ADHD), 41, 55, 143, 160

Baha'i, 108
behavioral intention, 125–126
benzodiazepines, 55
biopsychosocial changes, 156
boundaries, 10, 18, 57, 64, 156–157
brain fog, 42
Buddhist, 108–109, 138

cancer, 7, 17, 28, 39, 55, 133, 143
Canva, 36
carbon dioxide levels, 48
cardiovascular disease, 143
carpe diem, 51
Centers for Disease Control and Prevention (CDC), 9, 27, 31, 53, 55, 157, 159
child sexual abuse, 36
"Children's Reactions to Movie Horrors and Radio Crime," 15
chlamydia, 27–28
Chopra, Deepak, 116
Christian, 108–109, 138
chronic stress, 77, 84, 93–95, 104, 153
Clean Air Act, 49
climate change, 40, 48, 50–51, 160
cocaine, 55
cognitive behavior therapy (CBT), 96–97, 117–118
cognitive thinking, 156
Common Sense Media, 21, 29, 45–46
community: activities, 150; engagement, 72
compassion, 65, 68, 70–71, 73, 77–89, 92, 101, 113, 150, 164
confidence, 9, 27, 31, 53, 55, 157, 159
contempt, 63–66, 68, 97

COVID pandemic, 40, 132, 159–160
criticism, 31, 63–66, 71, 81–82, 91, 99, 134
Cyberbullying Research Center, 11
CyberWise, 21

defensiveness, 64–65
depression, 9–11, 36, 117–118, 120, 128, 156, 158, 160, 162–163; symptoms, 133, 157
digital devices, 9, 17–18, 20–21, 29, 40
dopamine, 157
drugs, 29, 37, 52–58, 69, 74, 103, 132, 157, 162

eating disorders, 36, 41, 118, 132
eco-anxiety, 48
Edison, Thomas, 14
Ekman, Paul, 96
emotional: experiences, 84; intensity, 157; lability, 131; peace, 139
empathy, 31, 65, 70–73, 77, 79–87, 89, 113, 133, 164
entertainment, 17–18, 32, 39
executive function, 80, 94, 141–143, 156
extracurricular activities, 6, 58, 61, 149–154

Facebook, 4, 10, 17, 39
fatigue, 10, 42, 94, 125, 133, 137
fondness and admiration, 66, 68
forced penetration, 30
forgiveness, 77–89, 109, 139, 154, 164
Four Horsemen, 63–66, 70
freedom, 61, 146, 163

Fridays for Future Organization, 51
functional MRI (fMRI), 139

GAIN: method, 21, 67, 73, 88, 105, 107, 144, 152; principles, 22, 47, 144
goals, 120, 123–124, 126–127, 152
Google's Be Internet Awesome program, 21
Gottman, John, 63–65
gratitude, 107–115
gratitude, acceptance, intention, and nonjudgment (GAIN), 21–22, 25, 33, 37, 47, 120, 126–128, 137–139, 152–153, 163
Greater Good Science Center, 112
gun violence, 43–45, 159
Gun Violence Archive, 45

hallucinogens, 55
happiness, 82–83, 93, 112, 115, 117–118, 121, 123, 131, 134, 137–138
healthy: internet use, 21; smartphone use, 20
herpes simplex virus (HSV), 28
Hindu, 108
honesty, 31, 112
HPV infection, 28
hypervigilance, 45

Illustrator, 36
immoral behavior, 14
independence, 61, 121, 163
inflammation, reducing, 143
insecurity, 44, 119, 131
Instagram, 4, 10, 12, 17, 39, 50–51
intention, 123–129
interpersonal problems, 36

Jewish, 108
Judaism worship, 109

Kabat-Zinn, Jon, 87, 91, 93, 123, 130, 138
Kardashian, Kim, 34

language, 3, 46, 66, 84
Leahy, Michael, 30
Learning Early about Peanut Allergy (LEAP), 161
LinkedIn, 39
Love Addicts Anonymous, 31
LSD, 55
Luskin, Fred, 78, 154
Luther, Martin, 109

maladaptive perfectionism, 132
mantra, 95, 138, 144
marijuana, 25, 52–53, 55–56, 157
Maslach Burnout Inventory, 110
media "influencers," 39
meditation, 37, 67–68, 72, 101, 103, 116–117, 127–128, 137–148, 154
Melvoin, Nick, 7
mental health, 4–5, 7, 9–10, 26, 36–37, 83, 86, 94, 120, 143, 158–159
metabolic syndrome, 143
meth, 54–55
mindfulness: meditation practice, 75, 117, 143–144; practice, 75, 86, 95, 100, 104, 109, 120, 126, 133, 152; role of, 162; training, 79, 89, 99, 132–133, 152–153
Mindfulness-Based Stress Reduction (MBSR) program, 138
movement meditation, 138

Murthy, Vivek, 7, 74
Muslim, 108
MySpace, 4

National Highway Traffic Safety Administration (NHTSA), 8–9
National Institute on Drug Abuse, 53
National Organization for Victim Advocacy, 37
National Sexual Assault Hotline, 37
National Sexual Violence Resource Center, 37
Negari, Shelly Ben Harush, 41
negative: affectivity, 131; thoughts, 77, 84, 94, 97–98, 111, 113, 117, 131, 152, 154
neurochemicals, 142–143; corticotropin-releasing hormone (CRH), 142; dimethyltryptamine (DMT), 142; dopamine, 5, 31, 142–143, 157; gammaaminobutyric acid (GABA), 142; glutamate, 142; N-acetylaspartyl glutamic acid (NAAG), 142; serotonin, 142
neurodegenerative diseases, 143
neuroplasticity, 66, 80, 87, 92–93, 104, 112, 118, 139, 141, 163
nonjudgment, 129–136

obesity, 10, 94, 143, 156
obsessive-compulsive disorder, 118, 132
One Tree Planted Organization, 51
online: bullying, 11; harassment, 21
opioids, 53–54

parental support, 37
Pepys, Samuel, 14

per- and polyfluoroalkyl substances (PFAS), 49
perfectionism, 132
personal growth, 109, 119
Photoshop, 36
physical attributes, 132
politics, 40, 46
*Porn University*, 30
pornography, 21, 29–32, 38, 160
positive emotions, 84–85, 111
post-traumatic stress disorder (PTSD), 36, 44–45
*The Power of Showing Up: How Parental Presence Shapes Who Our Kids Become and How Their Brains Get Wired*, 71
preeclampsia, 26
pregnancy, 25–26, 28, 38
psilocybin, 55
psychological skills training (PST), 152
psychotherapy, 37, 66–67, 72, 96

RAIN, 102–104
REACH, 4, 8, 43, 85, 125, 128
reading addiction/mania, 14
Reddit, 4, 17
relaxation, 17–18, 65, 67, 95, 112, 140, 145
risk-taking, excessive, 14
Ritalin, 55
role model, 6, 20, 40–41, 155
rumination, 92, 120, 131–132, 162

sadness, 12, 82–83, 92, 96, 146, 160, 162–163
safety, 8, 14, 16, 21, 36–37, 43, 45, 52, 70, 74, 118
school officials, 11, 19

science, technology, engineering, and math (STEM), 149
screentime, 19
self-acceptance, 109, 119
self-care, 72, 75, 111, 120
self-compassionate, 80
self-confidence, 51, 69, 97, 108, 119, 121, 151, 154, 162
self-esteem, 11–12, 26, 30, 36, 69–70, 77, 82–83, 86, 119, 150–154
self-exploration, 119
self-expression, 119–120
sex, 25–33, 35, 37, 39, 46, 157
Sex Addicts Anonymous, 31
Sexaholics Anonymous, 31
sexting, 21, 32–33, 35–36, 38
sextortion, 33–34
sexual: abuse, 34, 36–38; coercion, 30; risk-taking behavior, 36; violence, 36–37
sexually transmitted diseases (STDs), 27–29, 38
shame, 26, 31, 33, 35, 64, 91, 118, 132, 137, 139, 146, 162
Siegel, Daniel J., 157
Silver, Nan, 65
sleep: disruption, 9, 41; disturbance, 133
smartphones, 3–11, 13–23, 29, 32, 40, 51, 160
smoking, 52, 54–55, 77, 126
Snapchat, 4, 10, 13, 17
spiritual meditation, 138
Steyer, James P., 29
stonewalling, 64–65
substance abuse, 36, 56–57, 118, 132, 143

teen accounts, 12
teen pregnancy, 25, 38

teenage mothers, 26
teenagers, 3–6, 9–10, 13–14, 21, 99, 117–119, 126, 131–133, 156, 160, 164
teachers, 23
TikTok, 4, 13, 17, 39, 50
Tolle, Eckhart, 129
trauma, 45, 69, 158–159
Tumblr, 4
Twitter, 4, 51
type 2 diabetes, 143

validation, 70–73
Valium, 55
Van den Haag, Ernest, 15
VanDerveer, Tara, 154
violence, 30, 36–37, 39, 43–47, 78, 94, 146, 159
visualization, 154

Washington, George, 109
WhatsApp, 17
win-win protocol, 20

Xanax, 55

YGP curriculum key processes: building positive relationships, 113; capitalizing on strengths, 112; exploring identity, 112
Youth Gratitude Project (YGP), 112–113
YouTube, 4, 16, 18, 50–51

Zen Buddhism, 143

# ABOUT THE AUTHORS

**Greg Hammer, MD**, is a retired Stanford University School of Medicine professor. Dr. Hammer's clinical focus was pediatric cardiac anesthesia and critical care medicine. His research was in developmental pharmacology and immunology. Dr. Hammer won numerous accolades as a clinician, teacher, mentor, and research scientist.

Dr. Hammer has been a member of several professional organizations, including the American Society of Anesthesiologists, the American Academy of Pediatrics, the Society of Critical Care Medicine, and the International Anesthesia Research Society. He has published more than two hundred scientific articles and two books. He has had an active laboratory with ongoing studies in the areas of developmental pharmacology and immunology. He has lectured extensively on topics related to wellness and his scientific research and has been a visiting professor at more than forty institutions around the world.

Dr. Hammer is a longtime wellness enthusiast. He has been practicing Advaita and meditating daily for many years. He served as a member of the Stanford WellMD program and chair of the Wellness Task Force for the California Society of Anesthesiologists. His book, *GAIN without Pain: The Happiness Handbook for Health Care Professionals* won an independent book award and has been a bestseller. Dr. Hammer has done more than 450 television, radio, and podcast interviews. Many of these can be found on his website, https://greghammermd.com.

**Eric Wentworth** was a creative director at major advertising agencies in Chicago, New York, Los Angeles, and San Francisco, winning more than fifty top awards for creativity over the years. He has also worked for several internet startups in marketing communications and was a marketing adviser to Keiretsu Forum, the world's largest angel investor organization. He is also a serial entrepreneur, founding the first specialty international travel company, an advertising and public relations agency, cofounder of Arrangr.com, owner of two top-rated coffeehouses in Santa Barbara and Sausalito, California, and cofounder of a national executive recruiting firm, Wentworth Executive Recruiting. Eric graduated from the University of Missouri School of Journalism. He is an active supporter of Partnerships for Change and Citizens Climate lobby. Eric lives in the San Francisco Bay Area.

**John P. Rettger, PhD**, is a clinical psychologist, author, and expert on mindfulness-based approaches for mental health and well-being. He is in private practice in the San Diego area, where he cares for children, teenagers, and adults through individual, couples, and family therapy approaches. Dr. Rettger taught yoga and meditation professionally for nine years before transitioning to his full-time private practice. Dr. Rettger previously directed mindfulness programming and engaged in mindfulness research at the Stanford University Early Life Stress and Resilience Program for pediatric anxiety.

From an early age, he developed an interest in religious and spiritual experiences and has spent the past nineteen years learning about the intersection of spiritual practices with mental health interventions.